REVELATION

[MADE EASY]

A simple way to understand
end-time biblical prophecy

MICHAEL SEDGWICK

Lovingly dedicated to my wife Marcia Kay,

my son Jeremy,

and

my daughter Kayla.

Contents

Introduction

Christ: The Center of End-Time Prophecy

God wants all Christians to have at least a general understanding of the Book of Revelation. This is the only book of the Bible that contains a promised blessing for those who read it and obey its instructions (Revelation 1:3). Believers are urged to know and understand the Book of Revelation in anticipation of Christ's return. *Revelation Made Easy* is an easy to understand guide to end-time prophecy.

People are often surprised to learn that Revelation has become my favorite biblical book. Christians often associate this book with horrible judgments from God, combined with confusing symbols.

Why do I love the Book of Revelation? In addition to a promised blessing, Revelation reassures us that God is in control—no matter how desperate the times become. This book gives us wonderful glimpses into heavenly worship, points ahead to the Second Coming of Christ, and describes a wonderful eternity for believers. The Book of Revelation also reveals Jesus Christ more completely.

Many are intrigued with such topics as the seven-year tribulation, the antichrist, and the rapture (catching up) of believers. These subjects can lead to interesting discussions. But, the Book of Revelation contains much more than information about end-time events.

Christ Himself appeals to us not to compromise godly values and not to grow weary in our loyalty to God. The Spirit of God repeatedly expresses warnings to congregations to keep their spiritual lights shining bright while surrounded by spiritual darkness. We are encouraged to endure faithfully to the end, no matter how desperate the circumstances.

As you read this book, pray that the Holy Spirit will help you apply various biblical truths to your lifestyle. Also pray that God will help you share these warnings and encouragements with your family, congregation, and others that God brings into your life.

One

Why Should We Study Bible Prophecy?

Many Christians will advise other believers not to study Bible prophecy because such an endeavor may lead to confusion and even dissension concerning various interpretations. However, becoming familiar with many of the basics of biblical prophecy can and should produce positive spiritual results. For example, the Book of Revelation promises a blessing to those who read and study it (Revelation 1:3).

Twenty-eight percent of the Bible was prophetic when it was written.[1] Almost one-third of the Bible was prophetic in nature at the time of its writing. If a Christian does not believe in studying biblical prophecy, he or she has just discarded almost one-third of the Bible.

God has included many prophetic scriptures in the Bible for our benefit and even comfort. No one should study prophecy in order to make wild speculations. Believers should study this subject to better understand many of the things God has intended for us to understand in His word.

There are at least four reasons a Christian should study biblical prophecy:

(1) Fulfilled prophetic scriptures validate the divine origin of the Word of God. The Bible contains hundreds of prophecies that were written centuries before their fulfillment. According to Finis Dake, 3,268 verses containing thousands of details have already been fulfilled.[2]

Until recently, it was possible for unbelievers to contend that the prophecies concerning Christ could have been written after the fact—that is after Christ lived and died. Until the 1940's, the oldest Old Testament manuscripts dated from about 900 A.D. In 1947, many Old Testament scrolls and sectarian manuscripts were discovered in some remote caves in the Judean desert near the Dead Sea. They have come to be known as the Dead

Sea Scrolls. Most of the Dead Sea Scrolls have been determined to predate the Christ of whom they prophesy.[3] This has been done through paleographic, archaeological, and/or chemical analyses (the "carbon-14 test"), as well as through evidence from pottery, chronology, linguistic analysis, and coins.

Some of these scrolls range back as far as the mid-third century B.C., and some even further.

The Dead Sea Scrolls are one illustration of the divine inspiration of the Bible. There are 55 prophetic details concerning Christ the Messiah in the Book of Isaiah alone. A complete Book of Isaiah is included in the Dead Sea Scrolls. These documents have been scientifically determined to predate Christ by hundreds of years. The probabilities against these 55 prophecies about Christ being fulfilled just by chance have been calculated to be one in 36,028,797,018,963,968.[4]

Fulfilled prophecy is strikingly absent in the writings of all other world religions such as Buddhism, Hinduism, Confucius, or the Islamic Koran.[5] However, many biblical prophecies have been fulfilled concerning such things as the rise and fall of cities, nations, and empires. The Bible contains thousands of specific prophecies that have already been fulfilled! This is solid evidence that the Bible is divinely inspired and far superior to all other religious writings on earth.

(2)   Biblical prophecy reveals many of the purposes of God. Many of these purposes are included in the Book of Revelation.

(3)   Knowing basic information about biblical prophecy brings peace to believers. When referring to future things, Jesus told His disciples, "Let not your heart be troubled" (John 14:1). It is reassuring and comforting to know that God has everything under control.

(4)   An understanding of biblical prophecy motivates us to live holy lives; to more effectively serve God; and to share our faith with others as we await Christ's return.

A study of Bible prophecy can be very beneficial spiritually, as well as intellectually.

Two

Some Guidelines for Interpreting the Book of Revelation

The Book of Revelation was written to churches in the province of Asia to correct their errors and to encourage them to hold fast by explaining "the things to come."

The author, John, indicates that he was exiled to the island of Patmos (1:9) off the west coast of Asia Minor (modern Turkey). The Roman Emperor Domitian was persecuting the Christian community.[6] Apparently some Christians were sent into exile because of their faith in Christ. On the "Lord's Day," John was caught up "in the Spirit" (1:10) and saw the visions recorded in this book.

The Central Figure of the Book of Revelation

The central figure is Jesus Christ. The book begins with the words, "The Revelation of Jesus Christ" (1:1). It should not be referred to as the revelation of John the apostle. This book reveals Jesus Christ more fully.

There are three distinct views of Christ in the New Testament:

(1)   In the gospels, Jesus is presented as ***Savior***.
(2)   In the epistles, Jesus is presented as the ***head of the church*** who is in daily relationship with His followers.
(3)   In the Book of Revelation, Jesus is presented as ***triumphant Lord***, King of kings, ruling the earth. This last book in the New Testament completes the overall picture of Christ.

Throughout the Book of Revelation, Christ appears in various images. Each illuminates one of His special functions or characteristics:

- As a **lion** (5:5) representing royal power
- As a **root** (5:5; 22:16), He represents Davidic lineage
- As the **Lamb who was slain** (5:6)
- As the **white horse rider** (19:11) symbolizing victory over evil
- As the **Lord of the world** (2:26; 12:5; 19:15-16)

The main message of the Book of Revelation is that God reigns. Jesus Christ is portrayed as the fulfillment of the hopes of believers, no matter how grim circumstances may appear. The central theme of all biblical prophecy is the person and redemptive work of the Lord Jesus Christ. The Book of Revelation provides comfort by pointing ahead to the Second Coming of Christ.

Four Approaches to Interpreting the Book of Revelation

(1) **Preterist View:** The Book of Revelation has been largely fulfilled in the past.[7] This view holds that these prophecies were fulfilled in the struggles of Jews and early Christians during the Roman Empire, except for chapters 19-22, which await future fulfillment. Some preterists contend that the Book of Revelation refers to the destruction of Jerusalem and the nation of Israel in 70 A.D., and the later destruction of the Roman Empire.

(2) **Historicist View:** The Book of Revelation is symbolic of various stages of church history. This view also holds that the greater part of these prophecies has been fulfilled. However, there is a major problem with this view. Robert H. Gundry has stated that ". . . the explanations of individual symbols vary so widely among interpreters of this school that doubt is cast on the interpretive method itself."[8] In other words, the explanations of these various historical stages vary to such an extent that this method is called into question.

Nevertheless, it is a common belief that the seven churches mentioned in chapters 2 and 3 of Revelation represent seven periods of church history. Gary Cohen summarizes a popular view of the historical periods represented by the seven churches of Revelation:

- Ephesus – Apostolic church (A.D. 30 - 100)
- Smyrna – Persecuted church (A.D. 100 - 313)

- Pergamos – State church (A.D. 313 - 590)
- Thyatira – Papal church (A.D. 590 - 1517)
- Sardis – Reformed church (A.D. 1517 - 1790)
- Philadelphia – Missionary church (A.D. 1790 - 1900)
- Laodicea – Apostate church (A.D. 1900 - Present)[9]

There are various interpretations about the stages in church history that these seven churches may represent. Some believe it is mere speculation to view each of these churches as representing a stage in church history, and that the historical view is not suggested in the text.

(3) **Idealist (spiritual or symbolic) View:** The Book of Revelation is only symbolic of the continual struggle between good and evil. It does not refer to actual historical events, only to spiritual principles.[10]

(4) **Futurist View:** Except for the first three chapters, the Book of Revelation describes events that will occur at the end of this current age. The coming tribulation will immediately be followed by the visible return of Christ to set up His millennial reign on the earth. This will be followed by the final judgment of God, and the eternal state.[11] *Revelation Made Easy* interprets the Book of Revelation from the futurist perspective.

There is a Past, Present, and Future Tense to the Book of Revelation (1:19)

Past: John was instructed to write things that he had seen. This was the vision of Christ in the midst of the candlesticks (chapter 1).

Present: John was instructed to write things that are now (in John's time). This concerned the conditions of the churches in Asia Minor that the book was addressed to (chapters 2 and 3).

Future: John was also instructed to write about future things that would take place hereafter (chapters 4-22).

The events in chapters 4 through 19 take place during the seven-year tribulation period. This is a time when God will pour out judgments upon the earth. Nothing in chapters 4 through 19 have yet been fulfilled.

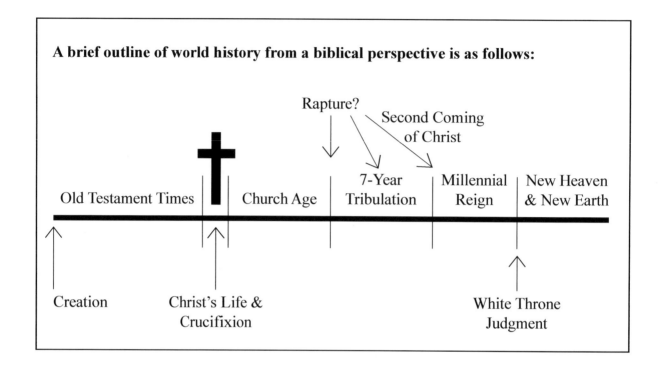

A brief outline of world history from a biblical perspective is as follows:

Division of the Chapters

There is a division of chapters with two stories being told at the same time: a heavenly story and an earthly story.

(1) The heavenly story is about the activities taking place around the throne of God (chapters 4, 5, and parts of 19 and 20).

(2) The earthly story is in chapters 6, 8, 9, 16, and parts of 19 and 20.

Both stories take place simultaneously over a seven-year period.

A few chapters go beyond the seven-year tribulation period into the millennial reign of Christ and into eternity (part of chapter 20 and all of 21 and 22).

There are also informational chapters. These do not necessarily continue the stories that are unfolding. Instead, these chapters are used to enlarge upon details concerning a person, group of people, or a particular event happening in either the heavenly or earthly stories. The informational chapters are 7, 10-15, 17 and 18.

The Series of Judgments in the Book of Revelation

Seven Seal Judgments: The opening of the seven seals on a scroll will initiate judgments of God on the earth. The first four seals are commonly known as the "four horsemen of the Apocalypse." The first six seals are described in chapter 6. The opening of the seventh seal in chapter 8 will introduce the seven trumpet judgments.

Seven Trumpet Judgments: The first four trumpet judgments are described in chapter 8. The fifth and sixth trumpet judgments occur in chapter 9. The seventh trumpet judgment is described in chapter 11. The fifth, sixth, and seventh trumpet judgments are also called the three woes.

Seven Vial (or Bowl) Judgments: These are described in chapter 16. The bowl judgments will be among the last events before the Battle of Armageddon and the Second Coming of Christ.

The Symbolism of Numbers in the Book of Revelation

The Book of Revelation emphasizes groups of threes, sevens and twelves. Three is the number that represents the trinity of God. Three, seven and twelve express perfection and completeness.[12]

John often uses phrases in groups of three (triplets). For example, in 1:5 John describes Jesus Christ as "the faithful witness . . . the first begotten of the dead . . . the prince of the kings of the earth." In 1:18, another triplet appears when Jesus refers to Himself as "he that liveth, and was dead; and . . . I am alive for evermore." We have already mentioned the triplet in 1:19. In that verse, Jesus told John to "Write the things which thou hast seen [past], and the things which are [present], and the things which shall be hereafter [future]." The Book of Revelation is filled with triplets.

The number four is the number of the world.[13] John often refers to the earth using four descriptions. For example, Revelation 5:9 refers to the earth using four expressions: "every kindred, and tongue, and people, and nation." In 10:11, the world is again referred to as "peoples, and nations, and tongues, and kings." Then, 7:1 mentions "the four corners of the earth," which refer to the four directions of north, south, east, and west (Isaiah 11:12).

The number six represents the weakness of man, the evils of Satan, and the manifestation of sin.[14] For example, man was created on the sixth day (Genesis 1:24-31). Man's days of labor each week are supposed to be six (Exodus 20:9-11). Since the number seven represents perfection, the number six falls short of perfection. In Revelation 13:8, the number six is associated with the Antichrist. It represents an incomplete and imperfect system that is associated with Satan (666).

As previously mentioned, the number seven is one of the numbers expressing spiritual perfection and completeness. For example, the seventh day was blessed and sanctified by God (Genesis 2:3). Noah took clean animals into the ark by seven's (Genesis 7:2). On the Day of Atonement, the high priest sprinkled the blood upon the mercy seat seven times (Leviticus 16:14). There are many such examples in scripture. Seven is the most important number in the Book of Revelation. Here are some examples:

- Seven spirits (1:4; 3:1; 4:5; 5:6)
- Seven churches (1:4,20)
- Seven stars (1:16,20; 2:1; 3:1)
- Seven candlesticks (1:12-13,20; 2:1)
- Seven seals (5:1,5)
- Seven eyes (5:6)
- Seven horns (5:6)
- Seven trumpets (8:2,6)
- Seven angels (8:2,6; 15:6-8; 17:1; 21:9)
- Seven thunders (10:3-4)
- Seven plagues (15:1,8; 21:9)
- Seven vials (bowls), (15:7; 17:1; 21:9)
- Seven mountains (17:9)

The number 12 and its multiples also represent completeness, divine authority, administration and governmental perfection. Some examples are Matthew 19:28; Numbers 1:5-16; and 1 Kings 4:7. Examples in the Book of Revelation include 24 thrones with 24 elders (4:4), and the 144,000 witnesses (14:1). In the last two chapters of the Book of Revelation, the descriptions and measurements of the city of New Jerusalem include many uses of the number 12, or multiples of 12:

- 12 gates (21:12,21)
- 12 angels (21:12)
- 12 tribes of Israel (21:12)
- 12 foundations (21:14)
- 12 apostles (21:14)
- 12,000 furlongs (21:16)
- 144 cubits (21:17)
- 12 pearls (21:21)
- 12 types of fruit (22:2)

The redeemed will spend eternity under the perfect leadership and administration of God.

Five Principles for Interpreting Bible Prophecy

(1) **Do not seek hidden or mystical meanings to scripture when this is not called for.**

For example, the mark of the beast probably does not refer to one number, but to a numbering system. In addition, this may not even be a literal mark. However, some Christians have attempted to transliterate the names of famous persons into Greek to see if these names equal "666" and if these persons could possibly be the Antichrist. This is foolish speculation.

(2) **The literal meaning should not be unnecessarily changed to spiritual or symbolic meanings.**

Give scripture a plain and literal meaning unless it is made clear that a double meaning is to be understood. Most of the time, we are to give the same meaning to the words of prophecy that are given to the words of history. Divine prophecy is literally history written beforehand. Simply because it is prophecy does not mean it has some mystical meaning and cannot be understood in the literal sense. For example, Revelation 6:12-17 refers to an earthquake. This is not to be interpreted symbolically as the breaking up of society, as some have suggested. This is a literal earthquake.

Another example is gold, which represents deity in the Bible. When the Book of Revelation mentions a street of gold and gates of pearls in the New Jerusalem (Revelation 21:21), these are literal, not figurative.

(3) **There are times when a word or phrase should be interpreted symbolically.**

Of course, there are metaphors. These are figures of speech that are not literal. Most of these should be easily recognized. For example, when Jesus said, "You are the salt of the earth" (Matthew 5:13), he was not referring to salt in our bodies. He meant that as salt preserves food, Christians are a type of preservative in the world.

Jesus is referred to as the cornerstone of our faith (Psalm 118:22; 1 Corinthians 10:4). He is also referred to as a lamb (Isaiah 53:7; John 1:29; Revelation 5:6). This is figurative language. Christ is not a literal rock or a literal lamb.

There are other types of symbols that may be more difficult to recognize; however, other scriptures help us to interpret these symbols. Although the Book of Revelation uses symbols and figurative language that some believe are difficult to interpret, these need not be a mystery. J. Dwight Pentecost has stated that "Scripture interprets its own symbols."[15] Here are some examples:

SEA: When not speaking about a specific body of water, a sea can be symbolic of great masses of people or nations (Daniel 7:2-3; Revelation 17:1,15).

BEAST: Beasts are sometimes used in scriptures as symbols of kings or kingdoms (Daniel 2:38-39; 7:2-7,17,23). The beast rising from the sea in Revelation 13:1 refers to the rise of a king out of masses of people.

WINDS: Winds can denote wars, strife or judgments (Daniel 7:2; Revelation 7:1-3).

HEADS: Heads can represent kings and kingdoms (Revelation 17:9-10).

HORNS: Horns can also represent kings or rulers (Daniel 7:24).

MOUNTAINS: When the words "mountain" or "hill" are used in Bible prophecy, and a geographic place is not referred to, a kingdom is being referred to. An example is found in Revelation 17:9-10.

THE MYSTERIOUS HARLOT SITTING ON A BEAST WITH SEVEN HEADS AND 10 HORNS in Revelation 17:3-5: The seven heads may refer to great kingdoms of history. The 10 horns refer to lesser future kingdoms. The harlot, associated with the word "mystery" or mystical, is a religious (spiritualistic) system shared by these past and future kingdoms.

(4) **Understand the law of double reference.**

This is where two distinct persons or events are referred to in a passage. For example, in Genesis 3:14-15, God declares judgment on the serpent. But since the serpent was a tool of Satan, God was also speaking to Satan. In other examples, Isaiah 14:12-14 and Ezekiel 28:12-17 address the kings of Babylon and Tyre. These scriptures also refer to Satan's ultimate defeat.

(5) **The prophetic perspective of time must often be noted for two or more events.**

J. Dwight Pentecost has written the following:

> *"Two events, widely separated as to the time of their fulfillment, may be brought together into the scope of one prophecy."*[16]

In other words, sometimes future events are described as if they are continuous when there may be thousands of years between these events. For example, some Old Testament prophecies refer to Christ's first coming, his suffering and crucifixion. Other prophecies in the same passages refer to Christ's Second Coming when he will visibly rule the nations. New Testament revelation makes it clear that some of these events prophesied side-by-side are at least 2,000 years apart. Other prophetic events are grouped together in the same passage, even though they may be separated by centuries. Examples from the Old Testament include prophecies about the Babylonian captivity side-by-side with events of the day of the Lord, the return from Babylon, another dispersion, and another regathering of the Jews to Israel.

Finis Dake has stated that "the prophets see things in the same vision as one would look at a distant range of mountain peaks, where the valleys between them are not seen."[17] In other words, it is as if most biblical prophets were looking at mountain peaks from a distance without observing the valleys in between.

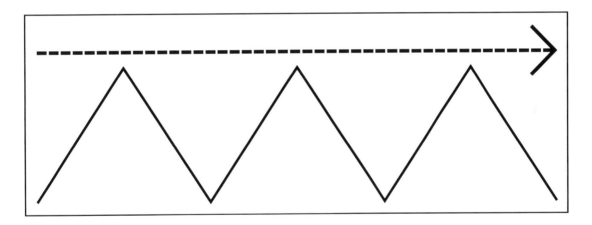

Bible prophecy often has both a near and distant fulfillment. For example, in Matthew, chapter 24, Christ predicted that the Jewish temple and the city of Jerusalem would be destroyed. This was fulfilled in 70 A.D. when the Romans destroyed the city and the temple after a Jewish revolt. However, this prophecy also refers to the destruction of the temple that will exist in Jerusalem during the seven-year tribulation. Jesus uses the tragic events surrounding the destruction of Jerusalem to illustrate the conditions preceding His return in the distant future. The destruction of Jerusalem in 70 A.D. foreshadows the conditions in Israel immediately before Christ's return at the end of the tribulation.

DOLPHIN: Christ's resurrection

Three

Revelation – Chapter 1

Brief Summary

The book begins by stating that this "Revelation of Jesus Christ" reveals future events. The first chapter offers a blessing to those who read and receive this prophecy. Christ's divinity gives believers comfort because He has future events under control. His promise to return is one of the themes of this book.

Christ appeared to the Apostle John. The hair of Jesus was "white as snow." His eyes were "as a flame of fire." His feet were like "fine brass." His voice was "as the sound of many waters."

Each of the seven local churches mentioned in the Book of Revelation received a unique message from Christ, which was part of chapters 2 or 3. All these churches also received a copy of the entire Book of Revelation (1:11).

Introduction

1   The Revelation of Jesus Christ, which God gave unto him, to shew unto his servants things which must shortly come to pass; and he sent and signified it by his angel unto his servant John:

2   Who bare record of the word of God, and of the testimony of Jesus Christ, and of all things that he saw.

3   Blessed is he that readeth, and they that hear the words of this prophecy, and keep those things which are written therein: for the time is at hand.

It is "The Revelation of Jesus Christ." This book reveals future events concerning the tribulation period and Christ's return to establish His kingdom on earth.

Verse 3 tells us that those who read this book will be blessed. It is the will of God for every believer to have at least a general understanding of the Book of Revelation. We are also instructed to keep the things that are in this book; therefore, we must know it and understand it. Most important of all, studying this book should draw us closer to Christ. The phrase "the time is at hand" is an urgent call to obedience.

> 4   John to the seven churches which are in Asia: Grace be unto you, and peace, from him which is, and which was, and which is to come; and from the seven Spirits which are before his throne;

The messages to these seven churches in Asia Minor are also meant for churches throughout the Church Age. The statement, "from Him which is, and which was, and which is to come" refers to the eternal nature of God.

Verse 4 includes the phrase "the seven Spirits which are before His throne." Revelation 4:5 and 5:6 also refer to "the seven Spirits of God." We know from Ephesians 4:4-6 that there is only one Holy Spirit. Why is the term "seven Spirits of God" used? Some believe this symbolizes the different manifestations, operations, and aspects of the Holy Spirit. In Isaiah 11:2, seven titles of the Holy Spirit are mentioned:

(1)   The Spirit of the Lord
(2)   The Spirit of wisdom
(3)   The Spirit of understanding
(4)   The Spirit of counsel
(5)   The Spirit of might
(6)   The Spirit of knowledge
(7)   The Spirit of the fear of the Lord

However, Revelation 1:4 does not symbolize seven titles of the Holy Spirit, since there are many more than seven titles given to the Spirit of God. Some additional titles of the Holy Spirit are the following:

- Spirit of grace (Hebrews 10:29)
- Spirit of adoption (Romans 8:15)

- Spirit of holiness (Romans 1:4)
- Spirit of supplication (Zechariah 12:10)
- Spirit of truth (John 16:13)
- Spirit of glory (1 Peter 4:14)

The number seven denotes completeness. When related to God the number seven also denotes spiritual perfection. Here the number seven represents the Holy Spirit and the perfection of His activities.

> 5   and from Jesus Christ, who is the faithful witness, and the first begotten
> of the dead, and the prince of the kings of the earth. Unto him that loved us, and
> washed us from our sins in his own blood,

God has raised others from the dead, but later those people died again. Jesus was the first to be raised from the dead with a body that would never die again (1 Corinthians 15:20). He is the first of millions who will come back to life someday. Christ loves us and His blood cleanses us from sin.

Jesus is represented in a threefold way:

(1)   Christ is a "faithful witness," which refers primarily to His ministry on the earth in teaching, preaching, and healing as the prophet and witness of God.

(2)   He is referred to as "the first begotten of the dead" (Colossians 1:15-18; 1 Corinthians 15:20-23). Christ was the first to rise from the dead with a glorified body. Neither Enoch, Moses, Elijah, nor anyone else was resurrected with glorifed bodies before Christ.

(3)   He is called "the prince of the kings of the earth." Prince, here, means "ruler" as in Daniel 10:13-20. This refers to Christ's eternal reign as Messiah and King.

> 6   And hath made us kings and priests unto God and his Father; to him be
> glory and dominion for ever and ever. Amen.

Believers are co-heirs with Christ (Romans 8:14-17). True Christians are also currently a "royal priesthood" (1 Peter 2:9). Our roles as kings and priests will be completely fulfilled in the future (2 Timothy 2:12; Revelation 5:10; 20:4, 6). With Christ, we shall own all things and administer the affairs of the universe (Daniel 7:18-22, 27; 1 Corinthians 6:2-3). We will reign with Him. This becomes more apparent toward the end of the Book of Revelation.

The Promise of Christ's Second Coming

> 7   Behold, he cometh with clouds; and every eye shall see him, and they also which pierced him: and all kindreds of the earth shall wail because of him. Even so, Amen.

This is not referring to the rapture. Instead, it is referring to Christ's Second Coming after the seven-year tribulation, when He returns to rule the earth for a millennium (1,000 years).

At the rapture, Christ appears personally in the air to meet the raptured believers. He does not touch the earth (1 Thessalonians 4:16-18). It appears that the rapture is hidden from the sight of undiscerning persons.

At the Second Coming, Christ appears visibly to people on the earth, along with the believers from heaven who return with Him.

- He will come in power and glory to judge His enemies, and He will be visible (Joel 3:11; Zechariah 14:5; Matthew 16:27; 24:29-31; Mark 13:26; Luke 21:27; Colossians 3:4; 1 Thessalonians 3:13; 1 John 3:2; Revelation 19:11-20:2).
- At the Second Coming, Jesus will stand on the Mount of Olives near Jerusalem (Zechariah 14:4-5; Revelation 1:7).
- He shall bring His saints with Him (Joel 3:11; 1 Thessalonians 3:13; Jude 14).
- Satan will then be bound in the Lake of Fire (Revelation 20:1-2; Romans 16:20).
- Seated upon a throne of glory, Christ will review the nations of the earth (Joel 3:11-17; Matthew 25:31-46; Acts 17:31; 2 Thessalonians 1:7-10).
- At the Second Coming, Christ will begin to rule the earth for 1,000 years. This is known as the Millennium (Revelation 20:2-7).

The Second Coming of Jesus is announced three times in the Book of Revelation. It is announced at the beginning (1:7), in the middle (11:15-18), and at the end (22:20). Christ's Second Coming is described in Revelation 19:11-21. At Christ's Second Coming, everyone on earth shall witness His return as it occurs (Matthew 24:30-31; Revelation 1:7).

John's Vision of Christ

> 8   I am Alpha and Omega, the beginning and the ending, saith the Lord, which is, and which was, and which is to come, the Almighty.
> 9   I John, who also am your brother, and companion in tribulation, and in the kingdom and patience of Jesus Christ, was in the isle that is called Patmos, for the

word of God, and for the testimony of Jesus Christ.

10   I was in the Spirit on the Lord's day, and heard behind me a great voice, as of a trumpet,

11   Saying, I am Alpha and Omega, the first and the last: and, What thou seest, write in a book, and send it unto the seven churches which are in Asia; unto Ephesus, and unto Smyrna, and unto Pergamos, and unto Thyatira, and unto Sardis, and unto Philadelphia, and unto Laodicea.

12   And I turned to see the voice that spake with me. And being turned, I saw seven golden candlesticks;

Alpha is the first letter of the Greek alphabet and Omega is the last letter. The Almighty God of the Old Testament is described as the beginning and the end, the first and the last (Isaiah 41:4; 44:6; 48:12). In Revelation 1:8, Jesus is claiming equality with the Father (Revelation 1:8,11,18; 22:13). Jesus is the Almighty Jehovah God of the Old Testament.

God seals this prophecy of the Book of Revelation with the authority of His own name.

John was a prisoner on the Island of Patmos, which was a small rocky island off the western coast of Asia Minor, about thirty miles southwest of Ephesus. The Romans used Patmos as a place to banish criminals.[18] These prisoners were forced to work in the mines and quarries of the island. John was sent to Patmos as a criminal for preaching the gospel of Christ.

The phrase "in the Spirit" refers to a special spiritual sensitivity. John was apparently seeking the Lord in prayer when Christ appeared to him.

The expression the "Lord's day" was used during the first century A.D. for the day set apart to worship the Lord.[19] It refers to Sunday, the day of the Lord's resurrection (Matthew 28:1; John 20:19). It also refers to the first day of the week when believers usually met (Acts 20:7; 1 Corinthians 16:2). Early Christians expressed their belief in Christ's resurrection by meeting on Sunday, not the Jewish Sabbath of Saturday.

Verse 20 tells us that the seven candlesticks represent the seven churches that the book addresses.

The messages to the churches are often incorrectly referred to as "letters." This implies separate communications to each church. In Revelation 1:11, John is commanded to send the entire contents of this book to these churches. This means that each church received the messages addressed to the other six churches, as well as the entire book.

> 13   And in the midst of the seven candlesticks one like unto the Son of man, clothed with a garment down to the foot, and girt about the paps with a golden girdle.

Since verse 20 tells us that the seven candlesticks are the seven churches, Christ is described as being in the midst of the churches. He is, in fact, head of the church (Ephesians 1:20-23; 2:19-22; 5:22-23). The term "Son of man" refers to the exalted Christ (Daniel 7:13; Matthew 26:64; Luke 21:27; John 1:51).

In verse 13, the New International Version states He had "a golden sash around His chest." Christ's clothing symbolizes priestly royalty. He is our high priest who intercedes for us in God's presence to obtain forgiveness for the sins of believers. His clothing represents royal priesthood.

> 14   His head and his hairs were white like wool, as white as snow; and his eyes were as a flame of fire;
> 15   And his feet like unto fine brass, as if they burned in a furnace; and his voice as the sound of many waters.

The white hair indicates His wisdom and divine nature (Daniel 7:9). His flaming eyes symbolize judgment of all evil, and possibly His infinite knowledge (omniscience). His bronze-like feet probably represent the judgmental activity of stomping on His enemies. The symbolism of the brass is consistent with the brazen altar of the Old Testament tabernacle, where sin was judged.

"His voice was as the sound of many waters." Several scriptures mention this attribute of God (Psalm 29:4,10; Ezekiel 1:24; 43:2; Revelation 19:6). Many waters represent His divine authority.

> 16   And he had in his right hand seven stars: and out of his mouth went a sharp two-edged sword: and his countenance was as the sun shineth in his strength.

Verse 20 also tells us that the seven stars represent the angels of the seven churches. The Greek word translated "angels" primarily means "messengers." The idea that these angels are actually the seven pastors is made clear in chapters 2 and 3. In these chapters, John is instructed to address these messages to the angel (messenger) of each church (2:1, 8, 12, 18; 3:1, 7, 14). The fact that the messages to the seven angels include rebukes supports the idea that these angels refer to the pastors of these churches, not heavenly messengers.

The two-edged sword represents Christ's word. Verse 16 states that "out of His mouth went a sharp two-edged sword." This sword is a symbol of the power of the Word of God (Ephesians 6:17; Hebrews 4:12). A two-edged sword cuts both ways. The Word of God will either cut away sin from the churches bringing them closer to Christ, or eventually bring judgment. The power of His spoken word is as sharp as swords (Isaiah 49:2; Hebrews 4:12).

Verse 16 also indicates that Christ's face was shining like the brilliance of the sun. This refers to the divine nature and glory of Christ. Here, John saw Jesus in all of his glory, just like on the Mount of Transfiguration (Matthew 17:1-2). His shining face represents the glory of His deity.

> 17   And when I saw him, I fell at his feet as dead. And he laid his right hand upon me, saying unto me, Fear not; I am the first and the last:
> 18   I am he that liveth, and was dead; and, behold, I am alive for evermore, Amen; and have the keys of hell and of death.

Verse 18 clearly identifies the person in this vision as Christ. In this verse, Christ refers to His own death and resurrection. The keys signify power and authority (Matthew 16:19; Isaiah 22:22). Jesus has authority over death and hell. Jesus is Lord over all the realms of life and death. Jesus is the only one who can deliver us from the bondage of sin.

God is "the first" and "the last" (Isaiah 44:6; 48:12). Since Jesus is also "the first and the last" (Revelation 1:17-18; 2:8; 22:13), the correct conclusion is that Jesus is God. Jesus is not a lesser-created being. He is Almighty God. We look to Christ Jesus for our salvation. It is only through Him that we can live in God's eternal kingdom.

The Past, Present, and Future in the Book of Revelation

> 19   Write the things which thou hast seen, and the things which are, and the things which shall be hereafter;

John was instructed to write things that he had seen. This was the vision of Christ in the midst of the candlesticks (chapter 1: The *past*).

John was instructed to write things that are now (in John's time). This concerned the conditions of the churches in Asia Minor that the book was addressed to (chapters 2 and 3: This was the *present* in John's time).

John was also instructed to write about *future* things that would take place hereafter (chapters 4-22).

> 20   The mystery of the seven stars which thou sawest in my right hand, and the seven golden candle sticks. The seven stars are the angels of the seven churches: and the seven candlesticks which thou sawest are the seven churches.

The candlesticks symbolize true Bible believing churches that hold forth the light of the Word of God in this darkened world (Matthew 5:14-16).

As previously mentioned, the Greek word translated "angels" primarily means "messengers" and refers to the pastors of these seven churches. The idea that the angels are actually the seven pastors is made clear in chapters 2 and 3. In these chapters, John is instructed to address these messages to the angel (messenger) of each church (2:1, 8, 12, 18; 3:1, 7, 14). As previously mentioned, the messages to the seven angels include rebukes. This supports the idea that these angels refer to the pastors of these churches, not heavenly messengers. Pastors and their churches must effectively manifest the light of Christ.

The Threefold Application of the Messages to the Seven Churches

(1) *An application to the churches addressed in chapters 2 and 3.*
These seven messages portray actual conditions in seven local churches that existed in John's day.

(2) *A prophetic application to many other churches.*
These messages address churches throughout the Church Age, revealing possible spiritual conditions in many churches. This point is clear from the fact that the book is a "prophecy." Like other New Testament epistles, these messages are applicable to situations in churches today.

(3) *An application to individuals.*
Individuals throughout the Church Age are warned so they may profit by looking at the failures of these seven churches

NOAH'S ARK: Symbolic of the Church

Four

Revelation – Chapter 2

Brief Summary of Revelation, Chapters 2 and 3

Chapters 2 and 3 contain messages that Christ dictated to the Apostle John, addressing seven actual churches in Asia Minor. These churches were located in the following cities: Ephesus, Smyrna, Pergamos, Thyatira, Sardis, Philadelphia, and Laodicea. With a few exceptions, the messages tend to follow the same pattern:

- *Praise* for good works or attitudes
- *Condemnation* for shortcomings
- *Instruction* with a call to repentance
- *Promise* to those who remain faithful

Christ had no praise for the church in Laodicea. He also had no condemnation for the churches in Smyrna and Philadelphia.

In chapter 2, Christ confronts the church at Ephesus with the fact that this congregation had lost its original spiritual fervor. There was no condemnation for the church at Smyrna, but Christ warned them of coming persecution. Christ appealed to the churches at Pergamos and Thyatira to repent of false and immoral teachings, exhorting them to overcome these temptations.

The Message to the Church at Ephesus

The city of Ephesus had one of the seven wonders of the ancient world, the temple of Artemis (Diana to the Romans).[20] The worship of this goddess included prostitution and mutilation rituals.

1   Unto the angel of the church of Ephesus write; These things saith he that holdeth the seven stars in his right hand, who walketh in the midst of the seven golden candlesticks;

2   I know thy works, and thy labour, and thy patience, and how thou canst not bear them which are evil: and thou hast tried them which say they are apostles, and are not, and hast found them liars:

3   And hast borne, and hast patience, and for my name's sake hast laboured, and hast not fainted.

4   Nevertheless I have somewhat against thee, because thou hast left thy first love.

5   Remember therefore from whence thou art fallen, and repent, and do the first works; or else I will come unto thee quickly, and will remove thy candlestick out of his place, except thou repent.

6   But this thou hast, that thou hatest the deeds of the Nicolaitans, which I also hate.

7   He that hath an ear, let him hear what the Spirit saith unto the churches; To him that overcometh will I give to eat of the tree of life, which is in the midst of the paradise of God.

Christ is described as holding the "seven stars in his right hand." These seven stars refer to the human messengers, or pastors, of the seven churches (see the comments under Revelation 1:20). Christ alone is the head of all true Bible believing congregations. Christ had several good things to say about this church. The people in this congregation:

(1)   Produced good works
(2)   Labored in patience without quitting
(3)   Resisted sin by not tolerating those who work evil
(4)   Discerned false apostles
(5)   "Hast borne," meaning they were bearing up, in patience, under resistance and persecution
(6)   Endured hardships

Unfortunately, most of the believers in Ephesus had lost their original spiritual fervor because they had lost their first love. Their spiritual health and enthusiasm had deteriorated into a mere routine. Many Christians have allowed this to happen in their lives. As we battle to maintain sound doctrine and moral purity, we must make sure our love and fervor for Christ does not decrease. We must strive not to become preoccupied with other things to the point that our relationship with Christ suffers.

As we saw in chapter 1, verse 20, these candlesticks represent the seven churches. Christ would remove their lamp stand because of sin unless they repented. For Jesus to remove their lamp stand meant that the church would cease to have an effective outreach to the surrounding culture. A congregation may continue to exist without being a light to its community. This removal may also refer to judgment and destruction. Every Bible believing church must strive never to let the light of the gospel go out in its congregation.

The Nicolaitans were probably Gnostics who denied Christ's humanity. They taught that salvation was received by attaining mystical knowledge. The Nicolaitans also believed that the sharing of wives, adultery and fornication in general was not sinful.[21] They denied the reality of sin.

The idea of overcoming suggests combat and spiritual warfare against the forces of evil (Ephesians 6:10-18). Eventually, believers will be totally delivered from evil and live in a paradise forever.

The tree of life symbolizes spiritual nourishment that supports and maintains eternal life. It also suggests the extremely close fellowship that God had with humans in the Garden of Eden, before sin entered the world. Overcomers are promised that they will eat of the tree of life in paradise (Revelation 22:2). This tree is a symbol of eternal life. Believers will eat, while in a glorified state, throughout eternity (Matthew 26:29; Luke 24:41-43; Revelation 19:9).

The Message to the Church at Smyrna

The city of Smyrna was one of the most beautiful cities in Asia Minor. Smyrna was a center of Caesar worship. This city was known for a perfume that was also called Smyrna.[22]

8   And unto the angel of the church in Smyrna write; These things saith the first and the last, which was dead, and is alive;

9   I know thy works, and tribulation, and poverty, (but thou art rich) and I know the blasphemy of them which say they are Jews, and are not, but are the synagogue of Satan.

10   Fear none of those things which thou shalt suffer: behold, the devil shall cast some of you into prison, that ye may be tried; and ye shall have tribulation ten days: be thou faithful unto death, and I will give thee a crown of life.

11   He that hath an ear, let him hear what the Spirit saith unto the churches; He that overcometh shall not be hurt of the second death.

Christ commended this church for three things:

(1)   Good works
(2)   Endurance in tribulation
(3)   Though many of them were poor financially, they were rich in the Lord.

There was a group of people in Smyrna who claimed to be Jews, but they were not. These people ended up serving Satan's purposes. This made it difficult for Christians in that city. The New Testament definition of a true Jew is one who is circumcised "in the spirit" (Romans 2:29). Apparently there were those in this city who pretended to be Jewish believers in Jesus Christ, but who eventually persecuted Christians.

Christ had no condemnation of this church. There was also no appeal for repentance. Ten days indicates that the coming persecution would last a relatively short time.

A crown of life refers to the eternal joy given to one who is victorious. A "crown of righteousness" is promised to all believers who remain true (2 Timothy 4:8). Instead of allowing difficulties to turn us away from God, we should firmly decide to draw closer to God during these times. It helps when we remember our heavenly reward (Revelation 22:12-14).

The second death is eternal separation from God (Revelation 20:6, 14-15; John 5:29; Daniel 12:2). The overcomer is promised eternal life. The one who overcomes is the one who trusts in Jesus. Overcomers will not be hurt by the second death. The second death and the lake of fire are synonymous (Revelation 20:14-15; 21:8).

The Message to the Church at Pergamos

Pergamos was the capital city of Asia Minor. It was also the site of the famous temple of Aesculapius, the Greek god of healing. People traveled long distances in the hope of being healed in this pagan temple.[23]

> 12   And to the angel of the church in Pergamos write; These things saith he which hath the sharp sword with two edges;
> 13   I know thy works, and where thou dwellest, even where Satan's seat is: and thou holdest fast my name, and hast not denied my faith, even in those days wherein Antipas was my faithful martyr, who was slain among you, where Satan dwelleth.
> 14   But I have a few things against thee, because thou hast there them that hold the doctrine of Balaam, who taught Balac to cast a stumbling block before the children of Israel, to eat things sacrificed unto idols, and to commit fornication.

15   So hast thou also them that hold the doctrine of the Nicolaitans, which thing I hate.

16   Repent; or else I will come unto thee quickly, and will fight against them with the sword of my mouth.

17   He that hath an ear, let him hear what the Spirit saith unto the churches; To him that overcometh will I give to eat of the hidden manna, and will give him a white stone, and in the stone a new name written, which no man knoweth saving he that receiveth it.

The phrase "Satan's seat" probably refers to a center of Satan worship. This may also refer to a 200-foot-high altar to the Greek god Zeus, or to the fact that Pergamos was a center of emperor worship. In addition, it may refer to the center of worship of Aesclepius, a god of healing. The symbol of this god was a serpent. In scripture, Satan is often symbolized as a serpent. Whatever the exact meaning of "Satan's seat," it is obvious that this church was surrounded by a culture of non-Christian values.

Antipas was apparently a Christian who was martyred for his faith.

This church was commended for three things:

(1)   Good works
(2)   Holding fast to Christ's name
(3)   Not denying the faith

Christ had four condemnations for this church.

First, some of them held to the doctrine of Balaam. In the Old Testament, Balaam was a false prophet who advised a heathen king, Balek, to encourage Moabite women to seduce the men of Israel. This produced a spiritual disaster for God's people (Numbers 22-25 and 31:15-16). In this church, there were corrupt teachers and preachers who were leading people into immorality by teaching the doctrine of Balaam.

Second, many of them were eating things sacrificed to idols. Apparently, this was mixed with the worship of demons and false doctrines. It was not just referring to food purchased in a market that may have been previously sacrificed to idols. Eating things purchased in a market that were previously sacrificed to idols was not wrong in itself; however, it could offend weaker believers, causing them to stumble (1 Corinthians 8:1-4, 7-13; Romans 14:2). Here in Revelation, chapter 2, the food being discussed was probably associated directly with demon worship by so-called believers and the practices of false teachers.

Third, at least some in this church were committing fornication, that is, they were engaged in sexual relationships outside the bonds of marriage.

Fourth, some of them were holding to the doctrine of the Nicolaitans. As previously mentioned, the Nicolaitans were probably Gnostics who denied the humanity of Christ while He was on the earth. They taught that salvation was received by attaining mystical knowledge. The doctrine of the Nicolaitans also contributed to their sins of fornication, because they believed that the sharing of wives, adultery and fornication in general was not sinful. They denied the reality of sin.

Repentance is required of all backsliders. We must always hold fast to the truth, desiring holiness. Christians who compromise with the world are sowing a negative harvest that they will severely regret. God will withhold His blessings from carnal Christians. Continual sin will produce much heartache, even in the lives of believers.

Only the overcomer is promised heaven (Revelation 2:7, 11, 17, 26; 3:5, 12, 21). Christ promises three things to believers who are overcomers:

(1)   Manna – Since manna is always a type of Christ in the scriptures, this refers to eternal spiritual life through the Son of God. Jesus is the bread of life that provides believers with eternal spiritual nourishment (John 6:51).

(2)   A white stone – The white stone had three meanings to ancient peoples.[24]

- It was known as a victory stone.
- White stones also symbolized a pardon, or an acquittal.
- Conquerors in the public games were sometimes given white stones with their name on them. This entitled them to be supported the rest of their lives at public expense.

   Perhaps all three meanings of the white stone apply, signifying the triumph that accompanies faith and devotion to Christ.

(3)   A new name – A new name is also referred to in Revelation 3:12; Isaiah 62:2 and 65:15. This new name refers to a new eternal identity with the character of Christ.

The Message to the Church at Thyatira

The city of Thyatira was a small town of little importance compared to the other six cities. It was known for its cloth industry.[25] Acts 16:14 states that the apostle Paul met a business woman, Lydia, who was a dealer in purple cloth from Thyatira.

18   And unto the angel of the church in Thyatira write; These things saith the Son of God, who hath his eyes like unto a flame of fire, and his feet are like fine brass;

19   I know thy works, and charity, and service, and faith, and thy patience, and thy works; and the last to be more than the first.

20   Notwithstanding I have a few things against thee, because thou sufferest that woman Jezebel, which calleth herself a prophetess, to teach and to seduce my servants to commit fornication, and to eat things sacrificed unto idols.

21   And I gave her space to repent of her fornication; and she repented not.

22   Behold, I will cast her into a bed, and them that commit adultery with her into great tribulation, except they repent of their deeds.

23   And I will kill her children with death; and all the churches shall know that I am he which searcheth the reins and hearts: and I will give unto every one of you according to your works.

24   But unto you I say, and unto the rest in Thyatira, as many as have not this doctrine, and which have not known the depths of Satan, as they speak; I will put upon you none other burden.

25   But that which ye have already hold fast till I come.

This church was commended for six things:

(1)   Good works
(2)   Charity (acts of love)
(3)   Service
(4)   Faith
(5)   Patience
(6)   Their good works had increased until they were more than their first works

A false teacher had declared herself to be a prophetess. She taught that it was acceptable to commit fornication. Either this woman was named Jezebel, or the Lord was comparing her symbolically to the evil Jezebel that lived during the time of Elijah. In any event, they were permitting this woman to teach in the church while she was seducing Christians to commit fornication. She also encouraged Christians to eat things sacrificed to idols.

As previously stated in our discussion about the church at Pergamos, this food was probably associated with demon worship by so-called believers, and the practices of false teachers. It is not just referring to food purchased in a market that may have been previously sacrificed to idols. The Lord said that He would judge Jezebel. She would be cast into "a bed" of suffering and sickness, as Job was (Job 33:19).

"Her children" refers to the followers of Jezebel. God searches the "reins and hearts." This is figurative language, meaning that God searches the innermost minds of people. "The depths of Satan" refers to the immoral teachings associated with the false teacher referred to as "Jezebel." When Christ exhorted believers to "hold fast until I come," His messages, warnings and promises to the seven churches also apply to all churches throughout the Church Age.

> 26   And he that overcometh, and keepeth my works unto the end, to him will I give power over the nations:
> 27   And he shall rule them with a rod of iron; as the vessels of a potter shall they be broken to shivers: even as I received of my Father.
> 28   And I will give him the morning star.
> 29   He that hath an ear, let him hear what the Spirit saith unto the churches.

During the Millennium, overcomers will rule and reign with Christ over the nations, crushing all resistance like pottery (Revelation 20:4-6; Daniel 7:18).

Overcomers will be given the morning star as their ultimate reward. A morning star appears just before dawn, when the night is the coldest and darkest. When the world is in its darkest hour spiritually, Christ will suddenly appear to visibly usher in the kingdom of God on earth. The morning star is Christ (Revelation 22:16). He is the light of salvation.

FLEUR-DE-LIS: The human and divine Christ, Philippians 2:5-8

Five

Revelation – Chapter 3

Brief Summary

Chapter 3 continues with the messages that Christ dictated to the Apostle John, addressing some actual churches in Asia Minor. Christ promises the church at Sardis that the overcomers will receive recognition in heaven, and their names will never be blotted out of God's Book of Life. He also encourages the church at Philadelphia to hold fast to the things of God, looking for Christ's return. Finally, Christ makes an appeal to the church in Laodicea not to be lukewarm spiritually, and not to refuse Him entrance into their midst.

The Message to the Church at Sardis

The city of Sardis was noted for its immorality.[26]

1   And unto the angel of the church in Sardis write; These things saith he that hath the seven Spirits of God, and the seven stars; I know thy works, that thou hast a name that thou livest, and art dead.

2   Be watchful, and strengthen the things which remain, that are ready to die: for I have not found thy works perfect before God.

3   Remember therefore how thou hast received and heard, and hold fast, and repent. If therefore thou shalt not watch, I will come on thee as a thief, and thou shalt not know what hour I will come upon thee.

4   Thou hast a few names even in Sardis which have not defiled their garments; and they shall walk with me in white: for they are worthy.

> 5   He that overcometh, the same shall be clothed in white raiment; and I will not blot out his name out of the book of life, but I will confess his name before my Father, and before his angels.
>
> 6   He that hath an ear, let him hear what the Spirit saith unto the churches.

Revelation 1:4; 4:5 and 5:6 also refer to "the seven Spirits of God." As previously discussed, the seven Spirits of God refer to the perfect ministry of the Holy Spirit (see the comments under 1:4).

Revelation 1:20 also makes it clear that the stars refer to angels of these churches. The Greek word translated "angels" primarily means "messengers." The idea that these angels are actually the seven pastors is made clear in Christ's instructions to address these messages to the angel (messenger) of each church (2:1, 8, 12; 3:1, 7, 14). The fact that the messages to the seven churches include rebukes supports the idea that these angels refer to the pastors of these churches, not heavenly messengers.

This church had a reputation for being spiritually alive, but many in the congregation were spiritually dead. Verse 4 indicates that this church only had a few godly members who remained faithful to Christ. Otherwise, Christ had nothing good to say about this church.

A church needs to remain alive by the power of God's Word and the Holy Spirit, and not become worldly. Also, when a church stops evangelizing and growing, it begins to die. Christ had five commands for this church:

(1)   Be watchful
(2)   Strengthen the things that remain
(3)   Remember your teaching
(4)   Hold fast
(5)   Repent

Christ's coming as a thief in the night refers to the rapture of the church (1 Thessalonians 4:16-17). For the church in Sardis, it may have also meant Christ sending sudden judgment if they did not repent.

The names of overcomers will not be blotted out of God's Book of Life (Exodus 32:32-33; Psalm 69:28; Revelation 22:18-19). The overcomer is promised that he will be clothed in white raiment and have his name confessed before God and the angels.

The Message to the Church at Philadelphia

The city of Philadelphia was located near much volcanic activity and was destroyed several times by earthquakes.[27] In verse 12, Christ gave them a promise that they would someday dwell in a city from which they would not have to flee – the New Jerusalem. This must have been a source of comfort to them.

> 7   And to the angel of the church in Philadelphia write; These things saith he that is holy, he that is true, he that hath the key of David, he that openeth, and no man shutteth; and shutteth, and no man openeth;
>
> 8   I know thy works: behold, I have set before thee an open door, and no man can shut it: for thou hast a little strength, and hast kept my word, and hast not denied my name.

In ancient times a key expressed the idea of authority, power or privilege (Isaiah 22:22; Matthew 16:19; Revelation 1:18). The "key of David" signifies the authority possessed by Christ. Jesus has the authority to open the door of invitation into His kingdom. After the door is opened, no one else can close it. After the door is shut, no one else can open it and judgment is certain. Christ controls all opportunities to serve Him.

God had set before them an open door. The door may have referred to opportunities of service and evangelization (1 Corinthians 16:9; 2 Corinthians 2:12). The door may have also referred to entrance into God's eternal kingdom. Perhaps both meanings are applicable.

Christ said three good things about this church. They had:

(1)   Some spiritual strength
(2)   Kept God's Word
(3)   Not denied the name of Christ

Christ had no condemnations of this church. However, this church was not as strong as it should have been. Many churches today are also not as strong in the Word of God and spiritual sensitivity as they need to be.

> 9   Behold, I will make them of the synagogue of Satan, which say they are Jews, and are not, but do lie; behold, I will make them to come and worship before thy feet, and to know that I have loved thee.

> 10   Because thou hast kept the word of my patience, I also will keep thee from the hour of temptation, which shall come upon all the world, to try them that dwell upon the earth.
>
> 11   Behold, I come quickly: hold that fast which thou hast, that no man take thy crown.

The believers in this church kept "the word of my patience," which refers to godly doctrine. This caused them to be persecuted. Although Jewish synagogues were supposed to be dedicated to the one true God, many local Jews were very hostile to the gospel of Christ. They unknowingly became tools of Satan in persecuting believers in Christ.

Verse 10 states that this church would be kept from the hour of temptation, which would come upon the entire world. Some believe that verse 10 refers to deliverance of the church from the seven-year tribulation by the rapture. Others believe that this refers to a local persecution, because chapters 2 and 3 are discussing events in John's time. However, verse 11 does refer to the future rapture of the church, since it implies heavenly rewards.

> 12   Him that overcometh will I make a pillar in the temple of my God, and he shall go no more out: and I will write upon him the name of my God, and the name of the city of my God, which is new Jerusalem, which cometh down out of heaven from my God: and I will write upon him my new name.
>
> 13   He that hath an ear, let him hear what the Spirit saith unto the churches.

Pillar here is used figuratively of stability and authority, as in Galatians 2:9 and 1 Timothy 3:15. "Temple" refers to the eternal household of the redeemed (Ephesians 2:19-22).

The New Jerusalem is later described in Revelation 21:2, 9-27; 22:1-5. It is the future dwelling place for the people of God.

The leaders of a city often honored someone by erecting a pillar in a temple with the name of the person inscribed on it. The Lord will honor those who are faithful to Him by inscribing on them the name of God, the New Jerusalem, and the name of Christ. Thus, faithful believers will be identified throughout eternity as priceless possessions of God.

The Message to the Church at Laodicea

The city of Laodicea was known as a rich banking center.[28] Laodicea was also a tourist center because of its hot mineral baths. In addition, this city manufactured an ointment that was thought to improve both eyesight and hearing.[29] In view of this, it is interesting that Christ instructed them to buy of Him "gold tried in the fire" and "to anoint thine eyes with eye-salve, that thou mayest see" (verse 18).

> 14   And unto the angel of the church of the Laodiceans write; These things saith the Amen, the faithful and true witness, the beginning of the creation of God;
>
> 15   I know thy works, that thou art neither cold nor hot: I would thou wert cold or hot.
>
> 16   So then because thou art lukewarm, and neither cold nor hot, I will spue thee out of my mouth.

The "beginning of creation" refers to the source of creation. Christ is not a created being. He is the origin, author and source of God's creation (John 1:3; Colossians 1:15-18; Hebrews 1:2).

Lukewarm water is a disgusting drink. The church at Laodicea had become lukewarm and therefore distasteful to the Lord. We must always be totally committed to God because He will reject the spiritually lukewarm. Lukewarm can be nauseating. "Spue" means to vomit, with sickening implied. That is how God feels about lukewarm Christians. Christ exhorted them to be really committed to the things of God.

The most common interpretation of this passage is that "cold" and "lukewarm" are both very bad spiritual conditions. However, in the context, "hot" and "cold" are both good conditions. Only "lukewarm" is bad. Laodicea was near the city of Hieropolis, which was known for its hot springs.[30] These hot springs were recognized for their powers to heal and restore health. Also nearby was the city of Colossae, known for its cold drinking water that came from mountains that were snow covered all year.[31] These cold waters were known to be refreshing and uplifting. The hot water of Hieropolis and the cold water of Colossae were both considered very good.

Laodicea had poor tasting mineral water that was neither cold nor hot. After flowing from the hot springs through an aqueduct to Laodicea, this water was tepid and nauseating.[32] God wants us to be like hot water to help heal and restore people. He also wants us to be like cool water that refreshes, uplifts and encourages people. God wants us to be both hot (healing) and cold (uplifting), but not lukewarm.

> 17 Because thou sayest, I am rich, and increased with goods, and have need
> of nothing; and knowest not that thou art wretched, and miserable, and poor, and
> blind, and naked:
> 18 I counsel thee to buy of me gold tried in the fire, that thou mayest be rich;
> and white raiment, that thou mayest be clothed, and that the shame of thy naked-
> ness do not appear; and anoint thine eyes with eyesalve, that thou mayest see.
> 19 As many as I love, I rebuke and chasten: be zealous therefore, and repent.

Their wealth had caused them to become proud and spiritually indifferent. Christ had no words of praise for this church. But he did say six condemning things about the Laodiceans. They were:

(1) Wretched
(2) Miserable
(3) Although financially rich and proud, they were spiritually poor
(4) Spiritually blind, (ignorant of their true spiritual condition)
(5) Naked (spiritually vulnerable)
(6) Lukewarm (sickening to God)

No matter how many possessions or how much money we have accumulated, it is all meaningless without an intimate relationship with Christ.

Christ counseled the members of this church to do five things:

(1) Obtain gold from God, which represents true faith (1 Peter 1:7) and would change their spiritual impoverishment.
(2) Obtain white raiment, which is clothing that represents righteousness (Revelation 19:8).
(3) Anoint eyes with eye-salve. Although Laodicea was a city that manufactured ointment for the eyes, most of the people in this church were spiritually blind. The ointment that Christ offers represents enlightenment by the Holy Spirit and the Word of God (Psalm 19:8; Ephesians 1:18; Hebrews 6:4; 1 John 2:27). This church desperately needed spiritual illumination to see things from God's perspective.
(4) Be zealous for the things of God, not lukewarm.
(5) Repent.

We can avoid God's discipline by pursuing an intimate relationship with Him through prayer, Bible study, worship, and service as led by His Holy Spirit.

> 20 Behold, I stand at the door, and knock: if any man hear my voice, and open
> the door, I will come in to him, and will sup with him, and he with me.

The door referred to is the door of each person's heart, as well as entire congregations. In the Bible, the heart symbolically refers to the center of one's emotions, thoughts, and character. Christ desires to have entrance to the hearts of individuals. He also desires to have intimate fellowship with groups of believers.

Verse 20 is customarily thought of as a verse for sharing salvation with unbelievers. But it was used by Christ to address believers. In its worldliness, the church at Laodicea had actually excluded Christ from its congregation. The invitation of Jesus, spoken from outside the door, is an appeal for fellowship with any person who will repent of their spiritual complacency and lukewarmness. It also implies personal responsibility to respond to Christ's appeal. Even born-again Christians are incomplete without continued intimate fellowship with Christ.

Christ's offer to dine with those who will receive Him is consistent with the marriage supper of the Lamb (Revelation 19:9). Whenever we sense the convicting power of the Holy Spirit drawing us closer to Christ, we need to open up to God and pursue fellowship with Him.

The church at Laodicea is similar to many apostate churches today.

> 21   To him that overcometh will I grant to sit with me in my throne, even as I also overcame, and am set down with my Father in his throne.
> 22   He that hath an ear, let him hear what the Spirit saith unto the churches.

Overcomers will share the joys and blessings of Christ's throne. The Holy Spirit represents Christ's lordship over the churches. The Holy Spirit will remain active in any church as long as the congregation remains faithful to Christ and His Word, and cultivates a sensitivity to the leading of God.

Before we continue our study in the Book of Revelation, we need to briefly discuss some of the prophecies in the Book of Daniel, which include references to the future seven-year tribulation period and the coming Antichrist.

Six

An Overview of the Seven-Year Tribulation

Brief Summary of Daniel's Vision of the 70th Week

Daniel, chapter 2, describes a dream that King Nebuchadnezzar had, and that the prophet Daniel interpreted. This dream included symbols that represented four successive empires:

(1)   Babylonian Empire
(2)   Medo-Persian Empire
(3)   Greek Empire
(4)   Roman Empire

A fifth empire, or an alliance of ten kingdoms, was also predicted. These 10 kingdoms will eventually come under the rule of a person referred to as the Antichrist.

The prophet Daniel also had a vision about a time span of 490 years concerning the nation of Israel (Daniel, chapter 9). This is referred to as Daniel's Vision of the 70 Weeks. In this vision, each day represents one year, and each week represents seven years. The first 69 weeks (483 years) would occur just prior to the death of the Messiah. After that, God's 70-week time clock would temporarily stop. But there is still one week of seven years left to be fulfilled. This future seven-year period is referred to as the seven-year tribulation period.

During the tribulation, the Antichrist will rise to great power. He will claim to be a god and set up a satanically inspired system that will be political, religious, and economic. At the three and one-half year mark, he will also begin to persecute the Jews. The details of these seven years are given in the Book of Revelation, chapters 4 through 19.

The Kingdoms in Nebuchadnezzar's Dream (Daniel, Chapter 2)

Daniel 2:1-13 tells about a dream that King Nebuchadnezzar of Babylon experienced. In Daniel 2:29-35, Daniel describes the king's dream of a great metallic image. In verses 36 through 45, Daniel reveals the interpretation of this dream as revealed by God. The statue, made up of different materials, symbolized four successive empires and the final rule of God's kingdom. Because the head was made of gold and the feet of iron and clay, the image was top-heavy and destined to crash. Using history, the majority of Bible scholars contend that the kingdoms predicted in the dream were as follows.[33]

(1)   **Head of gold:** Babylonian Empire (604-539 B.C.) under King Nebuchadnezzar
(2)   **Chest and arms of silver:** Medo-Persian Empire (539-334 B.C.). The two arms symbolize the two nations that would make up the kingdom of the Medes and the Persians.
(3)   **Belly and thighs of brass:** Grecian Empire of Alexander the Great and the subsequent four divisions of his empire (334-146 B.C.)
(4)   **Legs of iron:** Roman Empire (63 B.C. to 455 A.D.). The two legs of the image represent the separation of the Roman Empire into the eastern and western divisions. This occurred during the fourth century A.D. The toes would be a mixture of iron and clay.

Each kingdom, after punishing Israel, would be absorbed into the succeeding kingdom. The degeneration of world kingdoms is represented in the diminishing value of the metals used. Silver is worth less than gold, brass less than silver, iron less than brass, and clay less than iron.

The feet and toes of clay and iron represented the final breakup of the Roman Empire. The territory Rome ruled eventually divided into a mixture of strong and weak nations. The toes also represent a future alliance of ten kingdoms or ten zones. These will also be partly strong and partly weak.

The head of gold, breast and arms of silver, belly and thighs of brass, and the legs of iron are already history. We are living at a time represented on the image as near the feet and toes.

The Fifth Kingdom

The feet and toes of iron and clay represent a ten-kingdom coalition, or possibly ten zones of nations. Many have taught that the ten toes represent a revision of the Roman Empire around the Mediterranean Sea.

The 10 kingdoms, represented by the 10 toes on the image, will exist during the seven-year tribulation period. We know this because these 10 kingdoms will be destroyed when Christ visibly returns to the earth (Daniel 2:42-44). These kings will come under the rule of the Antichrist during the second half of the tribulation (Revelation 17:12-13).

The rock cut out of the mountain in Daniel 2:44-45 depicts God's kingdom, which will be ruled eternally by the Messiah. Nebuchadnezzar's dream revealed Daniel's God as the power behind all earthly kingdoms. The stone symbolizes the kingdom of heaven headed by the Lord Jesus Christ who will visibly reign on the earth. Christ is called a "stone" (Psalm 118:22; Matthew 21:44; Ephesians 2:19-22 and 1 Peter 2:6-8).

Daniel's Vision Of 70 Weeks (490 Years Concerning Israel)

Daniel studied the prophecy of the 70 years of captivity from the prophet Jeremiah (Daniel 9:2; Jeremiah 25:8-13). This led him to pray for God's intervention on behalf of His people. He called on God to shorten the time of their grief (Daniel 9:1-19). The Lord's answer came through the angel Gabriel, who gave Daniel the prophecy of the Seventy Weeks, or 70 sevens (Daniel 9:20-27).

Daniel 9:24:

> 24 Seventy weeks are determined upon thy people and upon thy holy city, to finish the transgression, and to make an end of sins, and to make reconciliation for iniquity, and to bring in everlasting righteousness, and to seal up the vision and prophecy, and to anoint the most Holy.

The Hebrew word translated as "week" is sheboah. This word refers to a period of seven years. The 70's as envisioned by Daniel are actually years. The vision that Daniel received about 70 weeks pertains to 70 units of seven years each, or 490 years.[34] It was as if the angel were saying, "the captivity of the Jewish people in Babylon has been 70 years; but the period between the captivity and the coming of the Messiah will be seven times that long."

In Daniel 9:24, the angel Gabriel stated that the Lord would send "70 weeks" of years for further punishment upon the Jewish nation. Each day here represents one year. Therefore, each week represents seven years (70 x 7 = 490 years). Thus, the prophecy deals with 490 years in the future of the Jewish people. All these years would occur after Daniel received this vision.

Daniel 9:25-26a:

> 25   Know therefore and understand, that from the going forth of the com-
> mandment to restore and to build Jerusalem unto the Messiah the Prince shall be
> seven weeks, and threescore and two weeks: the street shall be built again, and the
> wall, even in troublous times.
>
> 26a: And after threescore and two weeks shall Messiah be cut off, but not for himself:

Daniel 7:25 refers to a decree to rebuild the city of Jerusalem (not the temple). Seven weeks, added to threescore and two weeks (7 + 62) is 69 weeks. Note that 69 x 7 = 483. There would be 483 years between the decree to rebuild the city and the time of Messiah (Daniel 9:25).

These 483 years most likely began in 457 B.C. This is when Ezra returned to Palestine and began to direct the rebuilding of Jerusalem.

The latter part of verse 25 refers to the time when the city of Jerusalem would be rebuilt. Verse 26 tells us that sixty-two of the weeks (434 years) would occur between the time the reconstruction of Jerusalem would be completed and when Messiah would be "cut off" (killed).

The 69th week ended when Christ the Messiah entered Jerusalem, was rejected and crucified by His own people. Thus, the first 69 weeks have been fulfilled. God's 70-week time clock has stopped for the moment.

There is a break between the 69th and the 70th weeks. This break of time is the current Church Age. These prophetic weeks are stopped for the moment. But there is one week of seven years left to go. The 70th week refers to the future seven-year tribulation.

Daniel 9:26b:

> 26b: and the people of the prince that shall come shall destroy the city and the
> sanctuary; and the end thereof shall be with a flood, and unto the end of the war
> desolations are determined.

In the second part of verse 26, Daniel speaks of another prince (not Messiah). The Book of Revelation makes it clear this will be the Antichrist. Antichrist will be a satanically inspired person who will oppose God and deceive many.

The Seven-Year Tribulation

Daniel 9:27:

> 27 And he shall confirm the covenant with many for one week: and in the midst of the week he shall cause the sacrifice and the oblation to cease, and for the overspreading of abominations he shall make it desolate, even until the consummation, and that determined shall be poured upon the desolate.

Daniel 9:27 reveals the event that will mark the beginning of the seven-year tribulation period. Antichrist will make a seven-year peace treaty with the nation of Israel. He will later break this treaty; however, the establishment of this covenant will start this seven-year period.

At the end of the Church Age (usually thought to be at the rapture), God's 70-week time clock will start again. The 70th week (seven years) will begin. This will be the seven-year tribulation. During this period, God will severely deal with the nation of Israel, bringing her to a state of national repentance. The details of these seven years are given in the Book of Revelation, chapters 4 through 19. At the end of these seven years, the Jewish people will be reunited with Christ, their Messiah (Romans 11:25-27).

The 70th week, or seven-year tribulation, will be divided in half (two three and a half year periods – Daniel 9:27). The first half is referred to as the "lesser tribulation." The second half is referred to as the "great tribulation" (Matthew 24:21; Revelation 7:14). The Great Tribulation fulfills Daniel's prophecies (Daniel 7-12). It will be a time of evil from false Christ's and false prophets, when many natural disasters will occur (Matthew 24; Mark 13).

2 Thessalonians 2:11-12 states that "God shall send them strong delusion, that they should believe a lie: that they all might be damned who believed not the truth." Based on this passage, some have taught that no persons will be saved during the tribulation. However, we know that there will be people that receive salvation during the tribulation. It is more likely that only those who have previously heard and rejected the gospel will be sent a strong delusion. Many others who have never understood the simple gospel message about Jesus dying for our sins will choose to accept salvation through Christ.

The seven-year tribulation will be a time of great persecution of Jews and Christians. Many will suffer martyrdom. However, during these times of suffering, revivals and miracles from the true God will also spread. Many people will be saved (Revelation 7:13-14; 11:13; 14:1-3). The gifts of the Holy Spirit will also be very active on the earth until the end of the seven-year tribulation period (Acts 2:17-21).

The Antichrist

Antichrist will be a satanically inspired person who will oppose God and deceive many. He may begin as a world diplomat.

As previously mentioned, Antichrist will gain power over 10 kingdoms or zones of nations (Daniel 2:31-44). The Antichrist will overthrow three of the 10 kingdoms by force (Daniel 7:23-24). The remaining seven kingdoms shall submit to him without further war (Revelation 17:12-13).

These nations will have one common currency. The Antichrist will cause people to take what is known as the mark of the beast (Revelation 13:16-18; 14:9-11; 16:2; 19:20). This will be on each person's hand or forehead. Some speculate that these marks will be imbedded computer chips, not visible except through scanners. These imbedded computer chips will act as debit cards. However, others believe that this is symbolic language. The right hand represents actions and behaviors while the forehead represents thoughts, decisions and attitudes. These two views about the mark of the beast will be discussed later.

Antichrist will enter into a seven-year alliance with the nation of Israel (Daniel 9:27). The Antichrist will probably need Jewish financial support to help him rise in political power. He will lead the negotiation of a peace treaty with the Arabs. The Antichrist will also encourage the Jews to rebuild their temple in Jerusalem. This temple will exist during the seven-year tribulation period (Revelation 11:1).

Many Jews will embrace the Antichrist as a great leader. He is referred to as the "Beast" in Revelation 13. Only when it is too late will the Jews realize they have been deceived. In the middle of the 70th week (halfway through the seven year period), Antichrist will break his peace treaty with the nation of Israel (Daniel 9:27). He will then attempt to destroy the Jews (Daniel 12:1; Matthew 24:21-22).

The Antichrist will aspire to be a world dictator. Although he may not succeed in dominating the entire world, the tribulation and judgments of God will, for the most part, be worldwide (Revelation 3:10).

One representation of Antichrist is given in 2 Thessalonians. He is pictured as the embodiment of lawlessness (2 Thessalonians 2:3,8-9; Daniel 7:25). The Antichrist will eventually claim to be deity, with power to perform signs and wonders (2 Thessalonians 2:9-10). He will also speak great blasphemies (Revelation 13:5).

The system Antichrist will set up will be satanic. It will be political, economic, and religious. The personal identity of the Antichrist is currently hidden. Don't try to identify the Antichrist. Instead, watch for the system that will produce him.

The Antichrist, called "the son of perdition" in 2 Thessalonians 2:1-8, will be held back until a restraining force gets out of the way. The Holy Spirit is a restraining force against sin (Genesis 6:3). But when the Antichrist is revealed, the Holy Spirit will move aside, and not restrain Antichrist's evil activities.

It is important to note that the Holy Spirit will continue to be active on the earth after the Antichrist is revealed. He will still be a comforter to those who get saved during the tribulation (John 14:16). The Holy Spirit will continue to convict people of their sins, and many will be drawn to Christ (Revelation 7:9,13-14; 14:6-7, 12-13). No person can be saved except through the ministry of the Holy Spirit (John 3:5-8; 16:7-15; Romans 8:9; 1 Corinthians 6:11; Ephesians 2:18; Titus 3:5). The Holy Spirit will also continue to empower believers during this time.

On the Day of Pentecost, the apostle Peter preached to thousands of people in Jerusalem. He told them that the outpouring of the Holy Spirit would continue until the sun turned black and the moon to blood (Acts 2:16-21). These are events that will occur at the very end of the seven-year tribulation (Matthew 24:29-31). Thus, the Holy Spirit will continue His ministry on earth during the tribulation, even though He will not restrain the Antichrist.

Fulfillment of the Times of the Gentiles

Luke 21:24 contains the phrase "the times of the Gentiles." This phrase refers to the extensive period of history when the people of Israel are subject to Gentile powers.[35] This phrase does not rule out temporary times of Jewish control of Jerusalem. In recent times, the Jews have controlled Jerusalem since the Six Day War in 1967. However, this control is only temporary. Revelation 11:1-2 predicts that Antichrist will control Jerusalem during the last half of the tribulation.

Jesus gave us an indication of when the times of the Gentiles would be fulfilled. In Luke 21:24, Jesus said the Gentile Age would come to an end when the Jews gain permanent control of Jerusalem. We are now living in the closing of the Gentile Age. Prophetically, God is now shifting His attention away from the Gentiles and back to the Jews.

The city of Jerusalem will probably continue to be controlled by the Jews until the middle of Daniel's 70th week. Then Antichrist will break his seven-year covenant with Israel, take over Jerusalem, and start the beast worship (Daniel 9:27; 11:36-37; Matthew 24:15-21; 2 Thessalonians 2:1-12; Revelation 13:4;14:9-11).

Jerusalem will again be in Gentile hands for 42 months (Revelation 11:1-2; 13:5). The city will finally be liberated at the Second Coming of Christ (Revelation 19:11-21; Zechariah 14:2-4; 2 Thessalonians 2:8). The "fullness of the Gentiles" will be completed when the nation of Israel turns to Christ (Romans 11:25-26). This will occur at the end of the tribulation. Jesus said, "And when these things begin to come to pass, then look up, and lift up your heads; for your redemption draweth nigh" (Luke 21:28).

ACT OF GRACE COMPLETE: "Abide in me, and I in you," John 15:4

Seven

The Rapture of the Church and the Second Coming of Christ

Brief Summary of the Two Phases of Christ's Return

Christ's return is usually interpreted as having two phases: the rapture and the Second Coming.

At some point in the future, and without warning, all true believers in Christ alive at that time will be caught up to meet Christ in the air and escorted to heaven (1 Thessalonians 4:13-18). Their bodies will be instantly transformed into new immortal bodies. This event is commonly referred to as the rapture of the church. Just prior to this moment, the bodies of "the dead in Christ" will rise and be resurrected into new, immortal bodies (1 Thessalonians 4:16). In other words, the souls and spirits of those who have died in Christ and have previously gone to heaven will be united with their resurrected and glorified bodies.

There is much disagreement as to whether the rapture of the church will occur at the beginning, middle, or end of the seven-year tribulation. However, most believers seem to accept the teaching that the rapture will take place at the beginning of the tribulation.

Christ will also visibly return to the earth at the end of the seven-year tribulation. This is referred to as the Second Coming. At this event, Christ will judge the nations and begin to visibly rule the earth for a thousand years. The rapture and the Second Coming are usually interpreted as two separate events.

The Rapture of the Church

1 Thessalonians 4:13-18:

> 13   But I would not have you to be ignorant, brethren, concerning them which are asleep, that ye sorrow not, even as others which have no hope.
>
> 14   For if we believe that Jesus died and rose again, even so them also which sleep in Jesus will God bring with him.
>
> 15   For this we say unto you by the word of the Lord, that we which are alive and remain unto the coming of the Lord shall not prevent them which are asleep.
>
> 16   For the Lord himself shall descend from heaven with a shout, with the voice of the archangel, and with the trump of God: and the dead in Christ shall rise first:
>
> 17   Then we which are alive and remain shall be caught up together with them in the clouds, to meet the Lord in the air: and so shall we ever be with the Lord.
>
> 18   Wherefore comfort one another with these words.

The phrase "rapture of the church" is not found in scripture. It is simply a phrase commonly used to refer to this event. The rapture will be a catching up of all true believers in Christ to meet the Lord in the air. The Lord will descend from heaven to take out of the world, in an instant, all the dead and living in Christ. All Christians alive in the world at that time will instantly disappear from the earth, and be transported to heaven. The soul and spirit of every deceased Christian, currently in heaven, will be reunited with his or her resurrected glorified body.

At the rapture, Christ does not appear visibly to those on earth, nor does He touch the earth. He remains in the air. When Christ meets the believers in the air, He will take them to heaven and present them to the Heavenly Father.

There are several reasons for the rapture:

- It allows Jesus to receive the believers to Himself (1 Thessalonians 4:17).
- It will resurrect the dead in Christ from among the wicked dead (1 Thessalonians 4:15-16).
- It will change the bodies of believers to immortality (1 Corinthians 15:51-55). This event will make believers whole in body, as well as in soul and spirit (1 Thessalonians 5:23).
- It takes believers to heaven where their works will be judged, and they will receive their rewards (2 Corinthians 5:10; Romans 14:10; 1 Corinthians 3:11-15; Matthew 25:23; Revelation 22:12).
- It will enable believers in Christ to participate in the marriage supper of the Lamb (Revelation 19:9).

- Most Christians believe the rapture will allow many believers to escape all or part of the seven-year tribulation period.

Whenever the rapture occurs, it will take place in an instant.

1 Corinthians 15:51-55:

> 51 Behold, I shew you a mystery; We shall not all sleep, but we shall all be changed,
>
> 52 In a moment, in the twinkling of an eye, at the last trump: for the trumpet shall sound, and the dead shall be raised incorruptible, and we shall be changed.
>
> 53 For this corruptible must put on incorruption, and this mortal must put on immortality.
>
> 54 So when this corruptible shall have put on incorruption, and this mortal shall have put on immortality, then shall be brought to pass the saying that is written, Death is swallowed up in victory.
>
> 55 O death, where is thy sting? O grave, where is thy victory?

If the rapture occurs at or just before the beginning of the tribulation, there will probably be a great revival afterwards. However, there will also be intense persecution, and the cost of commitment to Christ will be great.

Some believe in a partial rapture. They believe that not all believers alive at that time will be raptured, only those who are living in close fellowship and obedience to the Lord. This idea is based on scriptures that exhort believers to be faithful and watchful (i.e., Matthew 24:45-51; 25:1-30; Luke 21:34-36; Hebrews 9:28). Others contend that such passages are really distinguishing between true believers and merely professing believers. The idea of a partial rapture is probably not true for the following two reasons:

(1) In 1 Corinthians 15:51-52, we are told that "all" believers shall be "changed, in a moment, in the twinkling of an eye."
(2) The idea of a partial rapture denies the full power of sins forgiven through Christ's death on the cross because it makes right standing with God dependent on good works.

Distinguishing Between the Rapture and the Second Coming of Christ

The Second Coming of the Lord is usually interpreted as having two phases: the rapture of the church (1 Thessalonians 4:15; James 5:7-8) and the visible return of Christ (Matthew 24:30). These are two different events. Those who believe in a pretribulation rapture contend that it can occur at any moment. According to this view, no events need to be fulfilled before the rapture.

But the Second Coming cannot occur until all the events in Revelation 4:1 through 19:10 are fulfilled. This would be seven years after the rapture, at the end of the tribulation.

There are three main views concerning the timing of the rapture, in reference to the seven-year tribulation period. Some believe the rapture will occur at the beginning, or just before the seven year tribulation. Others believe it will occur in the middle of the seven-year tribulation. Still others teach that the rapture will occur at the end of the seven-year tribulation at the same time as Christ's visible Second Coming. If the reader wishes to learn more about these various views, you may consult Appendix A at the end of this book.

According to the pretribulation view, the rapture and Christ's Second Coming are seven years apart. According to the midtribulation view, the rapture and Christ's Second Coming are three and one-half years apart. According to the posttribulation view, the rapture and Christ's Second Coming are a few moments, or perhaps a few hours apart.

Those who believe in a pretribulation rapture teach that it will usher in the seven-year tribulation. On the other hand, the Second Coming at the end of the tribulation will usher in Christ's visible rule on the earth for a thousand years (Revelation 20:2-7).

At the rapture, believers in Christ go up to heaven (1 Thessalonians 4:16-17). At the Second Coming, Christ will visibly bring His saints with Him back to earth (Zechariah 14:5; Colossians 3:4; 1 Thessalonians 3:13; Jude 14).

Whereas the rapture is hidden from the gaze of unbelievers, Christ will be visible to everyone at His Second Coming (Matthew 24:29-30; Mark 13:24-26; Luke 21:27; Acts 1:9-11; Revelation 1:7).

At the rapture, Christ meets believers in the air to escort them to heaven (1 Thessalonians 4:17). At the Second Coming, Christ touches the Mount of Olives near Jerusalem (Zechariah 14:1-4) and remains on the earth to judge and reign over the nations (Matthew 25:31-32). Those who teach a pretribulation or midtribulation rapture also teach that the rapture will be followed by an acceleration of evil. In contrast, at the Second Coming, Christ will judge His enemies and begin His visible reign on the earth (Joel 3:11-17; Matthew 25:31-32; 2 Thessalonians 1:7-10; Revelation 19:11-21).

Those who teach a pretribulation or midtribulation rapture contend that afterwards, Satan will continue to operate on the earth for the remainder of the tribulation. At Christ's Second Coming, the Antichrist will be destroyed with the visible "brightness of His coming" (2 Thessalonians 2:8), and Satan will be bound in the bottomless pit for 1,000 years (Revelation 20:1-3).

At the rapture, the saved are removed and the wicked remain on the earth (1 Thessalonians 4:16-18). At the Second Coming, the saved are gathered (Matthew 24:31); however, the wicked are removed and the saved remain on the earth (Matthew 25:31-46).

The author of this book believes in a pretribulation rapture and the likelihood of a second rapture around the middle of the tribulation. As previously mentioned, a discussion about the different views as to the timing of the rapture is included in Appendix A at the end of this book.

Eight

The Olivet Discourse:
Signs of the End of the Age and Christ's Return

Brief Summary of the Signs of the Times

One day, Christ and His disciples visited the temple area in Jerusalem. Jesus told them that the temple would eventually be destroyed. Afterwards, they left the city and sat on the Mount of Olives. It was there that the disciples asked Jesus three questions about the future destruction of Jerusalem and about Christ's Second Coming. The Olivet Discourse is the longest teaching that Jesus gave about prophetic events.

Matthew 24:4-14 describes conditions that will increase prior to the tribulation, and that will greatly accelerate during the tribulation. They parallel the first five seals of judgment in Revelation, chapter 6. These include false messiahs, a great increase in wars, food shortages, starvation, pestilence, earthquakes, and mass deaths. Christ's followers will be persecuted. Many will die for their faith. However, during the first half of the tribulation, the gospel will be preached to all nations.

The "abomination of desolation" in Matthew 24:15 marks the mid-point of the tribulation. At this event, the Antichrist will begin to publicly proclaim himself as a god in Jerusalem, demanding worship. Antichrist will greatly persecute the people of Israel, and the Jews will be forced to flee into wilderness areas. The events of the second half of the tribulation will culminate in Christ's visible return to the earth to set up His millennial kingdom.

Three Questions Posed to Jesus About the End of the Age

Matthew 24:1-3:

> 1   And Jesus went out, and departed from the temple: and his disciples came to him for to shew him the buildings of the temple.
>
> 2   And Jesus said unto them, See ye not all these things? verily I say unto you, There shall not be left here one stone upon another, that shall not be thrown down.
>
> 3   And as he sat upon the mount of Olives, the disciples came unto him privately, saying, Tell us, when shall these things be? and what shall be the sign of thy coming, and of the end of the world?

After the disciples showed Christ the beauties of the temple, Jesus mentioned that the temple would someday be destroyed.

In verse 3, the word "world" is better translated as "age". Christ's statement brought forth three questions from the disciples:

(1)   When will this happen?
(2)   What will be the sign of your coming?
(3)   What will be the sign of the end of the current age?

The disciples believed that all three questions were related to a single event: Christ's return. However, the first question relates to the destruction of Jerusalem, in 70 A.D. This is when the Romans destroyed the city and the temple after a Jewish revolt. Christ's response as recorded in Luke 21:20-24 specifically deals with the destruction of Jerusalem. Much of Bible prophecy has both a near and distant fulfillment. The destruction of Jerusalem in 70 A.D. also foreshadows the conditions in Israel immediately before Christ's return, at the end of the tribulation.

The second and third questions have yet to be fulfilled. Christ's answers to these questions focus on the Jews living in Israel just prior to Christ's return, at the end of the tribulation. In other words, this discussion primarily concerns the Jews living in the nation of Israel during the second half of the seven-year tribulation.

Remember that Christ's return will be in two phases: the rapture and the Second Coming. The date and time of His return is unknown and will occur at an unexpected time (Matthew 24:36-25:13; 1 Thessalonians 4:13-18; 1 Corinthians 15:51-55). During Christ's ministry on earth, the disciples did not understand about the rapture. The rapture was later clarified by revelation received by the apostle Paul (1 Thessalonians 4:13-18; 1 Corinthians 15:51-55).

The second stage of Christ's return is at the end of the tribulation (Revelation 19:11-20:4). The passage in Matthew 24:1-35 pertains to events leading up to Christ's visible return.

The Signs Preceding Christ's Return

Matthew 24:4-14 describes conditions that will increase prior to the tribulation, and that will greatly accelerate during the first half of the tribulation. In other words, verses 4 through 14 extend at least through the first half of the tribulation. We know this because the "abomination of desolation" in the 15th verse takes place in the middle of the seven-year tribulation (Daniel 9:24-27). Verses 4 through 14 also parallel the first five seals of judgment in Revelation 6:1-11.

Matthew 24:4-7:

> 4   And Jesus answered and said unto them, Take heed that no man deceive you.
> 5   For many shall come in my name, saying, I am Christ; and shall deceive many.
> 6   And ye shall hear of wars and rumours of wars: see that ye be not troubled:
> for all these things must come to pass, but the end is not yet.
> 7   For nation shall rise against nation, and kingdom against kingdom: and
> there shall be famines, and pestilences, and earthquakes, in divers places.

The number of false messiahs / false Christs will dramatically increase during the tribulation. Jesus is particularly warning the Jewish people not to be tricked by these religious deceptions.

There will be a great increase in wars and rumors of wars, particularly against the Jewish people. Many nations will engage other nations in military conflicts. This parallels the second seal in Revelation 6:3-4, which is war.

The famines, pestilences and earthquakes mentioned by Jesus are part of the third and fourth seals in Revelation 6:5-8. The third seal will be great food shortages. The fourth seal will be death and hell. Many people will die prematurely during the tribulation due to starvation, disease, and war.

Matthew 24:8-10:

> 8   All these are the beginning of sorrows.
> 9   Then shall they deliver you up to be afflicted, and shall kill you: and ye shall
> be hated of all nations for my name's sake.

> 10   And then shall many be offended, and shall betray one another, and shall hate one another.

The term "beginning of sorrows" in verse 8 refers to labor pains, which will mark the transition from this current age to the age to come. These birth pangs are the first five seal judgments of Revelation, chapter 6, indicating that the seven-year tribulation is just beginning. These severe labor pains will be followed by a time of deliverance and joy, at the end of the seven-year tribulation.

There will be a great persecution and betrayal of many of Christ's followers. These are people who missed the rapture, but were saved during the first half of the tribulation. Many Christians will die for their faith during the tribulation. This parallels the fifth seal in Revelation 6:9-11, which refers to martyrs for Christ. This state of lawlessness also parallels the description of the Antichrist as a "man of lawlessness" in 2 Thessalonians 2:3.

Matthew 24:11-14:

> 11   And many false prophets shall rise, and shall deceive many.
> 12   And because iniquity shall abound, the love of many shall wax cold.
> 13   But he that shall endure unto the end, the same shall be saved.
> 14   And this gospel of the kingdom shall be preached in all the world for a witness unto all nations; and then shall the end come.

The deceptive work of false prophets is again mentioned. Many will be deceived. Christ was so concerned that His followers would be aware of the coming worldwide spiritual deception that he referred to it three times in Matthew 24:4, 11, and 24. Throughout the world, many church people will increasingly become involved in the occult, astrology, witchcraft and spiritism. The influence of demons will increase (1 Timothy 4:1). Sin will become even more extreme and widespread. The spiritual fervor of many will disappear.

The gospel will be preached to all nations. In the midst of severe difficulties, the Lord's followers are to persevere in spreading the gospel. Even during the sufferings of the first half of the seven-year tribulation period, revivals and miracles from the true God will occur. Many people will be saved (Revelation 7:13-14; 11:13; 14:1-3). The gifts of the Holy Spirit will also be active until the end of the seven-year tribulation period (Acts 2:17-21). This great evangelization will occur during the first three and one-half years of the tribulation.

Matthew 24:15:

> 15   When ye therefore shall see the abomination of desolation, spoken of by

Daniel the prophet, stand in the holy place, (whoso readeth, let him understand:)

Verses 15 through 31 are special signs that will occur during the second half of the tribulation period. We know this because verse 15 mentions the "abomination of desolation." This phrase refers to the time when the Antichrist will turn against the nation of Israel, and desecrate the temple in Jerusalem. This event will occur in the middle of the seven-year tribulation (Daniel 9:25-27; 12:11).

The Antichrist will set up an image of himself in the Jewish temple, declaring himself to be God. This becomes clear as the following scriptures are pieced together: Daniel 11:31; 12:11; Revelation 13:14-15; 2 Thessalonians 2:3-4. This image in the Jerusalem temple will miraculously come to life (Revelation 13:15). The worship of the Antichrist will begin. Many who refuse to worship the Antichrist (also called the beast) and his image will be put to death (Revelation 13:15).

Since verse 15 mentions an event that will occur halfway through the tribulation, verses 16 through 31 describe signs that will occur during the second half of the tribulation. These signs will accompany the destruction of Jerusalem and will also foretell Christ's visible Second Coming.

Matthew 24:16-27:

16   Then let them which be in Judea flee into the mountains:

17   Let him which is on the housetop not come down to take any thing out of his house:

18   Neither let him which is in the field return back to take his clothes.

19   And woe unto them that are with child, and to them that give suck in those days!

20   But pray ye that your flight be not in the winter, neither on the sabbath day:

21   For then shall be great tribulation, such as was not since the beginning of the world to this time, no, nor ever shall be.

22   And except those days should be shortened, there should no flesh be saved: but for the elect's sake those days shall be shortened.

23   Then if any man shall say unto you, Lo, here is Christ, or there; believe it not.

24   For there shall arise false Christs, and false prophets, and shall shew great signs and wonders; insomuch that, if it were possible, they shall deceive the very elect.

25   Behold, I have told you before.

26   Wherefore if they shall say unto you, Behold, he is in the desert; go not forth: behold, he is in the secret chambers; believe it not.

27   For as the lightning cometh out of the east, and shineth even unto the west; so shall also the coming of the Son of man be.

Matthew 24:16-20 mentions the Jews in Judea who will be forced to flee for their lives. Jesus gives advice to the Jews who will be living in Israel during the second half of the tribulation. He advises them to flee the city of Jerusalem before escape becomes impossible. During the second half of the tribulation, the Antichrist will greatly persecute and kill many Jews in Israel, forcing them to flee into wilderness areas (Revelation 12:6,14). Many will flee to the areas of ancient Edom and Moab (Isaiah 16:1-4) which are in modern day Jordan. This is an area that will escape the Antichrist (Daniel 11:41).

Verses 21 and 22 indicate that there will be great distress, unequaled prior to that time (see also Mark 13:19). Many will die from the persecution of Antichrist. The "great tribulation" refers to the second half of the tribulation.

In verses 23 through 26, Christ again warns about the deceptions of false messiahs. This warning primarily concerns Israel. Many of these false Christ's will work great miracles that are not from God. These false deliverers will not deceive committed believers in the Lord Jesus Christ.

Verse 27 reveals that the events of the second half of the tribulation will culminate in Christ's visible return to the earth.

Matthew 24:28:

> 28 For wheresoever the carcass is, there will the eagles be gathered together.

This was an expression among the Jews, which meant that sin and corruption require divine judgment. The Second Coming of Christ at the end of the seven-year tribulation is connected to the Battle of Armageddon. An angel will stand in the sun crying for birds to gather and eat the carcasses of the people who have been slain by Christ (Revelation 19:11-21). Luke also connects the visible coming of Christ to the gathering of eagles to eat those who have died at the Battle of Armageddon (Luke 17:34-37).

Matthew 24:29-31:

> 29 Immediately after the tribulation of those days shall the sun be darkened, and the moon shall not give her light, and the stars shall fall from heaven, and the powers of the heavens shall be shaken:
> 30 And then shall appear the sign of the Son of man in heaven: and then shall all the tribes of the earth mourn, and they shall see the Son of man coming in the clouds of heaven with power and great glory.

> 31   And he shall send his angels with a great sound of a trumpet, and they shall gather together his elect from the four winds, from one end of heaven to the other.

Spectacular cosmic signs shall occur at some point during the second half of the tribulation, preceding Christ's Second Coming. These cosmic signs are part of the sixth seal in Revelation 6:12-13.

The "sign of the Son of Man" will probably be Christ Himself returning on the clouds of glory, surrounded by brilliant light. This verse portrays Christ's appearing in the sky at the end of the tribulation. All believers who have been previously resurrected will return with Christ (Revelation 19:14; 17:14; Zechariah 14:5; Joel 2:1-11; Jude 14-15). Christ will return to begin His visible reign on the earth.

Matthew 24:31 includes a gathering of those believers on the earth who have survived the tribulation, as well as those believers returning with Christ from heaven.

When Christ returns to earth at the end of the tribulation, the following events take place:

- God's separation of believers from nonbelievers (Matthew 25:31-45)
- God's judgment on the wicked (Matthew 25:46; Revelation 19:17-18, 21)
- God's judgment on the Antichrist (Revelation 19:20)
- God's judgment on Satan (Revelation 20:1-3)
- Christ begins His thousand-year reign on the earth (Revelation 20:4-6)

The millennial reign of Christ starts out with only saved believers on the earth. All the unsaved will be removed from the earth at the end of the seven-year tribulation (Matthew 25:31-46).

No unsaved person will be on the earth at the start of Christ's thousand-year reign. Those believers who remained on the earth and survived the tribulation will enter the Millennium still in their physical bodies. Isaiah 65:20 indicates that people will be born during the Millennium. Many of those born during the Millennium will not accept Christ and will eventually rebel against God at the end of Christ's thousand-year reign (Revelation 20:7-10).

Matthew 24:32-35:

> 32   Now learn a parable of the fig tree; When his branch is yet tender, and putteth forth leaves, ye know that summer is nigh:
> 33   So likewise ye, when ye shall see all these things, know that it is near, even at the doors.

> 34   Verily I say unto you, This generation shall not pass, till all these things be fulfilled.
>
> 35   Heaven and earth shall pass away, but my words shall not pass away.

This is an admonition for believers to be fruitful. This generation may refer to the generation that begins to see the intensification of the general signs leading up to the seven-year tribulation (Matthew 24:4-14). It more likely refers to the Jewish people living in Israel during the tribulation period.

The parable of the fig tree illustrates the nearness of Christ's coming. As the budding of a fig tree indicates that summer is coming, the signs described by Jesus will indicate that His Second Coming is near. The coming out of the leaves refers to events during the tribulation. The fig tree represents the restoration of the nation of Israel (Isaiah 27:6; Hosea 9:10; Luke 13:6-9). The generation that witnesses the events during the second half of the tribulation period will also witness Christ's return. The pivotal sign will be the abomination of desolation, which refers to the desecration of the temple by Antichrist and a persecution of the Jews (Matthew 24:15-22).

God knows the future. All of these predictions made by Christ will be fulfilled.

The parables in the remainder of Matthew, chapter 24 and all of chapter 25, illustrate what Jesus had just described. They refer to the need to be faithful to God at all times. Believers are to be watchful for Christ's return. Those who are faithful will receive eternal rewards. These parables use the following illustrations:

- A comparison of these times with the days of Noah (24:36-39)
- Two men and two women (24:40-41)
- The owner of a house (24:42-44)
- The wise servant (24:45-51)
- The ten virgins (25:1-13)
- The three servants and the talents (25:14-30)
- The sheep and the goats (25:31-46)

Some believe that the Olivet Discourse only refers to Christ's Second Coming at the end of the tribulation, and not to an earlier rapture of the church. They take this stand because the Olivet Discourse addresses the persecution of the Jews in Israel during the tribulation, particularly during the second half of the tribulation. According to this view, the Jews in Israel who will accept Jesus Christ as their Messiah will be unable to accurately predict the end of the tribulation and Christ's Second Coming. This is because they will be ignorant of the seven-year tribulation timetable that precedes His Second Coming.

Others believe that the Olivet Discourse includes warnings about a pretribulation rapture, as well as the Second Coming of Christ. If the church is not raptured until the end of the tribulation period, believers could set a definite time for the rapture – seven years after the Antichrist enters into a covenant with Israel. But, it is unscriptural to set such dates (Matthew 24:36), because the time of the rapture is a secret (Matthew 24:37-44). The date of the rapture cannot be accurately predicted. As a result, many believe that Christ's statements that no one will know the day or hour of His return (Matthew 24:36,42,44,50; 25:13) include references to a pretribulation rapture.

Christians will disagree about whether the Olivet Discourse only warns about the Second Coming, or includes warnings about a pretribulation rapture. However, all Christians should agree that we must maintain an attitude of watchfulness and faithfulness.

GOD: Omnipresent and omniscient, Hebrews 4:13

Nine

Revelation – Chapter 4

Brief Summary

Chapter 4 begins the heavenly story that is taking place around the throne of God. The Book of Revelation shows us heaven before showing us the frightening events of the tribulation period. We are encouraged and comforted by being reminded that God is in control.

This scene is one of magnificent worship. The worshippers include 24 elders, four unusual creatures, a multitude of angels, and a huge company of redeemed people. Together, angels and redeemed humans will worship and glorify God because He is the creator and sustainer of all things. Worshipping God is our ultimate calling throughout eternity.

God's Throne

1   After this I looked, and, behold, a door was opened in heaven: and the first voice which I heard was as it were of a trumpet talking with me; which said, Come up hither, and I will shew thee things which must be hereafter.

2   And immediately I was in the spirit: and, behold, a throne was set in heaven, and one sat on the throne.

3   And he that sat was to look upon like a jasper and a sardine stone: and there was a rainbow round about the throne, in sight like unto an emerald.

God says "Come up hither, and I will show you things which must be hereafter." This may have a twofold meaning. It is a message to the Apostle John. However, it may also be symbolic of the "catching away" (rapture) of the church (1 Thessalonians 4:16-17; 1 Corinthians 15:51-52). After Revelation 4:1, the church is not mentioned on earth during the tribulation. This has led many to conclude that the church is raptured at the beginning of chapter 4, prior to the seven-year tribulation. From chapter 4 until chapter 19, the earthly story focuses on the nation and people of Israel.

John had an experience in the spirit. This refers to a state of heightened spiritual sensitivity. John was given a vision and shown events that he could not have seen in the natural. He was caught up to heaven and stood before God's throne. The throne is the center of activities in the Book of Revelation. It is mentioned 40 times.

The one who sat on the throne is identified as God in verse 8. This is referring to the Heavenly Father. Although God is Spirit (John 4:24), He can also sit on a literal throne (Isaiah 6:1).

John saw God the Father, who was "to look upon like a jasper and a sardine stone." Jasper is semitransparent, "clear as crystal" (Revelation 21:11). It is probably a diamond, which represents purity, holiness, and the glory of God. In Revelation 21:11, the light of the New Jerusalem is compared to that of a jasper stone. Sardine stones are red,[36] and probably picture God's avenging wrath. John saw a rainbow around the throne that was green like an emerald. The rainbow symbolizes God's mercy, grace, and covenant promises (Genesis 9:12-16). The color green probably is a symbol of life, and the circle represents eternity, which is never ending.

Some Christians believe they will never see God the Father. John said that "No man has seen God at any time" (John 1:18). However, the word "seen" in the Greek means to "comprehend." It means to understand everything about Him. No man has ever understood everything about God. We will continue to learn more things about God throughout eternity.

John saw God. Believers will be able to see God face-to-face while in their glorified bodies throughout eternity (Revelation 22:4).

The Twenty-four Elders

> 4   And round about the throne were four and twenty seats: and upon the seats I saw four and twenty elders sitting, clothed in white raiment; and they had on their heads crowns of gold.

There are 24 elders seated on 24 seats around God's throne. An "elder" is one who ministers to believers as a servant, humbly contributing to their spiritual growth. The Greek word translated "seats" in this verse can also be translated "thrones" as it is in verse 2. Being seated on thrones suggests that these elders have status and responsibility. However, their crowns suggest victory and joy, not power or authority. The white robes of the 24 elders symbolize purity.

These elders are not angels. In scripture, angels are never described as sitting on thrones or wearing crowns. Thrones and crowns are reserved for humans (1 Corinthians 9:25; 2 Timothy 4:8; Revelation 2:10; 3:21). In addition, angels do not grow older. This also indicates that these elders are humans.

Jesus promised his disciples that they would sit on 12 thrones and judge the 12 tribes of Israel (Matthew 19:28, Luke 22:30). Except for Judas, Christ's immediate disciples will probably be included in this group of elders.

The 24 elders are probably a combination of spiritual leaders from the Old Testament and leaders from the Church Age. They represent God's people of both ages. Twelve of the elders may represent believers from the Old Testament and twelve of the elders may represent believers from the New Testament. We know that the names of the 12 tribes of Israel and the 12 apostles are written on the holy city, the New Jerusalem (Revelation 21:10-14).

The priesthood of the Old Testament was represented by 24 elders, giving the number 24 some significance (1 Chronicles 24:1-19). The number 24 symbolizes heavenly government.

The Spirits and Creatures Around the Throne

> 5   And out of the throne proceeded lightnings and thunderings and voices:
> and there were seven lamps of fire burning before the throne, which are the seven
> Spirits of God.

The lightning and thunder coming out of the throne represent the awesome power and majesty of God. Lightning and thunder may also represent judgment and are probably introductory to the judgments described in Revelation, chapters 6 through 19.

The seven lamps of fire symbolize the Holy Spirit, along with His illuminating and purifying ministries. This is consistent with Zechariah 4:2-6 where seven lamps represent the one Holy Spirit. The Holy Spirit is also depicted as a burning fire of purity, filled with judgment against sin (Isaiah 4:4; John 16:18).

The Holy Spirit is before the throne. Those who believe in a pretribulation rapture believe that the Holy Spirit is standing with those He has brought with Him in the rapture.

This doesn't mean the Holy Spirit's ministry is finished on the earth. He will now conduct His remaining ministry during the tribulation from His heavenly position. As previously noted, the Holy Spirit will remain active on the earth during the tribulation. We know that many people will be saved during this seven-year period (Revelation 7:13-14; 11:13; 14:1-3). Under the New Covenant, no person can be saved except through the ministry of the Holy Spirit (John 3:5; Romans 8:9). The gifts of the Holy Spirit will also be very active on the earth until the end of the seven-year tribulation period (Acts 2:17-21).

> 6   And before the throne there was a sea of glass like unto crystal: and in the midst of the throne, and round about the throne, were four beasts full of eyes before and behind.

Two Common Interpretations About the Sea of Glass

1. The sea of glass in heaven refers to a huge crowd of redeemed believers. In Scripture, when the word "sea" is used, if it is not specifically talking about a body of water, it refers to a great mass of people, such as in Revelation 15:2. This sea is an immense number of people that make up the believers. "Crystal" refers to the believers in a condition of perfection and glory, in a full stage of spiritual maturity.

2. The sea of glass is a beautiful pavement near the throne of God. It includes crystal and fire (Revelation 15:2). This sea of glass may function as a mirror, reflecting the brilliant colors flashing from God's throne.

> 7   And the first beast was like a lion, and the second beast like a calf, and the third beast had a face as a man, and the fourth beast was like a flying eagle.
> 8   And the four beasts had each of them six wings about him; and they were full of eyes within: and they rest not day and night, saying, Holy, holy, holy, Lord God Almighty which was, and is, and is to come.

No explanation is given about these creatures. Some translations refer to the second creature as an ox. The many eyes of these creatures indicate spiritual perception, insight, wisdom, knowledge, and unceasing watchfulness.

These creatures around God's throne were created for the purpose of magnifying God's glory and holiness. They also direct worship to God on His throne.

Two Interpretations of What the Four Creatures Represent

1. These creatures represent the entire *forces of creation*:

(1) The lion represents untamed animal life.

(2) The calf, or ox, symbolizes domestic animal life.

(3) The beast with a face as a man represents all humans, God's highest earthly creation.

(4) The eagle pictures the fowls of the air.

The primary function of all creation is to worship and give glory to God.

2. Four of *God's attributes* are symbolized in these creatures:

(1) The lion symbolizes God's majesty and power.

(2) The calf, or ox, symbolizes God's faithfulness.

(3) The man symbolizes God's intelligence.

(4) The eagle symbolizes God's sovereignty.

God's attributes are incomprehensibly perfect.

The creatures described in Ezekiel, chapter 1, are almost identical to the living creatures referred to here. Ezekiel names these living creatures "cherubim," which is a type of angelic being (Ezekiel 10:20).

Isaiah was given a vision in which he saw creatures above the throne of God (Isaiah 6:1-3). Isaiah refers to these angelic beings as seraphim. This literally means "burning ones." This implies that these creatures have a fiery color or appearance, probably reflecting God's holiness and glory.

The seraphim and cherubim may be different creatures. The cherubim are described as under God (Ezekiel 10:20), beside God (Psalm 99:1), and around the throne of God (Revelation 4:6). On the other hand, the seraphim are described as above the throne of God (Isaiah 6:1-2).

When Adam and Eve were forced to leave the Garden of Eden, God put cherubims with flaming swords at the entrance to the garden (Genesis 3:23-24). When the Ark of the Covenant was made according to God's directions, there were two figures on the lid, which represented two cherubim (Exodus 25:18-20). The cherubs at the ends of the mercy seat above the ark symbolized God's holiness and presence among His people.

The four creatures described in Revelation 4:6-8 are angelic beings, but they are distinguished from the other angels mentioned in chapter 5. These four creatures are guardians to the throne. Being angels, they are also messengers.

"Holy, holy, holy" is the same phrase that the prophet Isaiah heard when he received a vision of the Lord in the heavenly temple (Isaiah 6:1-3). The scene in Revelation, chapter 4, depicts angels and redeemed humans worshipping God together.

Heavenly Worship

9   And when those beasts give glory and honour and thanks to him that sat on the throne, who liveth for ever and ever,

10   The four and twenty elders fall down before him that sat on the throne, and worship him that liveth for ever and ever, and cast their crowns before the throne, saying,

11   Thou art worthy, O Lord, to receive glory and honour and power: for thou hast created all things, and for thy pleasure they are and were created.

The four creatures act as God's cheerleaders by signaling the masses when to worship. The elders cast down their crowns before the throne when they worship. By doing this, they acknowledge the supremacy of God. They also are showing that they have been redeemed and have their crowns by His blessings.

Moses observed God in His glory by only looking at His back parts. When we are in a glorified state, we will see God face-to-face, sitting on His throne (Revelation 22:4).

Verse 11 summarizes the theme of chapter 4: all the creatures in heaven and eventually on earth will worship and glorify God because He is the creator and sustainer of all things. Humans, angels, and all the rest of His creation were created for God's pleasure. Worshipping God is our ultimate calling throughout eternity.

ROYALTY of Christ: Isaiah 9:6-7

Ten

Revelation – Chapter 5

Brief Summary

Chapter 5 continues the heavenly story that is taking place around the throne of God.

There is no one worthy to open a scroll with seven seals, except the Lord Jesus Christ. When Christ appears, all of the inhabitants of heaven sing praises to the Lamb of God. This praise and worship recognizes Christ's deity. As a result of His redemptive work, Christ is exalted to the highest position of honor and glory.

This scroll resembles official documents in the Apostle John's day. The opening of the seals on the scroll will initiate judgments of God on the earth in chapter 6. These are part of the events that must take place before Christ visibly returns to the earth at the end of the seven-year tribulation.

The Sealed Book

1   And I saw in the right hand of him that sat on the throne a book written within and on the backside, sealed with seven seals.

2   And I saw a strong angel proclaiming with a loud voice, Who is worthy to open the book, and to loose the seals thereof?

3   And no man in heaven, nor in earth, neither under the earth, was able to open the book, neither to look thereon.

4   And I wept much, because no man was found worthy to open and to read the book, neither to look thereon.

God was holding a book in His right hand. The right hand is a symbol of power and authority. This book was actually a scroll. It contained writing on the inside and on the back, and was sealed with seven seals. This indicates that nothing could be added to or changed in this scroll. The seven seals also indicate the importance of its contents. As each seal is opened, a portion of the scroll will be revealed. Chapter 6 reveals that this document contains information about some of the coming judgments of God.

God was ready to give this book to anyone worthy to open it. The angel who asked, "Who is worthy to open the book" was probably Michael. No man or angel was worthy to open the book. As John was looking at this scene, he wept from suspense and anxiety. Perhaps John was concerned that God's purposes of judgment and blessing would go unfulfilled if the book was not opened.

The Lamb Who Opens the Book

> 5   And one of the elders saith unto me, Weep not: behold, the Lion of the tribe of Juda, the Root of David, hath prevailed to open the book, and to loose the seven seals thereof.

Only Christ is worthy to break the seals and reveal the contents of this scroll. Jesus' is referred to as the "Lion of Judah," which indicates that He is from the tribe of Judah (Genesis 49:9-10). A lion is a symbol of power and authority and refers to Christ's future and visible rule of the earth. As a lion, Christ will lead the battle that will finally defeat Satan (Revelation 19:11-21). Christ the lion will be completely victorious.

Jesus is also referred to as the "Root of David," meaning that humanly speaking, Christ is a descendant of King David. It was prophecied that the Messiah would come from the line of David and would be an ideal king, combining power and goodness (Isaiah 11:1-10; Jeremiah 23:5-6; Zechariah 3:8-10; Revelation 22:16).

> 6   And I beheld, and, lo, in the midst of the throne and of the four beasts, and in the midst of the elders, stood a Lamb as it had been slain, having seven horns and seven eyes, which are the seven Spirits of God sent forth into all the earth.
> 7   And he came and took the book out of the right hand of him that sat upon the throne.

Jesus appears as a lamb that still displays the marks in His body from His trial and crucifixion. John the Baptist called Jesus the Lamb of God (John 1:29). In the Old Testament, lambs were substitute sacrifices for the sins of the people. A lamb is a symbol of meekness and of sacrificial offering. Christ was the perfect sacrifice for the sins of humanity (Isaiah 53:7; Hebrews 10:1-12,18). This representation as a lamb emphasizes the complete and perfect triumph of Christ's sacrificial death. Christ is the ultimate expression of the power and authority of a lion and the humility of a lamb.

The Lamb (Christ) has seven horns and seven eyes, which are also the seven spirits of God. This represents the Holy Spirit and the overlap between the Holy Spirit and Christ (Romans 8:9) as members of the trinity. The complete anointing and power of the Holy Spirit is upon Jesus.

Notice the following additional symbols:

- The number seven is used several times in the Book of Revelation. As previously mentioned, the number seven in scripture represents perfection and completion. In this context, it speaks of the fullness of power and wisdom.
- The seven horns are symbols of strength and governmental authority (Daniel 7:8,24;8:8-9; Zechariah 1:18-21). Although Christ was a sacrificial lamb, He possesses perfect power as a divine ruler.
- The seven eyes signify complete and perfect insight, knowledge, and watchfulness.
- The number seven here also signifies the perfect characteristics of the Holy Spirit that rest on Jesus without measure (Isaiah 11:1-2; John 3:34).

Only Christ is worthy to open the seals. Those who believe in a pretribulation rapture believe that in this scene, Jesus has recently left heaven, gathered the church in the air, and has come back to the throne. He is now ready to begin opening the seals of the scroll.

The contents of the scroll are things that shall transpire during the tribulation. This is not the book of redemption that contains all the names of the redeemed, as some have taught. This book, or scroll, speaks of judgments.

Worship of God and the Lamb

8   And when he had taken the book, the four beasts and four and twenty elders fell down before the Lamb, having every one of them harps, and golden vials full of odours, which are the prayers of saints.

9   And they sung a new song, saying, Thou art worthy to take the book, and to open the seals thereof: for thou wast slain, and hast redeemed us to God by thy blood out of every kindred, and tongue, and people, and nation;

10   And hast made us unto our God kings and priests: and we shall reign on the earth.

Verse 8 refers to some of the many musical instruments in heaven. Since God allows musical instruments in heaven, it should not be considered wrong to have musical instruments in the church, as some have taught.

The golden vials, or bowls, full of sweet odors represent the prayers of the believers (Psalm 141:2; Revelation 8:4). Perhaps God, in some sense, stores up our prayers. The Lord does not answer all of our prayers immediately. Instead, He keeps them for the proper time of fulfillment.

Verse 9 describes the four creatures and the twenty-four elders singing a new song declaring that Jesus Christ, the Lamb, is "worthy." Since we are commanded to only worship God (Matthew 4:10), this worship of Christ emphasizes His deity. This song will be sung to Christ, praising Him for making redemption available to mankind.

Verse 10 indicates some of the status and responsibilities of resurrected believers during the millennial reign of Christ on the earth. Through Christ's death on the cross, all true believers have been made priests of God (1 Peter 2:5-9). We will also rule and reign with Christ on earth during the Millennium and in the new earth forever (Daniel 7:18; Revelation 2:26-27; 5:10; 20:4-6; 22:5).

> 11 And I beheld, and I heard the voice of many angels round about the throne and the beasts and the elders: and the number of them was ten thousand times ten thousand, and thousands of thousands;
> 12 Saying with a loud voice, Worthy is the Lamb that was slain to receive power, and riches, and wisdom, and strength, and honour, and glory, and blessing.
> 13 And every creature which is in heaven, and on the earth, and under the earth, and such as are in the sea, and all that are in them, heard I saying, Blessing, and honour, and glory, and power, be unto him that sitteth upon the throne, and unto the Lamb for ever and ever.
> 14 And the four beasts said, Amen. And the four and twenty elders fell down and worshipped him that liveth for ever and ever.

Verse 11 mentions that the angels worshipping God number "10,000 times 10,000, and thousands of thousands." If this is a literal number, it is referring to at least 100 trillion, which is much more than the mere billions of the earth's human population. The number of humans is very small compared to the number of God's holy angels. Heaven must be a gigantic place to accommodate this population. It is hard to imagine the wonderful praise and worship that comes forth from such a huge number of worshippers.

Verse 13 states that every creature in heaven, and on earth, and under the earth will eventually worship Christ. This verse jumps ahead past the tribulation and past the Millennium to the Great White Throne Judgment, when every living creature will be required to worship Christ (Philippians 2:9-11; Revelation 20:11-15). Even those who rejected Christ in this life will be forced to worship Him just before receiving their final judgment. Eventually, there will be universal recognition that Jesus Christ is Lord.

RED ROSE: Martyrdom

Eleven

Revelation – Chapter 6

Brief Summary

Chapter 6 begins the earthly story during the tribulation. The opening of the seven seals on the scroll will initiate judgments of God on the earth. The first four seals are commonly known as the "four horsemen of the Apocalypse." The first six seals are described in chapter 6:

First seal – A white horse rider representing the rise and conquests of the Antichrist

Second seal – A red horse rider representing war, bloodshed, and destruction

Third seal – A black horse rider representing food shortages and famine

Fourth seal – A pale horse rider representing mass death, accompanied by the forces of hell

Fifth seal – Martyrs slain for Christ

Sixth seal – The wrath of the Lamb, which includes great earthquakes, the sun turning black, the moon becoming red as blood, stars falling (meteors), and every mountain and island being moved

These first six seals are consistent with the judgments that Jesus foretold in the Olivet Discourse (Matthew 24:4-29).

The Sealed Book is Opened

> 1   And I saw when the Lamb opened one of the seals, and I heard, as it were
> the noise of thunder, one of the four beasts saying, Come and see.

Jesus is the Lamb of God (John 1:29). This book is actually a scroll, sealed with seven seals (5:1). Each seal that is broken introduces a tragedy on earth. One of the beasts near the throne instructs John to look at the seals. The first four seals are the four horsemen of the Apocalypse. Their activities will continue throughout the entire seven years of tribulation. The symbolism of four horses is also found in Zechariah 6:1-8.

The seals are the first of three groups of judgments. The seventh seal introduces the seven trumpets that occur in chapters 8 and 9. The seventh trumpet introduces the seven bowls, or vials, in chapter 16.

The First Seal: The Rise of the Antichrist

> 2   And I saw, and behold a white horse: and he that sat on him had a bow;
> and a crown was given unto him: and he went forth conquering, and to conquer.

This rider on a white horse cannot be Christ because Jesus is the one who is opening the seals. The first seal refers to a leader who is opposed to Christ. This illustrates the rise of the Antichrist.

Some believe that since all the other horsemen are symbolic, the rider of this horse does not represent a specific person, but the spirit of Antichrist in general. However, the scriptures point to a political leader who will emerge that will be the embodiment of the Antichrist spirit (Daniel 11:36-45; 2 Thessalonians 2:3-9; 1 John 4:3; Revelation 13:2-18; 17:9-12; 19:19-20).

Since the only similarity between the Antichrist and Christ is the color of the horse they ride, white, the rider in Revelation 6:2 is not Christ. The Antichrist stands in contrast to Christ.

Antichrist	Christ
• The white horse that the Antichrist rides is merely a symbolic horse. • Antichrist has a bow. • Antichrist has a crown given unto him (by Satan) • Antichrist sets out as a conqueror (a man of war). He has not conquered yet. • Antichrist begins a series of terrible events on earth.	• In Revelation 19:11, Jesus rides a white horse, which is literal. • Jesus has a two-edged sword (Revelation 1:16; 19:15, 21). • Jesus already has many crowns (Revelation 19:12). • Jesus has already conquered death, hell and the grave (Revelation 20:14). All power has been given to Him (Matthew 28:18). • Jesus ends these events (Revelation 19 and 20).

The Antichrist is portrayed as an ambitious conqueror. This fulfills Daniel 7:8, 24-26 and 11:36-46, which refer to the rise of the Antichrist over a ten-kingdom coalition.

As previously mentioned, the Antichrist will overthrow three of the ten kingdoms by force (Daniel 7:23-24). The remaining seven kings shall submit to him without further war (Revelation 17:12-13). The nations over which Antichrist rules will have one common currency. An identification number will be required on each citizen's hand or forehead (Revelation 13:16-17; 14:9, 11; 16:2; 19:20; 20:4). These may be imbedded computer chips not visible except through scanners. It is often speculated that they will act as debit cards. However, some contend that this mark is not literal. According to this view, the hand represents the actions and behaviors of people. The forehead represents a mental commitment of allegiance to the Antichrist.

Antichrist will gain control over these ten kingdoms by the middle of the tribulation. He will be king over these ten kings through the operation of satanic powers (2 Thessalonians 2:9-12; Revelation 13:1-4; Daniel 11:36-39). The only god he will honor is a god of fortresses, which probably refers to his ability to wage war (Daniel 11:38). He will redivide territories he conquers to promote his own gain (Daniel 11:39).

Many believe that Antichrist will initially pretend to be the Jewish messiah (Matthew 24:4-5; John 5:43; Daniel 9:27). He comes symbolically on a white horse, imitating Christ, and claiming to be Him. However, others believe that he will be seen as a messiah for the Muslims. This will be discussed in our commentary on Revelation, chapter 13. In any event, millions of people will probably be fooled into thinking that he is a representative of their god.

The Antichrist will be a dictator who will eventually present himself as greater than any god. He will speak blasphemies against the true God (Daniel 11:36). Antichrist will be allowed to prosper for a time (Daniel 11:36). The system the Antichrist will set up will be satanic. This system will be political, economic, and religious. Do not try to identify the Antichrist. Instead, watch for the system that will produce him.

In scripture, when a bow is used symbolically in connection with humans, it pictures evil designs and conquests. Notice that, although Antichrist has a bow, there is no mention of Antichrist having any arrows. This may indicate that Antichrist will initially conquer through diplomacy rather than war. He will probably initiate a temporary and false peace. The absence of arrows may also indicate a lack of resources. Although he aspires to be a world dictator, he may lack the resources to pull if off. Whether or not Antichrist will rule the entire world will be addressed when we discuss Revelation, chapter 13.

As previously mentioned, the Antichrist will enter into a seven-year alliance with the nation of Israel (Daniel 9:27). This will be the 70th week of Daniel's prophecy, which is actually seven years. He will break the covenant after three and one-half years and begin to persecute the Jews in Israel.

Only the first seal refers to a particular person (Antichrist). Seals 2, 3, 4 and 5 refer to the results of Antichrist's activities. He will cause the wars, famines, pestilence and death of the second, third, fourth and fifth seals (Revelation 6:3-11).

The Second Seal: War

3   And when he had opened the second seal, I heard the second beast say, Come and see.

4   And there went out another horse that was red: and power was given to him that sat thereon to take peace from the earth, and that they should kill one another: and there was given unto him a great sword.

Another horse appears that is red. Its rider has a great sword to take peace from the earth and bring death. These are clear symbols of war and bloodshed. This second seal is consistent with Christ's prediction of wars in Matthew 24:6.

War will result from the Antichrist's conquests (Daniel 7:24; 11:40-45; Matthew 24:6-7). The fact that peace will be taken from the earth may indicate a world war, perhaps a nuclear war. The Antichrist will desire to take over the world by the method of war. This seal of war will be in effect during the entire seven years of the tribulation.

The Antichrist and his military forces will even attempt to fight against Christ at the Battle of Armageddon at the end of the tribulation (Revelation 16:16; 17:8-14). This battle will conclude when Christ visibly returns to destroy the Antichrist and his armies (Revelation 19:11-21).

The Third Seal: Food Shortages

> 5   And when he had opened the third seal, I heard the third beast say, Come and see. And I beheld, and lo a black horse; and he that sat on him had a pair of balances in his hand.
> 6   And I heard a voice in the midst of the four beasts say, A measure of wheat for a penny, and three measures of barley for a penny; and see thou hurt not the oil and the wine.

The black horse rider represents famine and economic chaos. This rider held a pair of scales. This was to measure food. In Ezekiel 4:10-17, bread by measure and weight signifies food shortages. Famines often occur during and after times of war. Mass deaths from war produce a shortage of people to care for and harvest crops. There will be food shortages for the entire seven years of the tribulation (Matthew 24:6-7). Many will starve because food will not be grown in those areas devastated by war.

Many consumer goods will be scarce, causing prices to become extremely high. There will be much inflation and scarcity. In scripture, a penny, or denarius, represented an average daily wage (Matthew 20:2,9). Three measures of barley is barely enough daily food to sustain one person. Thus, most people will have to work a whole day to earn enough money to buy a very minimal amount of food.

The rider on the black horse is commanded not to damage "the oil and the wine." Oil and wine are symbolic of luxuries, which historically have been foods enjoyed by the wealthy. The continued existence of these luxuries may mean that this famine will not severely hurt the rich, but will be devastating to those who are not wealthy.

Perhaps this famine, in the aftermath of nuclear war, will result in calls for a tight regulation of the world's economy. In response, the Antichrist will introduce his system of economic control, including the "mark of the beast" (Revelation 13:16-18).

The Fourth Seal: Death and Hell

> 7   And when he had opened the fourth seal, I heard the voice of the fourth beast say, Come and see.
>
> 8   And I looked, and behold a pale horse: and his name that sat on him was Death, and Hell followed with him. And power was given unto them over the fourth part of the earth, to kill with sword, and with hunger, and with death, and with the beasts of the earth.

The rider of the pale horse symbolizes death. The light color of this horse represents a lack of warm skin color, characteristic of death. Hell (actually Hades in the Greek) closely followed him as a companion. It is not clear whether Hades and death are on separate horses or riding on the same horse. In any event, many people will die prematurely during the tribulation due to starvation, disease, and war. This is consistent with Christ's predictions in Matthew 24:6-7. Most of the people who die during this time will be lost and go to hell.

Death and hell will be given power over a fourth of the earth to kill with violence, hunger, and wild beasts. Some interpret this to mean that one fourth of the human race will be killed. Others interpret this to mean that this seal will only cover one fourth of the earth. In either case, great masses of people will die. Wherever dead bodies are fallen from wars, famines and plagues are a result. These situations will be made even worse by animals that will gather to eat the bodies (Matthew 24:28; Luke 17:34-37; Ezekiel 39:17-21). The fourth seal actually results from the judgments of the first three seals.

The reference to "the beasts of the earth" may indicate attacks by animals, even those that are domesticated. It may also symbolically refer to the leaders of governments. In Daniel, chapter 7, human kingdoms are pictured as beasts. Also, the Antichrist and his government are portrayed as a beast in Revelation, chapter 13.

The Fifth Seal: Martyrs for Christ

9   And when he had opened the fifth seal, I saw under the altar the souls of them that were slain for the word of God, and for the testimony which they held:

10   And they cried with a loud voice, saying, How long, O Lord, holy and true, dost thou not judge and avenge our blood on them that dwell on the earth?

11   And white robes were given unto every one of them; and it was said unto them, that they should rest yet for a little season, until their fellow servants also and their brethren, that should be killed as they were, should be fulfilled.

These verses refer to those believers in Christ who will be killed by the Antichrist in the areas that he rules. This is consistent with Christ's predictions in Matthew 24:9-10. Some believe that this group under the altar will include all those who were martyred in past ages. The white robes of the martyrs represent purity and victory. They were praying for the fulfillment of God's justice.

God will not avenge the martyrs until all of them have died. God will patiently delay the final judgment to give many unsaved an opportunity to repent. As a result, God will postpone final judgment even though His followers continue to suffer.

When a believer dies, that person's soul and spirit go to be with the Lord (2 Corinthians 5:8; Philippians 1:21-24). The physical body stays on the earth and sleeps, but the soul and spirit are conscious. In the same way, the martyred believers during the tribulation will be conscious before their resurrection, not asleep in their graves. This shows how people who have passed on in death are fully conscious before the future resurrection of their physical bodies.

Christians who have died prior to the rapture, or who will be alive on the earth at the rapture, will have their physical bodies resurrected or transformed during the rapture (1 Thessalonians 4:15-17; 1 Corinthians 15:51-55). Those who are saved during the tribulation and then killed by the Antichrist will have their physical bodies resurrected at the close of the tribulation (Revelation 20:4-6).

The first five seals of judgment in Revelation 6:1-11 parallel the predictions Christ made in Matthew 24:4-14. These first five seals of judgment begin during the first half of the tribulation. We know this because the "abomination of desolation" in Matthew 24:15 occurs at the mid-point of the seven-year tribulation (Daniel 9:24-27). Therefore, the first five seals in Revelation, chapter 6, and Matthew 24:4-14 begin during the first half of the tribulation. They also extend to the remainder of the tribulation.

The Sixth Seal: The Wrath of the Lamb

> 12   And I beheld when he had opened the sixth seal, and, lo, there was a great earthquake; and the sun became black as sackcloth of hair, and the moon became as blood;
>
> 13   And the stars of heaven fell unto the earth, even as a fig tree casteth her untimely figs, when she is shaken of a mighty wind.
>
> 14   And the heaven departed as a scroll when it is rolled together; and every mountain and island were moved out of their places.

The first five seals are the results of the conquering activities of the Antichrist and may be directed at specific geographic areas. The sixth seal will be worldwide. This parallels the natural upheavals mentioned by Christ in Matthew 24:29. These tremendous upheavals will include:

- A great earthquake
- The sun turning black
- The moon becoming red as blood
- Stars falling (meteors) like fruit falling from a tree in a wind storm
- Every mountain and island being moved

> 15   And the kings of the earth, and the great men, and the rich men, and the chief captains, and the mighty men, and every bondman, and every free man, hid themselves in the dens and in the rocks of the mountains;
>
> 16   And said to the mountains and rocks, Fall on us, and hide us from the face of him that sitteth on the throne, and from the wrath of the Lamb:
>
> 17   For the great day of his wrath is come; and who shall be able to stand?

Revelation 6:16 refers to these judgments as "the wrath of the Lamb." Some believe verses 15 and 16 imply that people on the earth will be able to look into heaven and see the throne of God. Some have contended that the sixth seal occurs at the very end of the tribulation, immediately preceding Christ's visible return. However, the sixth seal cannot begin at the end of the tribulation. The reason is that it is followed by the seventh seal, which introduces the trumpet and bowl judgments. The wrath of the sixth seal probably begins during the first half, or around the middle, of the seven-year tribulation. It continues through the trumpet and vial (bowl) judgments to the end of the seven years.

When the ungodly realize that the time of God's wrath has come, they will be terrified because they will know that God will judge them for their sins. The world will realize that this judgment is from Christ Jesus. Even the unsaved will refer to Him as "the Lamb." The unsaved will experience great fear and despair as they attempt to hide. They will call for the mountains to fall on them so they will not have to face judgment from the Lamb of God.

Twelve

Revelation – Chapter 7

Brief Summary

Chapter 7 is an informational chapter that enlarges upon the details in the earthly story. It is inserted between the sixth and seventh seals and contains some events that will occur after the sixth seal. This chapter refers to people who will accept Christ as their personal savior during the tribulation (Revelation 7:14).

Two groups of converts to Christ are described. The first group is 144,000 Jews who accept the Lord Jesus Christ as their messiah. They will be sealed and protected from the judgments that are initiated by God. The 144,000 will become Jewish evangelists who are given the assignment of preaching Christ to Israel.

The second group includes people from every nation who also have accepted Christ as their savior. This group is seen standing before the throne of God and may include the 144,000 Jews mentioned above.

It is possible that the 144,000 Jews may come to the realization that Jesus is their messiah shortly after an invading army from the north is miraculously defeated on the mountains of Israel. This battle will occur toward the beginning of the tribulation.

144,000 Jews Sealed

1   And after these things I saw four angels standing on the four corners of the earth, holding the four winds of the earth, that the wind should not blow on the earth, nor on the sea, nor on any tree.

2   And I saw another angel ascending from the east, having the seal of the living God: and he cried with a loud voice to the four angels, to whom it was given to hurt the earth and the sea,

3   Saying, Hurt not the earth, neither the sea, nor the trees, till we have sealed the servants of our God in their foreheads.

4   And I heard the number of them which were sealed: and there were sealed an hundred and forty and four thousand of all the tribes of the children of Israel.

5   Of the tribe of Juda were sealed twelve thousand. Of the tribe of Reuben were sealed twelve thousand. Of the tribe of Gad were sealed twelve thousand.

6   Of the tribe of Aser were sealed twelve thousand. Of the tribe of Nephthalim were sealed twelve thousand. Of the tribe of Manasses were sealed twelve thousand.

7   Of the tribe of Simeon were sealed twelve thousand. Of the tribe of Levi were sealed twelve thousand. Of the tribe of Issachar were sealed twelve thousand.

8   Of the tribe of Zabulon were sealed twelve thousand. Of the tribe of Joseph were sealed twelve thousand. Of the tribe of Benjamin were sealed twelve thousand.

The four angels mentioned in verse 1 may be the first four of the seven trumpet angels in chapter 8. The phrase "four corners of the earth" refers to the four directions (Isaiah 11:12; Matthew 24:31; Revelation 20:8). The winds of the earth may temporarily cease. However, these winds primarily refer to judgments of God that will be postponed a little while until the events of verses 2 and 3 occur. God will delegate control of these four winds of devastation to four angels. These four angels will hold back these four winds of judgment until the people of God are sealed as His own. After these believers are sealed, Christ will open the seventh seal (Revelation 8:1).

In 2 Thessalonians 2:11-12, it states that "God shall send them strong delusion, that they should believe a lie: that they all might be damned who believed not the truth." Based on this passage, some have taught that no persons will be saved during the tribulation. But we know that many will receive salvation during the tribulation (Revelation 7). Therefore, probably those who have previously heard and rejected the gospel will be sent a strong delusion. Many others who have never heard the simple gospel message about Jesus dying for our sins will choose to accept salvation through Christ.

Many people will be saved during the tribulation. The Holy Spirit will not be removed from the earth, but He will no longer restrain sin during the tribulation. The Spirit of God will continue to convict people of their sins, and many will be drawn to Christ (Revelation 7:9, 13-14; 14:6-7, 12-13). During the current dispensation, no person can be saved except through the ministry of the Holy Spirit (John 3:5; Romans 8:9; Titus 3:5; 1 Corinthians 6:11). The Spirit of God will continue to empower believers until the very end of the tribulation (Acts 2:16-21).

Revelation 7:4 states that the group receiving this seal will number 144,000. God will withhold some of His judgments until these believers have been sealed for their protection. In ancient times, a seal was a ring or tool that stamped an owner's mark of identification on an object. A seal would also guarantee protection of the object. God's seal on a believer identifies that person as belonging to God (Ephesians 1:13). This seal is the exact opposite of the mark of the beast that is mentioned in Revelation 13:16-17.

These sealed people will not be harmed by the trumpet judgments that come from God's wrath. They will be protected from God's direct judgment, as in Ezekiel 9:4-6. Those receiving the seal of God will also be protected from demonic affliction (Revelation 9:4).

Some speculate that the number 144,000 is not a literal number. If this is true, then it represents totality and completeness in the eventual conversion of the nation of Israel. However, this number is most likely literal. This group of 144,000 persons is a literal group of physical Jews, as opposed to spiritual Jews. The detailed listing of the twelve tribes shows this. There are no Gentiles in this group.

These will be 144,000 Jews who will accept Jesus Christ as their Messiah and will refuse to give their allegiance to the Antichrist. There will be 12,000 from each of the 12 tribes that will be represented in this group. These Jews will be saved during the first half of the tribulation, after the rapture of the church.

Revelation 7:2 mentions "the seal of the living God." This seal will protect these 144,000 Jews. Revelation 9:3-4 also refers to those people who do not have the seal of God for their protection.

Two Interpretations About God's Seal on the Foreheads of the 144,000

1. *The seal will not be a literal, visible mark.* Instead, the seal refers to decisions for salvation made by the 144,000. They will accept Jesus Christ as their Messiah. This involves a change in thoughts of the mind.

A mark on the hand and forehead is figurative language for behaviors and attitudes (Exodus 13:8-9, 14-16; Deuteronomy 11:18; Revelation 14:1; 22:3-5). The "right hand" is figurative for actions and behaviors. The "forehead" is figurative for thoughts, decisions, and attitudes. Thus the seal on the foreheads of the 144,000 will not be literal marks.

The seal referred to is spiritual, since the Holy Spirit is the mark or seal of God's ownership of believers (Ephesians 1:13)

2. *The seal will be a literal and visible mark on the 144,000.* The demonic locusts from the abyss that will torment those without the seal will be able to see it (Revelation 9:3-4).

There is a possibility that the visible seal of God on the foreheads of the 144,000 will anger the Antichrist. This may motivate the Antichrist to put a literal mark of the Beast, as identification, on the right hands or foreheads of his people.

Angels will search for those Jews who have an open attitude toward God and reveal to them that Jesus Christ is the true Jewish Messiah. As they accept, they are sealed with the name of God.

The number 144,000 is significant. As previously mentioned, the number 12 represents completeness in scripture.[37] The number 10 is a number of testimony.[38] The number 144,000 is a multiple of 12 and 10. Thus, the number 144,000 symbolizes completeness and testimony.

Revelation 14:4 tells us that the 144,000 "were not defiled with women: for they are virgins." Consequently, some believe that the 144,000 are all male virgins. However, others believe that this group is made up of both men and women because the term "virgin" can refer to either males or females. The phrase "not defiled with women: for they are virgins" may best be understood in a spiritual sense. Perhaps it refers to this group remaining pure and refusing to partake of worldly sins after their conversions to Christ.

What event will draw these 144,000 Jews to suddenly accept Jesus Christ as their Messiah? It could very well be a miraculous victory over an invading army from the north, combined with the ministry of two special witnesses.

An Invading Army From the North Defeated by Israel

Ezekiel 38 and 39 primarily refer to a battle that occurs at the beginning of the tribulation, or perhaps shortly before the tribulation. The Battle of Armageddon is another battle that occurs at the end of the tribulation (Revelation 16:16; 19:17-21). Many confuse both of these battles, referring to them as one battle: Armageddon.

There are two reasons for distinguishing this first battle from the Battle of Armageddon:

(1)   When the first battle occurs, the Jews of Israel will be dwelling "safely" (Ezekiel 38:8). Israel will be a "land of unwalled villages" (Ezekiel 38:11). The Israelis will have a false sense of security. Perhaps they will be trusting in an alliance with the European Union to protect them. This is not describing conditions at the end of the tribulation. Israel will not be dwelling in peace and safety during the second half of the tribulation (Revelation 12:6, 13-17; Matthew 24:15-22; Mark 13:14-20). This passage in Ezekiel is describing conditions toward the beginning of the tribulation, or perhaps shortly before the tribulation.

(2)   After this battle, the Israelis will be able to use the weapons and equipment of the defeated army for fuel for the following seven years (Ezekiel 39:9). It is doubtful that the seven years of clean up from this battle will extend into the Millennium. This first battle probably occurs toward the beginning of the tribulation, or perhaps shortly before the tribulation.

In this battle, God will give Israel a miraculous victory over an invading army from the north. This army from the north will come from the land of Magog (Ezekiel 38:2-3). Magog refers to the lands far to the north of Israel, which primarily are the lands of Russia, and some other areas of the former Soviet Union.[39] Ezekiel chapter 38 lists ten ancient names of lands that will be represented in this invasion force. In addition to Russia, these countries include Iran, Turkey, Sudan, and Libya.[40] These countries will invade Palestine to capture Israel's wealth (Ezekiel 38:11-12), and to control the Middle East.

John Hagee has written the following:

> *Ezekiel's war as described in chapters 38 and 39 will consist of an Arab coalition of nations led by Russia for the purpose of exterminating the Jews of Israel and controlling the city of Jerusalem. The Russian payoff will be the ability to control the oil-rich Persian Gulf.*[41]

Mr. Hagee further discusses the motivation for Russia to invade Palestine. In return for leading an alliance of Arab nations in a conquest of Israel, Russia will hope to gain more access to Middle East oil, will hope to gain a warm water port, and will hope to gain the vast amounts of mineral deposits in the areas around the Dead Sea. The Russians will also promise the nations of Islam total control of Jerusalem, including the temple mount.[42]

When this invasion begins, the response from many nations will simply be a passive diplomatic response (Ezekiel 38:13). America, after its war in Iraq, will be determined to stay out of the Middle East.

Russia and an alliance of Arab states will actually be drawn by God to invade Israel (Ezekiel 38:1-12,16). God will do this in order to supernaturally destroy these invading armies. This invasion force will be defeated in a single day of battle on the mountains of Israel (Ezekiel 39:2-4). A great earthquake will accompany this battle. Torrents of hailstones and burning sulfur will rain down on this invading army (Ezekiel 38:18-23). The soldiers in this great army will also turn against each other (Ezekiel 38:21). This will be a great object lesson to the world that the God of Abraham, Isaac, and Jacob is the one true God (Ezekiel 38:17-23; 39:21).

The slaughter will be so great that it will take seven months to bury the dead (Ezekiel 39:12). As previously stated, the Israelis will be able to use the weapons and equipment of the defeated army for fuel for the following seven years (Ezekiel 39:9). It is doubtful that the seven years of clean up will extend into the Millennium. This battle will probably occur toward the beginning of the tribulation, or perhaps shortly before the tribulation.

This miraculous victory over an invading army from the north will draw many Jews back to their God (Ezekiel 39:6-7,22,28). God will remove Israel's blindness about Jesus, starting with the 144,000. This revival in the nation of Israel will also be a response to the ministry of two witnesses ordained by God (Revelation 11:3-6). The two witnesses will be discussed as we study chapter 11.

After their fantastic victory over the invading army from the north, all of Israel will rejoice. Those who have an open attitude toward God will receive the witness of the sealing angels (Revelation 7:1-4) that Jesus is their Messiah. Some have speculated that much of the celebration about this miraculous victory will occur around the temple area in Jerusalem. If this is correct, then many of the 144,000 may be sealed on and around the temple mount.

The Mission of the 144,000

Zechariah 8:23 implies that most of Israel will eventually be converted, along with others as well. In addition, the gospel will be preached to all nations during the seven-year tribulation (Matthew 24:14; Mark 13:10). A likely scenario is that the 144,000 will become Jewish evangelists who are given the assignment of preaching Christ.

The 144,000 will attempt to evangelize those who have not yet been deceived into accepting the mark of the Beast. The followers of the Antichrist will probably attempt to denounce these 144,000 witnesses for Christ. Those who have embraced the beast system will try to persuade the undecided to accept the mark of the Beast. The 144,000 may consist primarily of unmarried persons without family responsibilities. This is because they have a huge task to perform and not much time to do it.

The 144,000 Jewish evangelists will evangelize Jews all over the world, wherever they were dispersed. Most of Israel, the natural seed of Abraham, will be saved, as Paul prophesied in Romans 11:26-27. Paul distinguishes between the natural seed of Abraham and the spiritual seed of Abraham. All born again Christians are the spiritual seed of Abraham. All Jews, by lineage, are of the natural seed of Abraham. God will graft the natural branches back into the olive tree (Romans 11:17-24).

The nation of Israel will be the primary vehicle through which the gospel will be preached during the tribulation. The preaching of these Jews will lead to great revivals. Unfortunately, this will also lead to severe persecution of believers, inspired by the Antichrist.

Some teach that the 144,000 Jews are also the manchild referred to in chapter 12. Others believe the manchild refers to Christ Himself. We will address this as we study chapter 12.

Unfortunately, after much of the military forces of Russia and the Arab states in the Middle East are destroyed, the Antichrist will be able to extend his power well beyond the European Union. In the middle of the tribulation, he will turn against Israel and persecute the Jews (Daniel 9:27; Matthew 24:16-20; Revelation 12:6,14). God in His mercy will hide away many Jews until the end of the tribulation.

A Great Multitude in White Robes

9   After this I beheld, and, lo, a great multitude, which no man could number, of all nations, and kindreds, and people, and tongues, stood before the throne, and before the Lamb, clothed with white robes, and palms in their hands;

10   And cried with a loud voice, saying, Salvation to our God which sitteth upon the throne, and unto the Lamb.

11   And all the angels stood round about the throne, and about the elders and the four beasts, and fell before the throne on their faces, and worshipped God,

12   Saying, Amen: Blessing, and glory, and wisdom, and thanksgiving, and honour, and power, and might, be unto our God for ever and ever. Amen.

13   And one of the elders answered, saying unto me, What are these which are arrayed in white robes? and whence came they?

14   And I said unto him, Sir, thou knowest. And he said to me, These are they which came out of great tribulation, and have washed their robes, and made them white in the blood of the Lamb.

15   Therefore are they before the throne of God, and serve him day and night in his temple: and he that sitteth on the throne shall dwell among them.

16   They shall hunger no more, neither thirst any more; neither shall the sun light on them, nor any heat.

17   For the Lamb which is in the midst of the throne shall feed them, and shall lead them unto living fountains of waters: and God shall wipe away all tears from their eyes.

Verse 9 states that this multitude of people standing before the throne of God is from "all nations, and kindreds, and people." In other words, believers from every nation and ethnic group will be represented in this multitude. We know that these people are saved because verses 9 and 10 tell us they are standing before the throne of God in heaven, singing praises and wearing white robes. They also have "palms in their hands," which symbolize victory and rejoicing. This great multitude is made up primarily of Gentiles, but may include the 144,000 Jewish converts.

The inhabitants of heaven offer great praises to God. Seven elements of this praise are mentioned in Revelation 7:12. They are: blessing, glory, wisdom, thanksgiving, honor, power, and might.

Possible Second Rapture Near the Middle of the Tribulation

When we study Revelation, chapter 14, we will see that the 144,000 Jewish converts will suddenly appear before the throne of God in heaven. The text does not say that the 144,000 have died. This sudden appearance of the 144,000 in heaven has led some to believe that this group will be caught up to heaven in a second rapture. This may take place after the seventh trumpet. After it sounds, this group suddenly is seen before the throne of God (Revelation 14:1-5).

We are told that Jesus will meet the 144,000 at Mount Zion (Revelation 14:1). This may refer to Jerusalem, where Jesus will meet them and escort them to heaven. On the other hand, it may refer to the heavenly mount Zion (Hebrews 12:22-23). In any event, some believe that when the Antichrist turns against the nation of Israel in the middle of the tribulation, God will protect the 144,000 from the wrath of Antichrist by catching them up in a second rapture.

The 144,000 will be given a seal of protection from the judgments of God. Some contend that this will not make them immune from martyrdom that comes from the wrath of Satan, and persecution from Antichrist. As a result, some believe that Revelation 14:1-3 refers to the martyrdom of the 144,000.

DEATH: *". . . and so death passed upon all men . . ."* Romans 5:12

Thirteen

Revelation – Chapter 8

Brief Summary

Chapter 8 picks up where chapter 6 left off in telling the earthly story. It starts with the seventh seal. The seventh seal is silence in heaven for one-half hour. The opening of the seventh seal will introduce the seven trumpet judgments. Chapter 8 describes the first four trumpet judgments:

(1) First trumpet judgment – A rain of hail, fire, and blood, destroying one-third of earth's vegetation

(2) Second trumpet judgment – A burning mountain that pollutes the sea

(3) Third trumpet judgment – A star called wormwood that pollutes drinking waters

(4) Fourth trumpet judgment – The sun, moon, and stars darkened

The first four trumpet judgments may be the result of nuclear explosions and fallout, chemical warfare, volcanic activity, or meteors and asteroids. Whatever their causes, these trumpet judgments will be devastating. They will bring economic chaos, governmental instability, tremendous suffering, and death throughout the world.

The last verse in chapter 8 is an announcement by an angel about the three woes. The three woes refer to the fifth, sixth, and seventh trumpet judgments. The fifth and sixth trumpets (first and second woes) are described in chapter 9. The seventh trumpet (the third woe) is described in chapter 11.

The Seventh Seal: Silence in Heaven

1   And when he had opened the seventh seal, there was silence in heaven about the space of half an hour.

The usual sounds of heaven are expressions of great joy and worship. Suddenly, there is silence in heaven for half an hour. In the Jewish temple, after a sacrificial lamb was killed, and while the altar of incense was being prepared, Jewish tradition required a great silence. This was a solemn worship. After the opening of the seventh seal, there will be a great silence in heaven, with somber worship. This silence will precede the horror of the judgments yet to come.

The seven seals and seven trumpets mark 14 consecutive events. The opening of the seventh seal will introduce the seven trumpet judgments.

The Seven Trumpet Angels and a Priestly Angel

2   And I saw the seven angels which stood before God; and to them were given seven trumpets.

3   And another angel came and stood at the altar, having a golden censer; and there was given unto him much incense, that he should offer it with the prayers of all saints upon the golden altar which was before the throne.

4   And the smoke of the incense, which came with the prayers of the saints, ascended up before God out of the angel's hand.

5   And the angel took the censer, and filled it with fire of the altar, and cast it into the earth: and there were voices, and thunderings, and lightnings, and an earthquake.

6   And the seven angels which had the seven trumpets prepared themselves to sound.

When the seventh seal is broken, there are seven angels that receive trumpets. The trumpet judgments and seal judgments are only partial. Perhaps these judgments are limited in order to warn many people and bring them to repentance. They will precede God's full wrath, which will be more encompassing and complete.

The prayers of all the saints are mentioned in verse 3. Prayers of believers are very important for the defeat of evil and the establishment of God's justice on the earth. Verse 3 implies that the prayers of the tribulation believers on the earth are joined with the intercession of all the redeemed people in heaven. These prayers apparently are stored up for this very day.

Verse 3 mentions a golden censer. The censer was a container for live coals on which incense was burned in worship (Numbers 16:17-18, 37-39, 46). It is associated with the ministry of a high priest (Leviticus 16:12; Hebrews 9:1-4). The censer was used in the purification ritual on the Day of Atonement (Leviticus 16:12-14). Incense was poured on the coals, causing a sweet-smelling smoke to drift upwards. This smoke symbolized the prayers of believers ascending to God (Exodus 30:7-9; Revelation 8:4).

Verse 3 also mentions a golden altar. The golden altar is the altar of incense that also symbolizes daily prayer to God. It is a type of Christ as our intercessor (Exodus 30:1-10).

Some believe this angel is an ordinary angel, like the seven angels with trumpets. But as previously mentioned, the censor is associated with the High Priest. The priestly angel mentioned in verse 3 may refer to Christ in his heavenly ministry as our great High Priest (Hebrews 4:14-16; 6:20; 7:24-28). After the ministry of the priestly angel at the altar, seven trumpets will be sounded.

Verse 1 of chapter 7 mentions four angels of God. These may be the first four of the seven trumpet angels in chapter 8. In 7:1-3, the four angels were told not to release their wrath until the 144,000 Jews could be chosen and sealed. Now that this has occurred, the angels are ready to begin their activities of wrath on the earth.

Verses 2 and 6 reveal seven angels with trumpets. Trumpets are a warning signal, combined with a call to repentance (Exodus 19:16,19). As each trumpet is blown, one at a time, it announces another judgment. These judgments are in response to the prayers of the redeemed.

The first four plagues released at the blowing of the trumpets are similar to some of the plagues of Egypt (Exodus 7:17-21; 9:22-26; 10:21-23). The first four trumpet judgments will affect the natural world. The last three trumpet judgments will specifically target those people who continue to be unrepentant.

The First Trumpet: Hail, Fire, and Blood

> 7   The first angel sounded, and there followed hail and fire mingled with
> blood, and they were cast upon the earth: and the third part of trees was burnt up,
> and all green grass was burnt up.

This judgment will effect vegetation. One-third of the earth's trees, and all grass, will be destroyed by fire and hail. This will cause agricultural disasters and famines. It will also greatly increase existing food shortages. The environmental impact will be incomprehensible. Oxygen in the earth's atmosphere will be greatly reduced. This could be the result of nuclear warfare, or much volcanic activity. The hail and fire will be mingled with blood. The blood may be a metaphor for a horrible disaster. If the blood is literal, this may become a common type of rain on the earth during the second half of the seven-year tribulation.

Whether or not actual blood rains on the earth, these trumpet judgments are real, not merely symbolic. Five of the plagues of Egypt resemble plagues in the Book of Revelation. Just as the plagues in Egypt were literal, so these judgments will be literal.

As horrible as these judgments are, they are probably partial. The reason there is a limit to these judgments is to warn the remaining undecided people, and to give many an opportunity to repent. These judgments will be followed by God's full wrath, which will be more encompassing and complete.

The Second Trumpet: A Burning Mountain

8   And the second angel sounded, and as it were a great mountain burning with fire was cast into the sea: and the third part of the sea became blood;
9   And the third part of the creatures which were in the sea, and had life, died; and the third part of the ships were destroyed.

This may refer to a large fiery meteor, asteroid, or volcano, or perhaps nuclear firepower. Whatever it is, it will pollute the sea. One-third of the sea will become blood. One third of the creatures in the sea will be killed. One-third of the ships on the sea will be destroyed.

Some teach that this will affect one-third of all the oceans. However, when the Bible refers to "the sea," it usually refers to the largest sea that borders Palestine, the Mediterranean Sea. This has led some to conclude that this judgment will target the Mediterranean area.

The Third Trumpet: A Star Called Wormwood

10   And the third angel sounded, and there fell a great star from heaven, burning as it were a lamp, and it fell upon the third part of the rivers, and upon the fountains of waters;
11   And the name of the star is called Wormwood: and the third part of the waters became wormwood; and many men died of the waters, because they were made bitter.

This could be a second meteor or asteroid, or it may refer to the radioactive pollution from a nuclear fireball. Since there is no mention of "the sea," this judgment appears to be worldwide. The gaseous vapors will poison a third of the earth's rivers and other domestic water supplies. These pollutants will have a devastating effect on entire populations and cities.

"Wormwood" is a term used in the King James Version to describe a very bitter tasting herb found in Palestine. It represents the bitterness of God's judgment, combined with human sorrow (Deuteronomy 29:18; Proverbs 5:4; Jeremiah 9:15; 23:15; Lamentations 3:15,19; Amos 5:7). Bitterness and sorrow are the results of sin. The star called "Wormwood" will cause drinking waters to become extremely bitter. Many people will die; however, God has promised true believers protection from the wrath of God (Revelation 7:2-3). Unfortunately, believers during the tribulation will not always be protected from the wrath of Satan, and many will die as martyrs for their faith (Revelation 12:9-12).

The Fourth Trumpet: The Sun, Moon, and Stars Darkened

> 12 And the fourth angel sounded, and the third part of the sun was smitten, and the third part of the moon, and the third part of the stars; so as the third part of them was darkened, and the day shone not for a third part of it, and the night likewise.

The sun, moon, and stars will be darkened. One-third of the daylight will be withdrawn and one-third of the light at night will be withdrawn. In addition to the reduced light, it appears that one third of the day and one-third of the night will include complete darkness from the heavens.

These conditions may refer to cosmic signs in outer space, where the light from these heavenly objects is weakened. If so, this will be a direct assault on witchcraft, New Age religions, and astrology. When God drastically affects the visibility of the sun, moon, and stars, this will greatly confuse all those who look to these things as a source of guidance. On the other hand, this could be referring to pollution in the atmosphere from nuclear fallout. This fallout would partially hide these bodies of light.

Whatever the cause, this is consistent with a prophecy that Joel made (Joel 2:30-31). Jesus also stated there would be signs in the sun, moon, and stars that will cause people to become terrified (Luke 21:26). However, these prophecies from Joel and Christ probably refer more to the conditions at the end of the tribulation, just prior to Christ's visible return (Matthew 24:29-30; Mark 13:24-26; Luke 21:25-27).

The length of darkness and reduced light from the fourth trumpet judgment will probably not be very long. The reason is that in the next trumpet judgment in chapter 9, the sun is darkened again by smoke from the abyss (Revelation 9:1-2).

An Announcement About the Three Woes

> 13   And I beheld, and heard an angel flying through the midst of heaven, saying with a loud voice, Woe, woe, woe, to the inhabiters of the earth by reason of the other voices of the trumpet of the three angels, which are yet to sound!

In verse 13, other translations of the Bible use the word "eagle" instead of "angel" to describe this heavenly messenger. But it is an angelic being.

An angel will fly through the heavens shouting warnings to the people on the earth. These warnings refer to the three woes, which will be the fifth, sixth, and seventh trumpets. The fifth and sixth trumpets, which are the first and second woes, will occur in chapter 9. The seventh trumpet, which is the third woe, will occur in chapter 11.

The cry of the angel is a warning that the next three trumpet judgments will be much more severe than the first four trumpet judgments. Each of the fifth, sixth, and seventh trumpets (the three woes) will probably be worse than all of the first four trumpets combined.

Fourteen

Revelation – Chapter 9

Brief Summary

In chapter 8, God used war and the forces of nature to cause the first four trumpet judgments. The last three trumpet judgments will be the result of the activities and influences of angels and demons.

The fifth, sixth, and seventh trumpet judgments are also called the three woes. The fifth and sixth trumpets (first and second woes) are described in chapter 9. The seventh trumpet (the third woe) is described in chapter 11.

The fifth trumpet (the first woe) – Refers to demonic oppression that will inflict a great deal of physical pain and suffering on humans for five months.

The sixth trumpet (the second woe) – Refers to 200-million demonic horsemen, invading the Middle East. Some teach that this army of 200 million only refers to demons that are released from the abyss. Others teach that this is a demonically inspired army of 200 million human soldiers, coming from either oriental countries or Muslim countries east of Israel.

The sixth trumpet judgment probably refers to both the release of demons from the abyss and to demonically inspired human armies that will kill multitudes of people.

The Fifth Trumpet: Demonic Oppression – The First Woe

1   And the fifth angel sounded, and I saw a star fall from heaven unto the earth: and to him was given the key of the bottomless pit.

2   And he opened the bottomless pit; and there arose a smoke out of the pit, as the smoke of a great furnace; and the sun and the air were darkened by reason of the smoke of the pit.

3   And there came out of the smoke locusts upon the earth: and unto them was given power, as the scorpions of the earth have power.

4   And it was commanded them that they should not hurt the grass of the earth, neither any green thing, neither any tree; but only those men which have not the seal of God in their foreheads.

5   And to them it was given that they should not kill them, but that they should be tormented five months: and their torment was as the torment of a scorpion, when he striketh a man.

6   And in those days shall men seek death, and shall not find it; and shall desire to die, and death shall flee from them.

7   And the shapes of the locusts were like unto horses prepared unto battle; and on their heads were as it were crowns like gold, and their faces were as the faces of men.

8   And they had hair as the hair of women, and their teeth were as the teeth of lions.

9   And they had breastplates, as it were breastplates of iron; and the sound of their wings was as the sound of chariots of many horses running to battle.

10   And they had tails like unto scorpions, and there were stings in their tails: and their power was to hurt men five months.

11   And they had a king over them, which is the angel of the bottomless pit, whose name in the Hebrew tongue is Abaddon, but in the Greek tongue hath his name Apollyon.

12   One woe is past; and, behold, there come two woes more hereafter.

As the fifth trumpet is sounded, a star falls from heaven to the earth. This is not a literal star. It refers to an intelligent being, an angel who is given the key to the bottomless pit. This star is referred to as "him" in verse 1, and "he" in verse 2. Angels are called "stars" in Revelation 12:4. This star must be an intelligent being because he is given a key and commanded to open the door of the pit.

Some believe that this star, or angel, that is given the key to the bottomless pit will be a demonic being, possibly Satan himself. However, in Revelation 20:1 an angel comes down from heaven "having the key to the abyss." This is probably the same angel of God who retains this key until the end of the tribulation period. God will not trust a fallen angel with the key to the bottomless pit where multitudes of demons are held. This holy angel will be allowed by God to release demons from the bottomless pit (verses 2 and 3). This will initiate the fifth trumpet judgment, which is also the first woe. After the tribulation, Satan will be bound in this pit for one thousand years (Revelation 20:3).

When the bottomless pit is opened, smoke like that from a great furnace will come out, darkening the sun and air. The bottomless pit, or abyss, is a place where certain demons are imprisoned (2 Peter 2:4; Jude 6). Most demons are currently free to roam the earth (Matthew 12:43-45; Luke 8:26-34; Ephesians 6:12). However, some have been imprisoned because they committed a terrible sin in the days of Noah (1 Peter 3:18-20). This sin involved sexual fornication (Jude 6-7). There were certain demons in the days of Noah who came to the "daughters of men" and had sexual relations with human women (Genesis 6:2-4). This produced a strange race that had to be destroyed in a worldwide flood (Genesis 6:5-7).

Those demons that have been imprisoned will be released on the earth. Their activities are seen in the descriptions of the fifth and sixth trumpet judgments, which are also the first and second woes.

The events described in verses 3 and 4 will apparently fulfill the prophet Joel's description of locust-type judgments and destruction that will precede the "day of the Lord" (Joel 2:1-11). In other words, these judgments will precede Christ's visible Second Coming at the end of the tribulation (Revelation 19:11-21).

The locusts in Revelation, chapter 9, will have the power to cause pain and misery (verse 10). They will have God's permission to torment unbelievers who do not have the "seal of God" (verse 4).

The power of God will prevent these locust type spirit beings from harming believers. This may encourage some uncommitted persons to acknowledge the power of the true God and to accept Jesus Christ.

These are not ordinary locusts for the following reasons:

- They arise from the infernal regions (verses 1-3), whereas ordinary locusts do not.
- They will not be burned or hurt by the smoke of the fire from the pit (verse 3).
- They will not eat vegetation (verse 4).
- They are intelligent because they receive commands not to hurt the people sealed by God (verse 4).

- Their description proves these are not ordinary locusts (verses 7-10).
- Their breastplates will seem to be like iron, indicating that man-made weapons cannot destroy them (verse 9). These locusts are indestructible and not mortal.
- They have a king (verse 11).

In this passage, locusts represent demonic beings, just like serpents and scorpions represent satanic forces in Luke 10:19. These locusts represent an increased number of demons and demonic activities unleashed on the earth from the bottomless pit. These demonic locust will be commanded not to harm those people with the seal of God in their foreheads. The 144,000, and perhaps their converts, have this seal.

Where did the demons come from? The best answer is that they are angels who fell with Satan during his rebellion against God (Ezekiel 28:11-19; Isaiah 14:12-15).

The pain from these locusts will be like that of a literal scorpion (verse 5). As previously stated, those with the seal of God will be protected from this demonic oppression. These demon locusts will be allowed to torment people for five months, but they will not be allowed to kill people (verse 6).

Many unsaved people who will be tortured by these locusts will want to die, but will not be able to die (verse 6). Death will take a five-month holiday. It will be impossible for people suffering from this plague to commit suicide. This will make them suffer more until the end of the five months, when death will claim them.

Some believe that these locusts will not be visible to humans. Others believe their description indicates that these locusts will be visible. If they will be visible to humans, their appearance and sounds will be terrifying. As previously mentioned, their breastplates will seem to be like iron, indicating that man-made weapons cannot destroy them. People will try to flee from them, even seeking death to avoid contact with them. The suffering from this judgment will last five months (verses 5 and 10).

Another Satanic angel is referred to in verse 11. His name in the Hebrew is Abaddon. In the Greek his name is Apollyon. Both names mean "destruction" or "destroyer." When the angel in verse one unlocks the bottomless pit, a king of the demons named destroyer, or "one who destroys," will lead these demon locusts in tormenting people. The demonic locusts were the first of the three terrible woes announced by an angel in chapter 8, verse 13.

Some have speculated that this particular leader of demons refers to Satan himself; however, this is not Satan because Satan is not currently imprisoned in the abyss. Currently, Satan rules in heavenly places surrounding the earth (Ephesians 2:2; 6:12). Satan is currently referred to as the God of this world or current age (John 12:31; 2 Corinthians 4:4). Satan will not be thrown into the bottomless pit until after Christ visibly returns to the earth (Revelation 20:1-3).

The Sixth Trumpet: An Invasion From the Euphrates (The Second Woe)

The sixth trumpet judgment, which is the second woe, refers to another army of demons that are released from the abyss. This judgment is even more severe. Whereas the demons of the fifth trumpet judgment inflicted pain, but were not allowed to kill people, the spirit-beings of the sixth trumpet will inflict death.

13 And the sixth angel sounded, and I heard a voice from the four horns of the golden altar which is before God,

14 Saying to the sixth angel which had the trumpet, Loose the four angels which are bound in the great river Euphrates.

15 And the four angels were loosed, which were prepared for an hour, and a day, and a month, and a year, for to slay the third part of men.

16 And the number of the army of the horsemen were two hundred thousand thousand: and I heard the number of them.

17 And thus I saw the horses in the vision, and them that sat on them, having breastplates of fire, and of jacinth, and brimstone: and the heads of the horses were as the heads of lions; and out of their mouths issued fire and smoke and brimstone.

18 By these three was the third part of men killed, by the fire, and by the smoke, and by the brimstone, which issued out of their mouths.

19 For their power is in their mouth, and in their tails: for their tails were like unto serpents, and had heads, and with them they do hurt.

Verse 13 refers to the Altar of Burnt Offering. The Altar of Burnt Offering at the entrance to the Jewish tabernacle and temple had four corners that jutted out at the top (Exodus 27:2). These projections looked like horns. They were called the horns of the altar.

In the tabernacle that Moses built, blood on the horns of the altar symbolized the mercy of God for those who had sinned in ignorance (Leviticus, chapter 4). But in this passage, God's attitude of mercy has changed to judgment.

As the sixth trumpet is sounded, the command is given to release "the four angels which are bound in the great river Euphrates" (verse 14). These have to be fallen angels because God's holy angels are never bound. God has held these fallen angels back until this appointed time, and they will only do what God allows them to do.

Perhaps those that are killed would never accept Christ, and would attempt to persuade those that are undecided to accept the mark of the beast.

The four fallen angels released from the pit will be allowed to kill a third of mankind. They will do this by leading an army of 200 million demon horsemen (verse 16). Whereas the demon locusts of the fifth plague were only allowed to torment people, the demon horsemen of the sixth plague will be allowed to kill people. One-third of the earth's entire population will die in this judgment. In Revelation 6:8, we saw that one fourth of the earth's population will be killed during the judgment of the fourth seal, the rider on the pale horse. That could be over 1.6 billion people, depending on when this judgment occurs. In addition, the sixth trumpet judgment (the second woe) will kill one third of the remaining population of the earth, perhaps another 1.6 billion people. Thus, nearly half of the world's population will be killed from the judgments of the fourth seal and the sixth trumpet. Even more would be killed if God did not set limits to this slaughter.

The four evil angels are bound in the area of the Euphrates River. In Old Testament times, God used invasions from the Euphrates area (Assyria and Babylonia) to punish Israel. This area is associated with military invasions by which God brings judgment. This river symbolizes Israel's enemies.

Human rebellion against God on a massive scale first occurred in this area of the world under the leadership of Nimrod (Genesis 10:8-12). It was also in this area that the Tower of Babel was built (Genesis 11:1-9). From this area of the Middle East, the worship of multiple gods and the practice of astrology began to spread around the world. This area has always been a stronghold of demonic activity.

As previously mentioned, the demonic locusts discussed in the fifth trumpet judgment were only allowed to torment people, not kill them. Under the sixth trumpet judgment, the 200 million horsemen will be allowed to kill multitudes of people.

Some believe that the descriptions in verses 17 and 18 refer to some type of modern weaponry. These phrases include "breastplates of fire," and "fire, smoke and brimstone." According to this view, the Apostle John was witnessing things he could not understand or describe. It is sometimes taught that he was attempting to describe nuclear firepower. In addition, it is sometimes taught that this refers to supernatural activities, such as when God sent judgment on the cities of Sodom and Gomorrah (Genesis 19:24-28).

The descriptions given in verses 17 and 19 indicate that the 200 million are not merely people. No human soldiers would fit this description. These horsemen represent demonic spirits from the pit under the leadership of the four evil spirits. However, the 200 million demonic spirits may inhabit 200 million humans. Most likely, 200 million troops of human armies, demonically inspired, will move toward the nation of Israel in preparation for the Battle of Armageddon.

The prophecy in Revelation 9:16-19 probably has a double meaning. It likely refers to a combination of armies of demons and armies of human soldiers. Four evil spirits will be released from the pit to lead an army of demonic spirits. These demons will also inspire human armies that will march against the nation of Israel. Thus, the manifestations described may be a combination of human weaponry and supernatural activities. Multitudes of people will be killed during this invasion.

Today there are nations and alliances that can gather this number of soldiers. Red China alone boasts that it is able to field an army of 200 million. It is also conceivable that an alliance of Muslim nations could field such an army in a so-called "holy war," or Jihad. This would be a demonically inspired army of 200 million human soldiers, coming from either oriental countries, or Islamic countries east of Israel.

Demonic spirits will go to the Orient, to Muslim nations, and to other countries to inspire these armies to be assembled. These demons will work deceptive miracles and manipulate many national leaders, causing them to send military forces against the nation of Israel (Revelation 16:13-16).

Revelation 16:12 states that the River Euphrates will dry up, allowing armies from the east to advance. As previously stated, the kings of the east are either oriental leaders, or leaders of Muslim nations east of Israel. According to Revelation 9:15, it will take the armies of the east one year, one month, one day and one hour to march to the Middle East. This great army will slowly sweep through southern Asia on the way to the Middle East. On this march, they will destroy one-third of the entire population of the earth. The horses that are mentioned may refer to military vehicles that have taken the place of horses. The horse was the most outstanding mode of transportation in John's day. John would have seen the relationship between the vehicles he saw and horses.

After crossing the Euphrates River, which has dried up, these troops will invade Israel toward the very end of the tribulation. This will occur at the Battle of Armageddon (Revelation 16:12-16).

Continued Refusal to Repent

> 20   And the rest of the men which were not killed by these plagues yet repented not of the works of their hands, that they should not worship devils, and idols of gold, and silver, and brass, and stone, and of wood: which neither can see, nor hear, nor walk:
>
> 21   Neither repented they of their murders, nor of their sorceries, nor of their fornication, nor of their thefts.

Even severe judgments from God will not persuade many to repent. Instead, the effect will be the hardening of their hearts (Exodus 8:15-19). Perhaps many people still undecided about Christ, who have not yet taken the mark of the beast, will be persuaded to repent and believe in Jesus.

Verses 20 and 21 mention six major categories of wickedness:

- The worship of demons
- Idolatry (the worship of images, such as money and nature)
- Murders (no regard for human life). Violent murders will be common place.
- Sorcery (witchcraft, the occult, magic arts) will be the leading religion. The Greek word for sorcery (pharmekeia) also indicates a widespread use of drugs and drug addictions in connection with spiritism. Many people will use drugs to escape the horrible conditions that surround them.
- Fornication (sexual immorality, lust, pornography) will abound even during these judgments.
- Thefts (referring to lawlessness and a breakdown of law and order). People will attempt to acquire money and things any way they can during the chaos of the seven-year tribulation.

This lack of repentance illustrates the depth of human depravity that will be very common.

TIME AND ETERNITY: Ecclesiastes 3:1-8, Isaiah 57:15, Revelation 10:6

Fifteen

Revelation – Chapter 10

Brief Summary

Chapter 10 is part of a parenthetical insert in the story. This chapter is another informational chapter. It is an interlude between the sounding of the sixth trumpet in chapter 9 and the seventh trumpet in chapter 11. This break in the story goes from 10:1 to 11:13.

The seven thunders are mentioned. These appear to be another set of judgments that are not revealed.

An angel announces that this present age will soon end, with no further delays. In other words, the remaining events and judgments of the tribulation period will unfold rapidly, bringing the current age to an end.

The Apostle John is instructed to take a little scroll, or little book, and eat it. Although it is sweet in his mouth, it becomes nauseous in his stomach. God's Word is sweet to believers because it brings them love, grace, and hope. But, when rejected, it brings judgment to unbelievers.

The Little Book and the Seven Thunders

1   And I saw another mighty angel come down from heaven, clothed with a cloud: and a rainbow was upon his head, and his face was as it were the sun, and his feet as pillars of fire:

2   And he had in his hand a little book open: and he set his right foot upon the sea, and his left foot on the earth,

> 3   And cried with a loud voice, as when a lion roareth: and when he had cried, seven thunders uttered their voices.
>
> 4   And when the seven thunders had uttered their voices, I was about to write: and I heard a voice from heaven saying unto me, Seal up those things which the seven thunders uttered, and write them not.

An angel comes down from heaven holding a little book, or scroll. This is the second scroll mentioned in Revelation.

This angel will place one foot on the sea and the other foot on the land. This probably signifies that the little book contains a message that will affect the entire surface of the world. Since the angel is standing on the earth, John is no longer in heaven. John has returned to the earth. This angel is referred to as "another mighty angel." Since the word "another" is used in reference to this angel, this is not one of the trumpet angels.

Two Interpretations About the "Mighty Angel" in Chapter 10

1. **This angel is Christ Himself.** In Revelation 11:3, this same angel is speaking and refers to the two witnesses as "my two witnesses." A common angel would not say this.

Also, this angel roars like a lion in verse 3. This connects him with the Lion of Judah, which is Christ (Revelation 5:5). Elsewhere, God is referred to as a lion (Isaiah 31:4-5; Jeremiah 25:30, 37-38; Hosea 11:10; Joel 3:16; Amos 3:7-8). This angel speaking in Revelation, chapters 10 and 11, is not a common angel, but Christ.

2. **This angel is *not* Christ.** Christ would not be referred to simply as "another mighty angel" (Revelation 10:1).

Although the angel of the Lord in the Old Testament was probably a preincarnate manifestation of Christ, the Son of God is never presented as an angel after His death, resurrection, and ascension. After He ascended into heaven, Christ always appears in His deity. The angel referred to in this passage is an unidentified angel, not the Lord Jesus Christ.

The little book contains God's final judgments and the events from this point on until Christ returns in Revelation 19:11. This little book probably also represents the gospel message that John and the two witnesses are called to proclaim (Revelation 10:11; 11:3).

Elsewhere in the Book of Revelation, thunder is associated with God's wrath and judgment (Revelation 8:5; 11:19; 16:18). The seven thunders represent additional judgments from God; however, we do not know what these will be. The seven thunders are an unknown. God would not permit the Apostle John to write about them. This tells us that not all of God's coming tribulation events have been revealed.

An Announcement of No More Delay

> 5   And the angel which I saw stand upon the sea and upon the earth lifted up his hand to heaven,
>
> 6   And sware by him that liveth for ever and ever, who created heaven, and the things that therein are, and the earth, and the things that therein are, and the sea, and the things which are therein, that there should be time no longer:
>
> 7   But in the days of the voice of the seventh angel, when he shall begin to sound, the mystery of God should be finished, as he hath declared to his servants the prophets.

Traditionally, many have interpreted the announcement in verse 6 to mean that chronological time would no longer exist. However, time will continue to exist after this event.

The Greek word translated here as "time" should really be translated "delay." The angel is announcing the end of any further delay. He is proclaiming that this present age will soon end, with no further delays. Time will continue for the remainder of the tribulation and into the Millennium. But the remaining events and judgments of the tribulation period will unfold rapidly, bringing the end of this current age.

Verse 7 refers to a seventh angel. This seventh angel will sound his trumpet in Revelation 11:15. The seventh trumpet involves events extending to the last day of the tribulation, when Christ will visibly return to establish His kingdom on earth. When the events following the seventh trumpet have been completed, all the remaining prophecies that God revealed to His prophets about the final days of this current age will be fulfilled.

The mystery referred to in verse 7 probably pertains to the mystery of the gospel (Colossians 1:26-27; Ephesians 5:32). God's final dealings with Israel will get them to respond positively to the mystery of the gospel (Romans 11:25-28).

The Bitter Sweetness of the Little Book

> 8   And the voice which I heard from heaven spake unto me again, and said, Go and take the little book which is open in the hand of the angel which standeth upon the sea and upon the earth.
>
> 9   And I went unto the angel, and said unto him, Give me the little book. And he said unto me, Take it, and eat it up; and it shall make thy belly bitter, but it shall be in thy mouth sweet as honey.
>
> 10   And I took the little book out of the angel's hand, and ate it up; and it was in my mouth sweet as honey: and as soon as I had eaten it, my belly was bitter.
>
> 11   And he said unto me, Thou must prophesy again before many peoples, and nations, and tongues, and kings.

John was instructed to eat the little book. This does not mean that John was told to eat parchment. Eating a scroll is symbolic of reading, accepting and applying its contents (Jeremiah 15:16; Ezekiel 3:1-4). John had to digest these messages from God mentally. Before a person can be God's spokesman and representative, that person must feed on the Word of God, study it, and digest it.

When John ate the little book, it was sweet in his mouth but nauseous in his stomach. When we feed on the Word of God, it is sometimes sweet like honey. At other times, its reproof and correction can be hard to swallow. The Word of God also has a mixture of blessings and curses. God's Word is sweet to believers because it brings them love, grace, and hope (Psalm 19:9-11); but when rejected, it brings judgment to unbelievers (Matthew 23:37-38; Luke 19:41-44; Jeremiah 20:8-9).

The sweet taste that John enjoyed probably referred to his looking forward to Christ's return. The bitterness that John endured came from the additional judgments he would declare.

Some people believe verse 11 means that John will return to earth in the future to be one of the two witnesses. This is not correct. In verse 11, the Greek word translated "before" should be translated "of" or "about." The verse means that John would prophesy again about peoples and nations.

Dominant church tradition records that John was released from his imprisonment on the island of Patmos, and he was allowed to continue his prophetic ministry in Ephesus.[43] Whether or not that is accurate, one thing is clear: John continued to prophesy about end-time events in the remainder of the Book of Revelation.

FISH in Greek: Jesus, Christ, Son of God, Savior

Sixteen

Revelation – Chapter 11

Brief Summary

Chapter 11 is another informational chapter. The break in the story, or interlude, between the sixth and seventh trumpets started in chapter 10 and continues though 11:13. The events recorded in the first 13 verses of chapter 11 occur in the city where "our Lord was crucified," that is, Jerusalem (Revelation 11:8). This chapter reveals that the nation of Israel will rebuild their temple and return to the Old Testament forms of worship. The temple will be desecrated by the Antichrist in the middle of the tribulation. This will temporarily reestablish Gentile control over the city of Jerusalem. Antichrist's military forces will control this city during the last three-and-one-half years of the tribulation.

This chapter also gives some insight into the ministry of two special followers of God, referred to as the "two witnesses" (Revelation 11:3). They will have a supernatural ministry and appeal to Israel to repent. God will protect the two witnesses for 1,260 days, after which Antichrist will be allowed to kill them. Three-and-one-half days after their deaths, they will be resurrected, and ascend into heaven.

The sounding of the seventh trumpet brings an announcement by angels in heaven that Antichrist's kingdom will be conquered by the kingdom of Christ. When this trumpet blows, there is still a period of 42 months left in the tribulation (Revelation 13:5). Thus, the seventh trumpet (the third woe) introduces the events of the last three-and-one-half years of the tribulation. These events will be revealed in the following chapters and will extend to Christ's return at the end of the tribulation.

The Abomination of Desolation in the Jerusalem Temple

> 1   And there was given me a reed like unto a rod: and the angel stood, saying, Rise, and measure the temple of God, and the altar, and them that worship therein.
>
> 2   But the court which is without the temple leave out, and measure it not; for it is given unto the Gentiles: and the holy city shall they tread under foot forty and two months.

The temple referred to is not the temple that existed in Jesus' day. That temple was destroyed in 70 A.D., about 25 years before John wrote the Book of Revelation. It is also not the millennial temple described in Ezekiel 40-48 because that will not be built until Christ visibly returns to set up His rule on the earth (Zechariah 6:12-13).

The temple referred to in Revelation 11:1-2 will be rebuilt by the Jews either before or during the first half of the tribulation. We know this because this temple will exist at the middle of the tribulation when Antichrist breaks his covenant with the Jews (2 Thessalonians 2:3-4). Although the Muslim Dome of the Rock currently sits on the ancient temple mount, this structure may be destroyed – perhaps by warfare or an earthquake. However, some archaeologists and biblical scholars contend that the Muslim Dome of the Rock is not on the exact spot of the ancient Jewish temple. If this is confirmed, the Israelis could build their temple without disturbing the Muslim Dome of the Rock. Several groups in Israel have prepared materials to be used in the temple when it is rebuilt. When the temple is completed, Israel will return to the Old Testament form of worship.

John was told to measure the temple with a rod. The reed, or rod, referred to here may also be the same reed that is referred to in Revelation 21:15-16, where an angel measures the city of New Jerusalem. It is like a rod or scepter. A scepter was the official staff of a ruler symbolizing his authority and power.

During the first half of the tribulation, most Jews will continue to reject Jesus as their Messiah. This is why they will desire to rebuild their temple and reinstitute an Old Testament type of worship. A holy angel will instruct John to measure this temple. This probably indicates that this Old Testament worship is not a satisfactory thing to God. Nevertheless, there are various interpretations about what this act of measuring means.

Three Interpretations About the Measuring of the Temple

1. *The measuring is for destruction.* There are scriptures that associate a rod with chastisement and even judgment (2 Samuel 7:14; Psalm 2:9; 89:32; Isaiah 11:4; Ezekiel 20:36-37; 1 Corinthians 4:21).

2. *The measuring is for construction of the temple and preservation of the Jews.* The context indicates preservation. The rod and the act of measuring are positive, as it is in Revelation 21:15-16.

3. *The measuring of the temple represents God's measuring of the spiritual condition of the Jewish people in the nation of Israel*

Regardless of the purpose of the measuring of the temple, the temple will be built before or during the first half of the tribulation. At the midpoint of the seven-year tribulation period, Antichrist will break his covenant with Israel (Daniel 9:27) and conquer Jerusalem. Antichrist will also desecrate the Jewish temple in Jerusalem. He will stand in the temple, declaring himself to be a god. Antichrist will speak great blasphemies against the true God and set up an image of himself in the temple, demanding worship (Daniel 11:31, 36-38; Matthew 24:15-16; Mark 13:14; 2 Thessalonians 2:3-4; Revelation 13:4, 8, 12, 14-15; 14:9; 16:2). Antichrist will also begin to persecute the Jews in Israel (Matthew 24:15-21; Mark 13:14-20).

The abomination that causes desolation will be followed by a period of 1,290 days (Daniel 12:11). In other words, when the Antichrist desecrates the temple in Jerusalem, there will be about three-and-one-half years of the tribulation remaining. As previously mentioned, this indicates that the abomination in the temple will occur around the midpoint of the seven-year tribulation.

The 42 months mentioned in verse 2 refer to the final three-and-one-half years of the tribulation (Daniel 7:25; 12:7; 9:27). During these three-and-one-half years, Gentiles (non-Jews) will control Jerusalem under the authority of the Antichrist.

The part of the temple referred to as the court of the Gentiles will not be measured for judgment. Only the things pertaining to the Jewish Old Testament type of worship in the temple will be placed under a rod of judgment. The purpose is to break the spirit of Israel as God calls the Jews to national repentance.

The second half of the tribulation will be the last period of time known as the times of the Gentiles, which are defined as when Gentiles (non-Jews) control the city of Jerusalem. Between 586

B.C. and 1967 A.D. Gentiles primarily controlled the city of Jerusalem. Jesus gave us an indication as to when the times of the Gentiles will be fulfilled. In Luke 21:24, Jesus said the Gentile Age would come to an end after the Jews again control the city of Jerusalem. The initial fulfillment of Jewish control of Jerusalem occurred in 1967 during the "six-day war." Thus, we are now living in the closing of the Gentile Age. God is now shifting His prophetic attention away from the Gentiles and back to the Jews.

The Jews will lose control of the city of Jerusalem in the middle of Daniel's 70th week, when Antichrist will break his seven-year covenant with Israel. Jerusalem will again be in Gentile hands for 42 months (Revelation 11:1-2; 13:5). Antichrist will also begin to persecute the Jews, particularly those who have come to accept Jesus as their Messiah, under the ministry of the 144,000 and the two witnesses. While Gentile forces under the command of the Antichrist control the city, the Israelis will flee to the wilderness for protection (Revelation 12:6,14). This will occur during the second half of the tribulation after the seven seals of judgment and the first six trumpet judgments have begun.

The city will finally be liberated at the Second Coming of Christ (Revelation 19:11-21; Zechariah 14:2-4; 2 Thessalonians 2:8). The times of the Gentiles will then end. Speaking primarily for the benefit of Jews living in Israel during the second half of the tribulation, Jesus said, "And when these things begin to come to pass, then look up, and lift up your heads; for your redemption draweth nigh" (Luke 21:28).

The Two Witnesses

3   And I will give power unto my two witnesses, and they shall prophesy a thousand two hundred and threescore days, clothed in sackcloth.

4   These are the two olive trees, and the two candlesticks standing before the God of the earth.

5   And if any man will hurt them, fire proceedeth out of their mouth, and devoureth their enemies: and if any man will hurt them, he must in this manner be killed.

6   These have power to shut heaven, that it rain not in the days of their prophecy: and have power over waters to turn them to blood, and to smite the earth with all plagues, as often as they will.

7   And when they shall have finished their testimony, the beast that ascendeth out of the bottomless pit shall make war against them, and shall overcome them, and kill them.

8   And their dead bodies shall lie in the street of the great city, which spiritually is called Sodom and Egypt, where also our Lord was crucified.

9   And they of the people and kindreds and tongues and nations shall see their dead bodies three days and an half, and shall not suffer their dead bodies to be put in graves.

10   And they that dwell upon the earth shall rejoice over them, and make merry, and shall send gifts one to another; because these two prophets tormented them that dwelt on the earth.

11   And after three days and an half the Spirit of life from God entered into them, and they stood upon their feet; and great fear fell upon them which saw them.

12   And they heard a great voice from heaven saying unto them, Come up hither. And they ascended up to heaven in a cloud; and their enemies beheld them.

13   And the same hour was there a great earthquake, and the tenth part of the city fell, and in the earthquake were slain of men seven thousand: and the remnant were affrighted, and gave glory to the God of heaven.

It is important to note that the two witnesses are two men. They are not two covenants or two dispensations as some teach. Verse 3 indicates these are two individuals. Sackcloth symbolizes a call to repentance.

God will anoint these two witnesses to preach the gospel and prophecy about the future. They will be His spokesmen and ministers on the earth for 1,260 days. This is about 42 months, or three-and-one-half years. It appears that God is using prophetic years, which only contain 360 days per year. Thus, these may be three-and-one-half prophetic years (see notes under Revelation 12:6 and 12:14). The number three-and-one-half is half of the perfect number 7. Thus, three-and-one-half can represent incompletion, imperfection and evil.

The two olive trees and the two candlesticks represent the two witnesses. They will be empowered by the Spirit of God to reveal the light and truth of God. This is consistent with Zechariah 4:3, 11-14, where the two olive trees represented two godly individuals: Zerubbabel the governor (representing the civil authority) and Joshua the high priest (representing the religious authority). In the Book of Zechariah, the olive trees are also types of the kingly and priestly ministries of Jesus Christ. In addition, Zerubbabel and Joshua are types of the two witnesses that will appear during the seven-year tribulation period. As a result, some believe that the two witnesses will be Zerubbabel and Joshua. However, this is mere speculation and cannot be supported in scripture. These olive trees are figures of speech and can also apply to any individual who stands before God on behalf of others.

Malachi 4:5 indicates that Elijah will return before the last judgment. As a result, many believe that Elijah will be one of the two witnesses. John the Baptist is referred to in Malachi 3:1, indicating that he would have a similar ministry to that of Elijah. However, Elijah must appear again to completely fulfill Malachi 3 and 4. The remaining verses in that passage refer to the future ministry of Elijah. This will be during the tribulation, prior to the visible return of Christ. It is commonly accepted that Elijah will be one of the two witnesses. However, some contend that the scriptures do not require the literal return of Elijah. Instead, this may be someone who has a ministry with power similar to that of Elijah.

Some believe that John will be one of the two witnesses because he was told in Revelation 10:11 that he would have a future ministry. As previously mentioned, that verse means that John would prophesy again concerning peoples and nations. That is what John did in the remainder of the Book of Revelation. The idea that John will be one of the two witnesses is not supported in scripture.

Some believe the two witnesses will be Elijah and Moses. Revelation 11:6 tells us that the two witnesses will have power to shut up the sky so it will not rain (resembling Elijah) and to call plagues down upon the earth (resembling Moses). But the more compelling reason why Moses may be one of the two witnesses has to do with an account in the gospels. Both Moses and Elijah appeared with Christ on the Mount of Transfiguration. This event was a special revelation of Jesus' divinity and glory (Matthew 17:1-5; Mark 9:2-4; Luke 9:28-31). The Transfiguration was also a preview of the glorious return of Christ.

There was a special reason Moses and Elijah were chosen to appear with Jesus at His Transfiguration. Moses represented the Old Testament Law. Elijah represented the prophets. Together they confirmed the abolition of the Law and the fulfillment of prophecies of the suffering Messiah. In addition, Moses and Elijah together represent the entire Old Testament to the Jewish nation. At the Mount of Transfiguration, Moses and Elijah, representing the Law and the prophets, transferred the authority of the offices they represented to the Lamb of God. Perhaps Moses and Elijah, as representatives of the entire Old Testament, will once again be selected by God to be witnesses to the nation of Israel during the seven-year tribulation. Moses may be one of the two witnesses, but this is not certain.

Enoch may be one of the two witnesses. This view is based on the fact that Elijah and Enoch were both taken to heaven without experiencing death (2 Kings 2:11; Hebrews 11:5). Hebrews 9:27 states that all people are destined to die once, and to face judgment afterwards. According to this view, Elijah and Enoch will both eventually be required to experience death on earth, as all other humans before the rapture have done. In addition, Jude 14-15 reveals that Enoch prophesied about the Second Coming of Christ. As a result, many associate Enoch with events during the tribulation that precede Christ's visible return.

The fact that Enoch did not die does not prove he will be one of the two witnesses. All believers who are alive at the rapture will also be exceptions to Hebrews 9:27, for they too will be taken up to heaven without experiencing death (1 Thessalonians 4:13-18). On the other hand, the fact that Antichrist will eventually "kill" the two witnesses probably indicates that these will be two natural men who have never died. They will still be in their natural bodies as mortals. Otherwise, the Antichrist would not be able to kill them.

Some argue that since the two witnesses will be killed, this excludes Moses from being one of these witnesses. The reason is that Moses, in his spiritual state, could not be killed by the Antichrist. Elijah may be one of the two witnesses. Enoch may be the other. But in the final analysis, the identities of these two witnesses are not certain.

Verse 5 indicates that God will protect the two witnesses from assassination attempts. The two witnesses will be given power from God to call down judgments on anyone attempting to hurt them. They will also have the power to send fire out of their mouths and kill anyone that would attack them. They will defy the Antichrist. The purpose of their power will be to glorify God.

Whereas the 144,000 Jewish evangelists will be witnesses for God throughout the earth, the two witnesses will most likely focus on the nation of Israel. These special witnesses will attempt to convince the Jewish nation to return to the one true God and to accept His son Jesus as their Messiah.

The two witnesses will have great supernatural power to exercise some of the judgments mentioned in chapters 8 and 9. They will be a great threat to the Antichrist and his system for three-and-one-half years.

The Antichrist will aspire to be a world dictator and attempt to gain the following of the entire world. This will be discussed as we study chapter 13. However, Antichrist will not be able to control the two witnesses in Jerusalem, or the ministry of the 144,000. There will also be plagues everywhere that will be hard for him to explain.

Verse 7 reveals that the two witnesses cannot be killed until they finish the work God has assigned to them. After three-and-one-half years of ministry, God will allow the two witnesses to be killed. "The beast" that will come out of the bottomless pit will kill them.

The phrase in verse 7, "the beast," is used for the first time in the Book of Revelation. Some have interpreted this beast to be Satan, or a system inspired and controlled by Satan. It actually refers to the Antichrist, who is called a beast in Revelation 13:1-7. His coming out of the abyss either refers to the source of Antichrist's inspiration, or it refers to a death and resurrection of the Antichrist. We will discuss these two views as we study Revelation, chapter 13.

After the two witnesses have finished their testimony, God will allow the beast to kill them.

Two Interpretations About When the Two Witnesses Will Conduct Their Ministries

1. **The two witnesses will minister during the second half of the tribulation.** During the time of their preaching, the Gentiles will control the city of Jerusalem for three-and-one-half years (Revelation 11:2-3). These 42 months refer to the last three-and-one-half years of the tribulation (Daniel 9:27).

The death of the two witnesses in Revelation 11:7 jumps ahead to the last several days of the tribulation. The two witnesses will probably be counting off the months and days until Christ returns. This will add to the Antichrist's anger.

In Revelation 11:3, God gives the two witnesses their power after the sixth trumpet, at the middle of the tribulation. Since the two witnesses are not mentioned until after the seals and first six trumpets, at midtribulation, their public ministry occurs during the second half of the tribulation.

The Antichrist will be allowed to kill the two witnesses when they have finished their three-and-one-half year ministries during the closing days of the tribulation.

2. **The two witnesses will minister during the first half of the tribulation.** In Revelation 11:1, the Apostle John was told to measure the temple of God. The two witnesses are mentioned immediately after this. The ministry of the two witnesses will begin during the rebuilding of the temple, toward the beginning of the tribulation.

The ministries and deaths of the two witnesses in Revelation 11:1-13 take place before the seventh trumpet (the third woe) in 11:14. When the seventh trumpet is sounded, there is still a period of 42 months left in the tribulation (Revelation 13:5). Revelation 12:6 also mentions 1,260 days.

Thus, the seventh trumpet blows in the middle of the seven-year tribulation period. The two witnesses conduct their ministries during the first half of the tribulation, and die before the seventh trumpet, at midtribulation.

Revelation 11:7 jumps ahead to the middle of the tribulation period. When Antichrist conquers Jerusalem at midtribulation, God will allow him to kill the two witnesses.

Verse 8 mentions the "great city, . . . where also our Lord was crucified." This refers to the city of Jerusalem. Jerusalem will be severely judged because of her rejection of Christ. In verse 8, Jerusalem and Israel are seen as being immoral like ancient Sodom, and worldly and materialistic like ancient Egypt.

We are told in verse 9 that the dead bodies of the two witnesses will lie in a street in Jerusalem for three-and-one-half days without burial. The whole world will witness this through the mass media. No one will be permitted to touch their bodies or to put them in a grave as they decompose.

Most of the world will rejoice at the death of the two witnesses (verse 10). This is because the two witnesses will have confronted the world about its sin and the need for repentance. The witnesses will have also proclaimed the coming judgments of God. Even a majority of those undecided about the Antichrist will be happy about the deaths of the two witnesses.

Verse 11 tells us that the two witnesses will be resurrected three and one-half days after they are killed. Fear will come upon unbelievers throughout the world and pandemonium will break out. This occurs after they have completed their three-and-one-half years of ministry, and after they have been dead for three-and-one-half days.

The two witnesses will be caught up to heaven while their enemies watch them (verse 12). Their resurrection will be a sign that they were representatives of the one true God.

During the same hour that the two witnesses are resurrected and raptured, a great earthquake will occur (verse 13). One-tenth of the buildings in Jerusalem will be destroyed and 7,000 people will be killed. This is an upheaval of nature that may have been withheld since the opening of the sixth seal in Revelation 6:12-17.

The "remnant" refers to those Jews who survive the earthquake. Some of these Jews may have come to believe on the Lord Jesus Christ. This remnant will begin to display a great reverence for God. This event may start a revival throughout the nation of Israel. Because of the resurrection of the two witnesses (Revelation 11:11-12) and God's judgment on Jerusalem (Revelation 11:13), many of the surviving Jews in Israel will accept the gospel message that had been preached by the two witnesses. A sizeable number of Jews in Israel will eventually turn to Jesus as their Messiah, giving glory to God (Romans 11:25-27).

Many of the Jews in Israel will be hidden from the Antichrist during the second half of the tribulation. We will discuss this as we review Revelation, chapter 12.

The Seventh Trumpet: The Beginning of Events During the Second Half of the Tribulation (The Third Woe)

> 14   The second woe is past; and, behold, the third woe cometh quickly.
>
> 15   And the seventh angel sounded; and there were great voices in heaven, saying, The kingdoms of this world are become the kingdoms of our Lord, and of his Christ; and he shall reign for ever and ever.

Perhaps Handel, the great composer, incorporated words from verse 15 into his great masterpiece, *The Messiah*. It is customary for audiences to stand when they hear the words of the closing chorus: "and He shall reign forever and ever."

The seventh trumpet is sounded shortly after the Antichrist breaks his covenant with the Jews, in the middle of the tribulation.

The third woe has to do with the sounding of the seventh trumpet. This is an announcement that anticipates the glory of the coming reign of Christ on the earth. This announcement also precedes the next set of judgments, the seven bowls, or vials. The seventh trumpet (the third woe) introduces the events of the last three-and-one-half years of the tribulation. When this trumpet blows, there is still a period of 42 months left in the tribulation (Revelation 13:5). These 1,260 days are also mentioned in Revelation 12:6. Thus, the seventh trumpet blows in the middle of the seven-year tribulation period. The seventh trumpet introduces events that extend to Christ's return at the end of the seven years.

This is an announcement by angels in heaven that Antichrist's kingdom will be conquered by the kingdom of Christ. This will be fulfilled when Jesus visibly returns to the earth to reign forever. Christ's rule will become visibly manifest on the earth, beginning in Revelation 19:11.

The events resulting from the seventh trumpet (the third woe) carry over into Revelation, chapters 12 and 13. The main event under the seventh trumpet is the casting out of Satan and his forces from the heavens (12:13). The seventh trumpet also includes some events in Revelation, chapter 16.

> 16 And the four and twenty elders, which sat before God on their seats, fell upon their faces, and worshipped God,
>
> 17 Saying, We give thee thanks, O Lord God Almighty, which art, and wast, and art to come; because thou hast taken to thee thy great power, and hast reigned.
>
> 18 And the nations were angry, and thy wrath is come, and the time of the dead, that they should be judged, and that thou shouldest give reward unto thy servants the prophets, and to the saints, and them that fear thy name, small and great; and shouldest destroy them which destroy the earth.

The 24 elders sing a song of thanksgiving. In this song, they prophesy four things that will occur, if not during the tribulation, then afterwards:

(1) The nations will be enraged because they have experienced God's wrath.
(2) The dead will be judged.
(3) God's servants will be rewarded.
(4) God will destroy those who destroy the earth, that is, those who are evil.

Believers and unbelievers will be judged separately.

The Judgment Seat of Christ: All believers will stand before the judgment seat of Christ. Those who are raptured will be judged in heaven during the tribulation. This will occur after Christ comes for His church (Revelation 22:12), which applies to both the rapture and the Second Coming. This is not a judgment of sin, for believers have had their sins judged and forgiven at the cross (Romans 8:1). It will not determine whether or not believers will enter heaven. Instead, it will determine their degrees of rewards throughout eternity (2 Corinthians 5:10; Romans 14:10; 1 Corinthians 3:11-15; Matthew 25:23). Believers on earth who survive the tribulation will be judged at Christ's glorious appearing. This will occur at the end of the tribulation when He brings rewards for His followers (Revelation 22:12). God judging His own people is also referred to in Psalm 50:3-6.

The Great White Throne Judgment: Unbelievers will be judged a thousand years later at the end of the Millennium (Revelation 20:11-15). Those who die before the Millennium without a faith in the true God will be sent to a place of torment (called Hades in most translations – Luke 16:19-31). At the Great White Throne Judgment, they will be transferred from Hades to the Lake of Fire (Revelation 20:14-15).

Despite God's judgments, verses 15-19 look forward to the time of Christ's glorious reign on the earth.

> 19   And the temple of God was opened in heaven, and there was seen in his temple the ark of his testament: and there were lightnings, and voices, and thunderings, and an earthquake, and great hail.

The temple of God in heaven was revealed to John. The ark referred to is not the one that Moses built, but the original ark in heaven. This glimpse of the Ark of the Covenant is a reminder to Israel and all believers in Christ that God is a covenant keeper. God has initiated several covenants. Humans have enjoyed the benefits of these covenants as long as they were obedient to the terms that God set forth.

The lightning and thunder represent the terror and confusion that people on the earth will experience during the last half of the tribulation.

Events of the seventh trumpet extend into Revelation, chapters 12 and 13. These include the casting out of Satan from the heavens; the persecution of the remnant; the flight of the woman into the wilderness; the rise of the beast out of the sea; and the rise of a second beast out of the earth.

Seventeen

Revelation – Chapter 12

Brief Summary

The seventh trumpet (also the third woe) was sounded in chapter 11. This initiated the seven bowl judgments, which carry over into Revelation, chapters 12, 13, and 16. The main event under the seventh trumpet is the casting out of Satan and his forces from the heavens (Revelation 12:13).

Chapter 12 is another informational chapter. It gives insight into the woman that brings forth a male child. After she gives birth to this male child, the child will be caught up to heaven (12:5). The woman will flee into the wilderness (12:6). The dragon will be cast to the earth where he will persecute the woman (12:13). These are symbols that obviously represent other things:

(1)   The dragon clearly represents Satan (12:9).

(2)   Some have speculated that the male child represents the 144,000 Jewish evangelists or the church. However, Revelation 12:5 states that this male child will "rule all nations with a rod of iron." Thus, the male child refers to the Lord Jesus Christ (Revelation 19:11-15).

(3)   Some have speculated that the woman refers to the Virgin Mary or the church. These teachings are inaccurate for the following reasons:

Brief Summary, continued

A.   The events described in the Book of Revelation concerning the woman and the male child are not consistent with the stories in the gospels about Jesus and the Virgin Mary. This woman is not the Virgin Mary.

B.   The woman gave birth to the male child. The woman does not represent the church, because Christ gave birth to the church. The church did not give birth to Christ.

The woman represents the people and nation of Israel, which gave birth to the Messiah.

What does all this mean? The dragon (Satan) will persecute the woman (the nation of Israel) who brought forth a male child (Christ). This persecution of Israel will intensify in the middle of the tribulation, when Satan and his demons are cast out of the heavens, and restricted to earth.

The Woman, Man Child, and Dragon

1   And there appeared a great wonder in heaven; a woman clothed with the sun, and the moon under her feet, and upon her head a crown of twelve stars:

2   And she being with child cried, travailing in birth, and pained to be delivered.

3   And there appeared another wonder in heaven; and behold a great red dragon, having seven heads and ten horns, and seven crowns upon his heads.

4   And his tail drew the third part of the stars of heaven, and did cast them to the earth: and the dragon stood before the woman which was ready to be delivered, for to devour her child as soon as it was born.

5   And she brought forth a man child, who was to rule all nations with a rod of iron: and her child was caught up unto God, and to his throne.

6   And the woman fled into the wilderness, where she hath a place prepared of God, that they should feed her there a thousand two hundred and threescore days.

Verse 1 states that a great wonder (better translated sign) appeared in heaven. This indicates that the woman is not a literal woman, but represents something else. The woman is "clothed with the sun, and the moon under her feet." On her head is "a crown of twelve stars."

In Joseph's dream, in Genesis 37:9-11, stars represented the forefathers (patriarchs) of the Israelite nation and the 12 tribes. In the same way, the 12 stars in Revelation 12:1 represent the 12 tribes of Israel. This woman represents Israel. The sun is a source of light, and the moon is a reflector of that light. God intended for the nation of Israel to reflect His light to all the other nations. She largely failed in this mission. But, the nation of Israel will reflect God's light and message during the tribulation, primarily through the 144,000 Jewish evangelists.

The number of the tribes (12) represents God's divine administration and governmental perfection. This was what God intended for the nation of Israel.

Some teach that this woman represents the Virgin Mary who gave birth to a male child: Jesus Christ. However, the events described in the Book of Revelation concerning the woman and the male child are not consistent with the stories in the gospels about Jesus and the Virgin Mary. For example, in Revelation 12:6 the woman flees into the wilderness for 1,260 days. But, the gospels do not state that the Virgin Mary fled into the wilderness. Also, Revelation 12:16 states that the dragon will pursue the woman like a flood, but the earth will swallow up the flood. This woman is not the Virgin Mary.

Some teach that this woman represents the church (all true believers in Christ). But, the church did not give birth to the Jewish Messiah. Jesus gave birth to the church.

In the Old Testament, the nation of Israel is sometimes represented as a woman (Isaiah 66:7-8; Jeremiah 2:32) and as a married woman (Isaiah 54:5-6; 62:5; Jeremiah 3:1-14, 20; Hosea 2:2-23). Israel is also pictured as a woman in pain (Isaiah 26:17-18; Jeremiah 4:31; 13:21; Micah 4:9-10; 5:3). The nation of Israel will greatly suffer during the tribulation (Daniel 12:1; Matthew 24:15-22).

The woman is a symbol of the nation of Israel, which gave birth to the Messiah. The symbolism refers to the struggle of the Jews in producing, and being identified with, the Messiah. The woman represents those Jews living in Palestine during the tribulation. In Revelation 12:2, the pain of childbirth also represents the misery of the nation of Israel during the second half of the tribulation (Revelation 12:13).

Verse 3 refers to Satan.

(1) The dragon is a symbol of Satan (Revelation 12:9).
(2) He is red because he has greatly inspired most of the bloodshed in world history.
(3) The heads represent complete authority. These seven heads may also represent seven great kingdoms. We will discuss these kingdoms in Revelation, chapters 13 and 17.

(4)   Horns are a symbol of political and physical strength. Ten represents completeness. Here, it represents an earthly completeness, which is limited. The 10 horns represent 10 lesser kingdoms, which we will also discuss in Revelation, chapters 13 and 17.

(5)   Seven crowns represent political authority.

Verse 4 states that one-third of the stars of heaven were cast to the earth. These are not literal stars that were cast to the earth because stars are generally larger than the earth. Also, in the Book of Revelation, both men and angels are called stars (1:20; 9:1). The stars in 12:4 symbolize the angels of God.

Satan was originally created as an angelic being of great beauty (Ezekiel 28:15). However, he eventually developed a strange self-infatuation (Ezekiel 28:17). In the ancient past, Satan rebelled against God and was cast out of heaven (Isaiah 14:12-16; Ezekiel 28:11-17; Luke 10:18). He sought to exalt his "throne above the stars of God," so as to be like the most high. There was war in heaven (Revelation 12:7-9) and Satan was cast out of heaven (Luke 10:18). Revelation 12:4 indicates that one-third of the angels also rebelled against God and fell with Satan. These fallen angels became the demonic principalities mentioned in Ephesians 6:12.

Two Interpretations About the Male Child

1. **The male child refers to Christ.** Verse 5 states that the male child will rule all nations with a rod of iron. This is a reference to Christ's millennial reign on the earth (Revelation 19:11-15). The snatching up of the child in verse 5 refers to Christ's past ascension into heaven after his resurrection (Luke 24:51; Acts 1:9-11). Revelation 12:4 also indicates that the dragon (Satan) wanted to devour the woman's "child as soon as it was born." This male child is Jesus Christ. The dragon (Satan) wanted to devour (kill) Jesus shortly after He was born. Consequently, Satan inspired King Herod to order that all the babies in Bethlehem age two and under be killed (Matthew 2:7-16).

2. **The male child refers to the 144,000** saved Jews. Satan will desire to "devour" them when they are converted to Christ. Verse 5 does not refer to the historical birth and ascension of Christ. The snatching up of the child in verse 5 refers to a midtribulation rapture, which occurs just before Revelation 14:1-5. This is when the 144,000 suddenly appear before God's throne in heaven. This male child (the 144,000) will also be part of the company of believers that will assist Christ in ruling with a rod of iron during the Millennium (Daniel 7:18, 27; Revelation 2:26-27; 5:10; 20:6).

The Antichrist will persecute believers in Christ and the Jews in Israel (Daniel 7:21-25; 8:24). Much of the nation of Israel (the woman) will flee from the Jerusalem area into the wilderness (Matthew 24:15-22). God will prepare a place where the Jews will be protected for 1,260 days. Many of these Jews will begin to sincerely search the scriptures and will accept Jesus Christ as their Messiah (Zechariah 13:8-9). They will be divinely protected (Revelation 12:13-16).

Daniel 11:41 mentions three ancient countries (Edom, Moab, and Ammon) that will escape the Antichrist's rule. These three ancient countries make up modern day Jordan. The nation of Jordan may be the place where most of the Jews who flee Palestine will hide.

God will protect many of these Jews by diverting the Antichrist's attention. The Antichrist will become distracted by threats from the north and east (Daniel 11:44-45). The nations to the north and east will move against the Antichrist to bring an end to his conquests. This will keep him occupied during most of the last half of the tribulation, and divert his attention from Israel (the woman), whom he is trying to persecute.

Eventually, the nations under the influence of Antichrist will be inspired by Satan to move their military forces against Israel and the remaining Jews that did not flee into the wilderness. This will be the second attempted invasion of Israel during the tribulation. In this second invasion, half of the city of Jerusalem will be destroyed (Zechariah 14:1-2).

The Jews will cry as they never have before for their Messiah to come. Many Jews will turn to Christ (Romans 11:25-26). Were it not for the direct intervention of God, the Antichrist's armies would completely annihilate the Jews in Palistine.

Christ will intervene from heaven (Zechariah 14:3-5; Rev. 16:16-21; 19:11-21) at the Battle of Armageddon. The woman (Israel) will be delivered at the end of the tribulation. Most of the nation of Israel will be converted to Jesus just prior to His return (Romans 11:26-27; Revelation 19:11-20:6).

Revelation 12:6 indicates that the woman will flee into the wilderness for 1,260 days. However, Revelation 12:14 states that the woman will flee into the wilderness for "a time, and times, and half a time," which is usually interpreted as three-and-one-half years. The 1,260 days in verse 6 is slightly less than the three-and-one-half years in verse 14. This indicates that God is using the traditional Jewish prophetic years of 360 days each (360 x 3 1/2 = 1,260).

A Future War in Heaven

7   And there was war in heaven: Michael and his angels fought against the dragon; and the dragon fought and his angels,

8   And prevailed not; neither was their place found any more in heaven.

9   And the great dragon was cast out, that old serpent, called the Devil, and Satan, which deceiveth the whole world: he was cast out into the earth, and his angels were cast out with him.

10   And I heard a loud voice saying in heaven, Now is come salvation, and strength, and the kingdom of our God, and the power of his Christ: for the accuser of our brethren is cast down, which accused them before our God day and night.

11   And they overcame him by the blood of the Lamb, and by the word of their testimony; and they loved not their lives unto the death.

12   Therefore rejoice, ye heavens, and ye that dwell in them. Woe to the inhabiters of the earth and of the sea! for the devil is come down unto you, having great wrath, because he knoweth that he hath but a short time.

Revelation 12:7-10 appears to have a double meaning. It refers to a past war when Satan and the angels that rebelled with him were cast out of heaven. It also refers to a future war in heaven. We know this because after this war, Satan will only have a short time left to exercise his wrath on the earth (Revelation 12:12). This short time is later described as "a time, and times, and half a time" (Revelation 12:14). This is usually interpreted to mean the last three and one-half years of the tribulation. This future heavenly battle will take place at the midpoint of the tribulation.

As a result of Christ's death on the cross, Satan has already been defeated (Revelation 12:10-12). Although Satan was previously cast out of heaven (Isaiah 14:12-15; Ezekiel 28:11-17; Luke 10:18), he has continued to have access to heaven where he accuses the believers before God (Job 1 and 2; Revelation 12:10). Satan also still has power in the heavens immediately surrounding the earth (Ephesians 2:2; 6:12). In addition, Satan is very powerful on the earth (John 12:31; 14:30; 16:11).

Satan and his angels may attempt to invade heaven where God lives. This attempted invasion will be defeated. In this future war in heaven, Michael, the archangel, will be in command of the angels of God (Revelation 12:7). The devil and his angels will be cast down to earth (Revelation 12:9-13). After this, Satan will no longer have access to heaven to accuse believers (Revelation 12:10). In addition, Satan will no longer have power in heavenly places. This will occur in the middle of the tribulation.

After Satan and his angels are cast out of the heavens, they will be restricted to this world. The inhabitants of heaven will rejoice (verse 12). However, those that live on the earth will experience great wrath from Satan during the remainder of the tribulation period. The casting of Satan to the earth begins the second three-and-one-half years of the tribulation, known as The Great Tribulation.

Realizing that he only has a short time – three-and-one-half years (Revelation 12:6,14) – Satan will exercise great wrath against the woman (Israel) who gave birth to the child (Christ). The earth will receive not only wrath from Satan, but also the wrath of God in the seven trumpet and seven bowl judgments.

Faithful believers on the earth will be able to overcome Satan, even if this means dying for their faith. They will be empowered to do this because of the delegated power and authority they receive from Christ's shed blood on the cross. These believers will be anointed to testify about their faith in Christ, even in the face of martyrdom.

God Protects the Woman

13   And when the dragon saw that he was cast unto the earth, he persecuted the woman which brought forth the man child.

14   And to the woman were given two wings of a great eagle, that she might fly into the wilderness, into her place, where she is nourished for a time, and times, and half a time, from the face of the serpent.

15   And the serpent cast out of his mouth water as a flood after the woman, that he might cause her to be carried away of the flood.

16   And the earth helped the woman, and the earth opened her mouth, and swallowed up the flood which the dragon cast out of his mouth.

17   And the dragon was wroth with the woman, and went to make war with the remnant of her seed, which keep the commandments of God, and have the testimony of Jesus Christ.

As previously mentioned, Satan will inspire the Antichrist to break his covenant with Israel (Daniel 9:27) and to persecute the Jews living in Palestine (verse 13). Many of the Israelis will be forced to flee into the wilderness (Revelation 12:6,14; Matthew 24:15-22; Mark 13:14-20). Those Jews in Israel, particularly those who have accepted Christ, will be hunted by the forces of the Antichrist (Revelation 12:13-14). As previously mentioned, God will protect many Jews from the Antichrist (Revelation 12:14-16).

God will help the Jews in Israel who take flight by giving them a special hiding place. This flight is symbolized by "two wings of a great eagle" (verse 14). Some speculate that since the eagle is the national emblem of the United States, verse 14 refers to an American air lift for many of the Jews that will flee from Antichrist's wrath.

Verse 14 states that the woman will flee into the wilderness for "a time, and times, and half a time," which is usually interpreted as three and one-half years. However, Revelation 12:6 states that the woman will flee into the wilderness for 1,260 days, which is slightly less than three-and-one-half years. This indicates that the 490 years in Daniel's 70-week prophecy are the traditional Jewish prophectic years of 360 days each (360 x 3 1/2 = 1,260).

When the serpent (Satan) realizes that the woman (the nation of Israel) is fleeing, Satan's wrath will pursue her like a flood (verse 15). God will provide a way of escape for the woman by causing the earth to swallow the flood (verse 16).

Two Interpretations of the Satanic Flood

1. **The flood refers to the armies of the Antichrist pursuing the Jews** in the wilderness to kill them.

In scripture, armies are sometimes depicted as floods (Jeremiah 46:7-9; 47:2-3; Daniel 9:26; 11:21-22, 26). God uses the earth to swallow up these pursuing armies.

2. **The flood is symbolic of words.** Satanically inspired words will come out of the mouth of the Antichrist while trying to persuade the nations to exterminate the Jews.

Much of the remnant of Israel will be hidden among the nations of the world. This flood of words is designed to convince the nations to destroy the Jews wherever they may be found. But, the nations of the earth help the woman (Israel) by largely ignoring Antichrist's oratory about destroying the Jews.

Perhaps both of these interpretations are true. This Satanic flood may stand for pursuing armies of the Antichrist in Palestine, and for satanically inspired oratory of anti-Semitism.

Satan will motivate the Antichrist to search for the local remnant of Jews who remain in Palestine. Toward the end of the tribulation, many of these Jews will have taken on the testimony of Jesus as their Messiah (verse 17). But, they will not flee into the wilderness. Antichrist's persecution will particularly focus on this remnant of the woman's seed.

As previously mentioned, Antichrist will be distracted from his persecution of the Jews because of news he receives from the east and the north (Daniel 11:44-45). It appears that several nations in Asia and Eastern Europe will form an alliance against the conquests of the Antichrist. This will keep him occupied for much of the last three-and-one-half years of the tribulation. For the most part, Antichrist will leave Israel alone while he is busy conquering his new enemies.

Some believe that Isaiah 16:1-5 is a prophecy of the persecution and flight of the woman (the nation of Israel). This passage may indicate she will flee to a place called Sela, also called Petra by the Romans. Sela means "rock" or "stronghold." This is a rock shaped fortress city in the mountains of ancient Edom. As previously mentioned, many Jews will take shelter in Edom, Moab, and Ammon (modern day Jordan). These are territories that will not be controlled by the Antichrist (Daniel 11:41). The Jordanians will not betray the Israelites to Antichrist.

SATAN, and Sin: Genesis 3:14

Eighteen

Revelation – Chapter 13

Brief Summary

Chapter 13 is another informational chapter. This chapter describes some of the conditions resulting from Satan being cast out of the heavens. Two beasts are mentioned. The first beast will rise out of the sea, having seven heads and ten horns. This beast represents the Antichrist. These terms are symbolic:

Sea: In scripture, when the word sea is used, and it is not referring to a specific body of water, it can be symbolic of great masses of people or nations. The Antichrist will suddenly arise out of the great masses of humanity.

Seven Heads: Some believe that the seven heads represent seven large kingdoms, mainly in the past. All of these kingdoms, or empires, were controlled by a satanic beast system. Others believe that these seven heads refer to the Seven Hills of Rome, where Antichrist will set up his headquarters. Perhaps the "seven heads" have a double meaning and both views are correct.

10 Horns: Horns can also represent kings or rulers. The 10 horns of the Antichrist represent an alliance of 10 kingdoms. Antichrist will gain control of these 10 kingdoms.

Brief Summary, continued

The second beast in chapter 13 will rise from the earth. The word "earth" represents peoples of the earth, similar to the word "sea" representing masses of people. The second beast represents a religious leader, later referred to as the false prophet. He will be a prophet of the Antichrist, deceiving many to accept the Antichrist as God. The false prophet will be a miracle-worker, using demonic deception. He will attempt to force everyone to receive the mark of the beast on his or her right hand or forehead.

Whereas the first beast will have great political power over an anti-Christian government, the second beast will preside over an anti-Christian religion. Whether or not Antichrist's government will preside over the entire world is debatable. But, Antichrist will probably dominate the global economy.

Chapter 13 should be seen as connected with chapter 17 for the best continuity of thought.

Chapter 13 sheds more light on the person known as the Antichrist. The term Antichrist appears only in 1 John 2:18-22; 4:3; and 2 John 7. The Apostle John uses this expression to describe those persons who oppose Christ and deny His deity. However, the scriptures also teach that one person will rise to leadership during the end times that will personify, more than anyone else, opposition and hatred for Christian values. He will oppose everything that Christ represents. He will also be a man of lawlessness (2 Thessalonians 2:3-8), with great occult powers (2 Thessalonians 2:9).

Antichrist will have a forceful and even dynamic personality (Daniel 7:20). He will blaspheme God and declare himself to be God (2 Thessalonians 2:3-4). One of his primary characteristics will be deceptiveness (Daniel 8:25). His power will come from Satan (2 Thessalonians 2:9). Antichrist will eventually persecute the Jews in Israel (Daniel 8:24).

The beast and the false prophet that are described in Revelation, chapter 13, are individuals. This is made clear in Revelation 19:20, when each is thrown into the lake of fire.

As previously mentioned, the Antichrist will enter into a covenant with the nation of Israel for seven years (Daniel 9:27). He will break this peace treaty with the Israelis in the middle of the tribulation. Although Antichrist may initially rise to power by diplomatic means, he will soon reveal himself as a man of war.

In addition to the term "Antichrist," this individual is also referred to as a "little horn" (Daniel 7:8; 8:9), the "man of sin" (2 Thessalonians 2:3), "son of perdition" (2 Thessalonians 2:3), and "a beast" rising up "out of the sea" (Revelation 13:1).

The Beast Rising From the Sea

> 1   And I stood upon the sand of the sea, and saw a beast rise up out of the sea, having seven heads and ten horns, and upon his horns ten crowns, and upon his heads the name of blasphemy.

There are times in scripture when words or phrases should be interpreted symbolically. Since there are no animals with seven heads, this description of a beast is not literal, but symbolic. The beast rising out of the sea must be treated symbolically.

Beasts are sometimes used in scripture as symbols of kingdoms or kings (Daniel 2:38-39; 7:2-7, 17, 23). Some of the details given about the beast in Revelation 13 apply to a kingdom. Other details about the beast apply to a person, such as the beast opening his mouth and speaking blasphemies (Revelation 13:5-6).

Unless a specific body of water is referred to, the scriptures sometimes use the word "sea" to symbolize great masses of people or nations (Daniel 7:2-3; Revelation 17:1, 15). The beast rising from the sea in Revelation 13:1 refers to the rise of a king out of masses of people and a kingdom out of the Gentile nations. During chaotic political events, the Antichrist will rise to power from the sea of people. Since scripture often uses "the sea" to refer to the Mediterranean, perhaps the Antichrist will arise from the masses of people in the Mediterranean area.

Horns can also represent kings or rulers (Daniel 7:24). Notice that the 10 horns in Revelation 13:1 have crowns. This indicates that the 10 horns are 10 kingdoms (Revelation 17:12). The 10 horns, crowned with political power, will receive their authority from a satanic system. These 10 horns correspond to the 10 toes in Daniel, chapter 2 and the 10 horns in Daniel, chapter 7. They are 10 kings who will give their power to the Antichrist.

Dwight Pentecost believed that these ten kingdoms will cover the approximate territory of the old Roman Empire. He wrote the following:

> "As the Roman Empire had been the agency through which Satan attacked Christ at His first advent, that empire in its final form will be the agency through which Satan works against the Messiah at His second advent."[44]

As previously mentioned, others teach that the ten horns refer to ten other kingdoms, or perhaps ten zones of nations, that report to the Antichrist.

The term "beast" is used in the Book of Revelation to represent at least two and possibly three different things:

(1)   A human being (the Antichrist) who comes out of the sea of people (13:1; 17:11)
(2)   A political/governmental system opposed to God (Daniel 7:3-7, 17, 23; Revelation 17:12-17)
(3)   Some believe the term "beast" may also refer to a supernatural being (a demon) that is allowed to come out of the bottomless pit (Revelation 11:7; 17:8). This demon will help inspire the beast system that Antichrist will set up.

Thus, the human beast out of the sea of humanity (Antichrist) and the beast government system are two different things. In addition, some believe that the beast from the bottomless pit is a demonic prince. If this is true, these three things are all represented by one symbol: the beast.

Two Interpretations About the Seven Heads

1. **The seven heads of the beast refer to the Seven Hills of Rome.** Revelation 17:9 states that the "seven heads are seven mountains, on which the woman sitteth." This refers to the city of Rome, the City of Seven Hills.

According to this view, the system that Antichrist will preside over will have its headquarters in Rome.

2. **The seven heads of the beast in Revelation 13:1 represent seven kingdoms, or empires, controlled by a recurring satanic system.** The seven heads are also called mountains in Revelation 17:9-10. When the word "mountain" is used in scripture, and it is not referring to a specific geographic place, it refers to a great kingdom. Examples include Jeremiah 51:25 and Daniel 2:35. Each of the seven heads also had a crown, indicating kingdoms (Revelation 12:3). Since these heads are called "mountains" (Revelation 17:9-10), these heads also represent kings or kingdoms. Most of these seven empires are in the past. These are kingdoms that God has used, or will use, to chasten Israel.

Revelation 17:10 tells us that by the Apostle John's time, five had fallen, one existed, and one was yet to come. This is referring to seven kingdoms in history.

In Daniel 2:29-45, five kingdoms predicted in Nebuchadnezzar's dream were as follows: Babylonia, Medo-Persia, Greece, Rome, and the future revised Roman Empire.

Revelation 17:3 and 17:7 refer to seven heads, which are seven mountains or kingdoms (Revelation 17:9-10). This list of seven kingdoms is as follows: Egypt, Assyria, Babylonia, Medo-Persia, Greece, Rome, and the future revised Roman Empire. John is considering two previous empires that Daniel's account did not consider (Egypt and Assyria).

The seven heads refer to seven empires controlled by a satanic beast system. The seventh kingdom, the revived Roman Empire, is yet to come and will be led by the Antichrist.

> 2 And the beast which I saw was like unto a leopard, and his feet were as the feet of a bear, and his mouth as the mouth of a lion: and the dragon gave him his power, and his seat, and great authority.

Both the beast system and the leader of this system will be empowered by the dragon, which is Satan (Revelation 12:9). The leader of the beast system will have great political power over an anti-Christian government.

The symbolism of animals allows us to identify the beast with the prophecies of Daniel, chapter 7. The Antichrist will be as cruel as a wild beast.

> 3 And I saw one of his heads as it were wounded to death; and his deadly wound was healed: and all the world wondered after the beast.

One of the heads was wounded, died, and came back to life. Revelation 17:8 also indicates that the beast, which was seen by people, and then not seen, will again appear after he comes up out of the abyss.

Two Interpretations of the Head Wounded to Death

1. **The Antichrist will be given a deadly wound to the head,** that is, he will be assassinated. Revelation 17:8 indicates that the beast, which was seen by people, and then not seen, will again appear after he comes up out of the abyss. This refers to the death and resurrection of the Antichrist.

Antichrist will be resurrected through Satan's supernatural power (Revelation 13:14). This may be Satan's method for deceiving much of the world (2 Thessalonians 2:9-10).

Some feel that Antichrist will portray a phony resurrection (Revelation 13:14). This will be inspired by the abyss. His alleged miraculous powers will convince many to follow and worship him (Revelation 13:3-4).

2. One of the beast's heads, a great kingdom, will be wounded to death (come to an end) and then revived.

In other words, this deadly wound, said to be healed, refers to the resurrection of a former great empire thought to be extinct. This beast governmental system was once in existence, but went out of existence. Through satanic powers, this system will be brought back into existence.

The beast in Revelation 17:8 cannot refer to the human Antichrist because the bottomless pit, or abyss, is not a place for human beings. It is a prison for certain demonic spirits (Luke 8:31; Revelation 9:1-11). There are certain satanic princes confined there (Revelation 11:7; 17:8).

Another reason that Revelation 13:3 cannot refer to a literal resurrection of the Antichrist is because God alone, through Christ, has the power of resurrection (John 11:25). Satan cannot raise anyone from the dead.

The resurrection of the beast represents the persistence of evil. This beast may be a resurrected kingdom that receives inspiration from the abyss.

In addition, the beast from the abyss in Revelation 17:8 may refer to a demonic being that is released in order to help with the formation of Antichrist's government system. Some teach that this demon "was, and is not, and shall ascend out of the bottomless pit" (17:8). This refers to the fact that this spirit was on the earth before John's lifetime, was imprisoned in the bottomless pit, but will be released again during Antichrist's reign.

It is often taught that the resurrection of a former kingdom refers to the revised Roman Empire. However, some teach that this resurrected kingdom will be the literal Babylon, which is in modern day Iraq.

The head that was wounded may represent Satan's attempt, through the Antichrist, to duplicate Christ's resurrection. If this is true, this will be a poor imitation of the Lamb of God who died and rose from the dead. Regardless of which of the previous interpretations is correct, those who are unsaved will marvel and be astonished at the beast and his system.

> 4   And they worshipped the dragon which gave power unto the beast: and
> they worshipped the beast, saying, Who is like unto the beast? who is able to make
> war with him?

Antichrist's power and possible resurrection will lead many people to worship Satan and the beast. Those who choose to receive the mark of the beast will knowingly associate themselves with things that are satanic. People who receive the mark of the beast will probably understand that they are rejecting the God of the Bible. But, they will not understand that this seals their fate in hell because they are deceived. Multitudes will swear allegiance to this satanic system. The worship of the beast will probably be both political and religious. It will be primarily enforced economically.

Antichrist will exalt himself as a god, and speak great blasphemies against the true God (Daniel 11:36-37; 2 Thessalonians 2:1-4). He will probably have occultic and supernatural powers given to him by Satan. This will make him appear to have godlike qualities. Antichrist will probably be deceived about himself, and really believe that he is God. As a result, he will demand everyone's worship.

Antichrist will create a religion centered on himself. Daniel 11:38-39 also indicates he will give honor to a god of forces, or fortresses. This probably refers to his love of war and conquests.

> 5   And there was given unto him a mouth speaking great things and blasphe-
> mies; and power was given unto him to continue forty and two months.

Antichrist will speak great things and blasphemies. This man does not openly take on the image of the Antichrist until the last three and one-half years of the tribulation. During the first three-and-one-half years, this man will be a great diplomat. He will reassemble the beast system that was in operation in the previous empires referred to in the Book of Daniel. The Antichrist will bring the beast system back into existence, making himself the head. God will limit the time that the beast will rule. Antichrist will be allowed to persecute believers for 42 months (the last three-and-one-half years of the tribulation).

> 6   And he opened his mouth in blasphemy against God, to blaspheme his
> name, and his tabernacle, and them that dwell in heaven.

Near the middle of the tribulation, the Antichrist will start to publicly blaspheme God, the holy things of heaven, and those that dwell in heaven. Perhaps he will be aware that there are many who have escaped him in a pretribulation or midtribulation rapture.

Speculation About the Nation That Will Produce the Antichrist

Daniel 7:23-24 indicates that in the last days, the Antichrist will come from one of the 10 small kingdoms that will occupy the approximate area of the fourth kingdom. We know from history that the fourth kingdom prophesied in Daniel, chapter 7, was the Roman Empire. Therefore, it appears that Antichrist will come from an area that was once part of the ancient Roman Empire. Many believe that Daniel 9:25-27 indicates that Antichrist will come from among the people who would destroy the second temple (the Romans destroyed the second temple in 70 A.D.). Consequently, some teach that the Antichrist will come from Italy, perhaps Rome. Others claim that Antichrist will merely come from an area that was in the former Roman Empire.

Others contend that Daniel, chapter 8, reduces the nations that Antichrist could come from down to four. In the vision in Daniel, chapter 8, the "he-goat" symbolizes the Grecian Empire. The "he-goat" had his horn broken off and in its place grew four horns (Daniel 8:8). This refers to the death of Alexander the Great. After Alexander died, his empire was divided into four kingdoms. These four divisions are modern day Greece, Turkey, Syria, and Egypt. Daniel 8:9 tells us that out of one of these four smaller kingdoms came another horn, which started out small. This refers to the Antichrist. According to this view, the little horn (Antichrist) must come from one of these four countries (Daniel 8:8-12). These four countries were all once part of both the ancient Grecian and Roman empires. Perhaps the Antichrist will come from Greece, Turkey, Syria, or Egypt. None of this is certain.

The Extent of Antichrist's Reign

> 7   And it was given unto him to make war with the saints, and to overcome them: and power was given him over all kindreds, and tongues, and nations.

Antichrist will enjoy great power and reverence. He will even proclaim himself to be a god (2 Thessalonians 2:4). This will be consistent with New Age teachings that all persons can become gods. Antichrist will also have satanic power to work signs and wonders to deceive many (2 Thessalonians 2:9-10).

Antichrist's satanically inspired system will be political, economic, and religious. He will persecute as many persons as possible who have accepted Christ. Many of these will be the converts of the 144,000 Jewish evangelists.

Will Antichrist Rule the Entire World? Two Interpretations

1. **Antichrist will rule the entire world.** He will force nearly everyone on earth to take the mark of the beast or be killed. This appears to be supported by the following verses from Revelation, chapter 13:

> 7   "… power was given him over all kindreds, and tongues, and nations."
>
> 8   "… all that dwell upon the earth shall worship him."
>
> 16 "… he causeth all, both small and great to receive a mark in their right hand, or in their foreheads."
>
> 17 "… that no man might buy or sell, save he that had the mark, or the name of the beast, or the number of his name."

2. **Antichrist will never succeed at conquering and ruling the entire world.** Here are some indications of this from scripture.

Daniel 11:41 mentions three ancient countries: Edom, Moab and Ammon. These three ancient countries make up modern day Jordan. Daniel 11:41 tells us that these areas will escape the Antichrist's rule. These ancient countries will not be controlled by the Antichrist, even though they will border his empire.

Daniel 11:44-45 tells us that countries to the north and east of Antichrist's kingdoms will make war on him. This will keep Antichrist occupied during most of the second half of the tribulation. This indicates that Antichrist will not be ruling the entire world, even in the second half of the tribulation.

Revelation 16:13-16 mentions unclean spirits that will work miracles of diplomacy through ambassadors. These spirits will seek the cooperation of many nations to help the Antichrist at the Battle of Armageddon. This is at the very end of the tribulation. Thus, even at the end of the tribulation Antichrist will not rule the entire world. He will be forced to rely on diplomacy to influence many nations.

Concerning the scriptures that seem to indicate that Antichrist will rule the entire world, it must be understood that the concept of "all" is often used in the scriptures in a figurative and limited sense.[45] Here are some examples:

- Daniel 2:38 states that King Nebuchadnezzar, king of Babylon, was a ruler, ". . . whereso-ever the children of men dwell,. . . ." But, we know that the Babylonian Empire did not rule the entire earth.
- Daniel 2:39 refers to the third kingdom (the Greecian Empire), "which shall bear rule over all the earth." But, we know that the Greecian Empire did not rule over all the earth.
- Daniel 7:23, referring to the fourth kingdom (the Roman Empire), states that this king-dom would ". . . devour the whole earth. . . ." But, we know the Roman Empire only covered a small part of the earth.
- Luke 2:1 states, "And it came to pass in those days, that there went out a decree from Cae-sar Augustus, that all the world should be taxed." This, of course, only referred to the areas inside the Roman Empire.
- In Romans 1:8 the apostle Paul stated, ". . . your faith is spoken of throughout the whole world." He really meant primarily throughout the Roman Empire, not literally the entire world.
- In Acts 11:28, we read about a severe famine ". . . throughout all the world: which came to pass in the days of Claudius Caesar." History tells us that this famine did not cover every part of the Roman Empire, much less the entire world.

There are hundreds of examples where the concept of "all" is used in scripture in a limited and figurative sense, pertaining to a particular region or area.[46] Sometimes the word or concept "all" only includes those individuals or groups for which the purpose was intended, not everyone, everywhere. It appears that the use of the concept "all" in Revelation 13 should be taken to mean all that God has in mind as far as the decrees of Antichrist are concerned.

Whether or not the Antichrist will rule the entire world as a dictator, his kingdom and reign will definitely exert great influence and have a huge impact worldwide. Perhaps Antichrist will not conquer the whole world by force. Instead, he may control most of the world by controlling the global economy and global communications. Although Antichrist may not rule the entire world, the tribulation will definitely be worldwide (Revelation 3:10).

> 8   And all that dwell upon the earth shall worship him, whose names are not written in the book of life of the Lamb slain from the foundation of the world.

People throughout the world will be followers of the Antichrist, whether or not he rules the entire world. Verse 8 states there are names not written in the Book of Life. This does not mean that God predestines some to be saved and some to be lost. It is God's will that all be saved (2 Peter 3:9). However, a person's name can be erased from the Book of Life (Psalm 69:28). The names of those who overcome will not be blotted out (Revelation 3:5).

Verse 8 also refers to the fact that Christ's death on the cross, which purchased salvation for believers, was decreed before the creation of the world (1 Peter 1:19-20).

> 9   If any man have an ear, let him hear.
> 10   He that leadeth into captivity shall go into captivity: he that killeth with the sword must be killed with the sword. Here is the patience and the faith of the saints.

Those who imprison or kill believers in Christ will eventually be imprisoned in hell and experience eternal spiritual death. Those who are persecuted by the Antichrist are to maintain a patient trust in God while refusing to adopt the methods of the beast system. Christ encourages the tribulation believers to remain faithful to God, even if it costs them their lives.

Will the Antichrist Be a Jew or a Gentile?

Three Interpretations About the Identity of the Antichrist

1. **The Antichrist will be a Jew.** Daniel 11:37 in the King James states that he will not "... regard the God of his fathers, ..." The context of this passage suggests that Antichrist will be a Jew. Perhaps he will pose as a Gentile and, at least initially, attempt to keep his Jewish ancestry a secret. Primarily a man of peace during the first half of the tribulation, Antichrist will negotiate a seven-year peace treaty with Israel (Daniel 9:27). He will also negotiate a peace treaty between the Jews and the Muslims. Antichrist will appear to be a friend to Israel during the first half of the tribulation, and will encourage the Jews to rebuild their temple in Jerusalem. Many Israelis will be tempted to think of him as their Jewish Messiah.

2. **The Antichrist will be a Muslim.** Although Antichrist will negotiate an uneasy seven-year peace treaty with Israel (Daniel 9:27), he will never appear to be a friend to Israel, much less a Jewish Messiah. This is because he will be a man of war from almost the beginning of the tribulation (Revelation 6:2-4, 7-8; 13:4, 7). The little horn in Daniel, chapter 8, has a dual fulfillment. Not only does it refer to an ancient king of Syria, Antiochus Epiphanes, but also to the future Antichrist.

Daniel 8:9 tells us that the small horn (Antichrist) will grow in power to the south and to the east. To the south of Israel is North Africa and Arabia. To the east of Israel are the countries of Jordan, Iran, Iraq, Afghanistan, and Pakistan. These are all Muslim countries. The Muslims of these countries would never accept the leadership of a non-Muslim. They would certainly not accept the leadership of a Jewish person.

Although he may not rule these nations, Antichrist will be very influential in these areas. In order for Antichrist to be accepted as a leader in these countries, he will have to be a Muslim. This may explain why the Antichrist will invade Israel at midtribulation and desire to kill the two witnesses. Antichrist will want to take over the temple mount in Jerusalem and give it back to Islamic powers. The Antichrist will gather together the forces of Islam in a holy war against the nation of Israel.

It is of interest that Islamic prophecy teaches that an Islamic leader will arise who will convert the world to Islam. The Muslims believe he will come out of Iraq.[47] Some believe that ancient Babylon will be rebuilt in oil-rich Iraq, and become the capital city of Antichrist's kingdom. Whether or not the ancient city of Babylon is rebuilt, the Antichrist will be able to economically bring all the industrialized nations to their knees by denying them oil from the Middle East.

This may also explain why many of the Jews in Israel (referred to as the woman in Revelation 12:6) will flee into the desert. Once the nation of Israel falls, the Jews will flee from a fanatical Muslim dictator who will want to kill any Jew that does not confess allegiance to Allah.

3. **The Antichrist will not be a Muslim or a Jew.** In the original language, Daniel 11:37 states that the Antichrist will not regard the "gods" of his fathers – plural.[48] The plurality of gods that his fathers embraced is not a Jewish reference. This can also be used to argue that the Antichrist will not be a Muslim. In addition, Daniel 11:40 speaks of the king of the south and the king of the north. According to one view, the king of the north is the Antichrist. The king of the south is an Islamic leader.

According to this view, the king of the north (Antichrist) will conquer Israel and the Islamic nations south of Israel. It is true that some Muslim nations have engaged in war against each other. However, if Antichrist makes war against both Israel and several Islamic nations, this may imply that Antichrist will not be a Muslim or a Jew.

A Second Beast Coming From the Earth

> 11   And I beheld another beast coming up out of the earth; and he had two horns like a lamb, and he spake as a dragon.

While the first beast that came out of the sea of people represents the Antichrist, the second beast coming out of the earth is later called the "false prophet" (Revelation 16:13; 19:20; 20:10). This second beast will be a prophet of the Antichrist, deceiving many to accept the Antichrist as God. He will also be a miracle-worker, using demonic deception. Christ specifically warned about the coming of false prophets during this time period (Matthew 24:24; Mark 13:22).

Some believe that the word "sea" is representative of Gentile nations, whereas the word "earth" is symbolic of the Jewish people. If this is true, then the first beast (Antichrist) will be a Gentile. The second beast, the false prophet, will be an apostate Jew. His apostasy will not be obvious to the Jews until the middle of the tribulation.

It is clear that both of these beasts are men, because both will eventually be cast alive into the Lake of Fire (Revelation 19:20). The first beast (Antichrist) is a governmental leader. The second beast is a religious leader who will persuade many to worship the first beast. His speech will be inspired by the devil, who is also portrayed as a dragon (Revelation 12:3-4, 7-9, 13, 17).

This second beast will have the appearance of a lamb. He will portray himself as a loving and caring religious leader. This implies he will use religious deception, perhaps as a counterfeit Christ. When he opens his mouth, he will speak as a dragon, that is, as a devil.

Christ warned us about false prophets who will come in sheep's clothing (Matthew 7:15). This false prophet will initially deceive Israel by coming in sheep's clothing. However, this lamb is symbolically described as having two horns. Lambs do not have horns. His horns reveal his true character as a wild and dangerous beast.

> 12   And he exerciseth all the power of the first beast before him, and causeth the earth and them which dwell therein to worship the first beast, whose deadly wound was healed.

> 13   And he doeth great wonders, so that he maketh fire come down from heaven on the earth in the sight of men,
>
> 14   And deceiveth them that dwell on the earth by the means of those miracles which he had power to do in the sight of the beast; saying to them that dwell on the earth, that they should make an image to the beast, which had the wound by a sword, and did live.

Whereas the first beast will have great political power over an anti-Christian government, the second beast will preside over an anti-Christian religion, ideology, and philosophy.

The second beast will be a false prophet who will deceive millions of people through his miracles (Revelation 13:13-14; 19:20). He will use great deception to cause people to worship the first beast. Many Bible scholars teach that people will worship a person, the Antichrist. However, some teach that people will, in effect, worship the beast system. This system will be economic, political and religious in nature. Many people will probably worship both the Antichrist and his system.

The Antichrist will trick people by performing deceptive miracles (2 Thessalonians 2:9). Revelation 13:13 tells us that the false prophet will be able to call down fire from heaven. Through miracles, the second beast will promote the Antichrist's false religion. Christ warned that there will be false messiahs performing miracles during this time (Matthew 24:24).

You may ask why God would allow Satan to exercise such miraculous powers during the tribulation. God puts a very high value on faith. If all of the miraculous signs were coming from God, such as through the two witnesses, it would no longer take faith to believe in God. It would simply be a logical response from people. Since both God and satanic forces will display supernatural power, faith will still be required to believe in the one true God.

All supernatural manifestations and spiritual teachings should be evaluated to determine if they are consistent with God's word (the Bible). During this dispensation, if a miracle or philosophy does not exalt the Jesus Christ of the Bible, it is not from the one true God.

Verse 14 states that the second beast will have an image created of the first beast for all to worship. This image will be set up in the temple in Jerusalem to be worshipped (Daniel 9:27; Matthew 24:15). Revelation 13:14-15 indicates that special powers will be given to the image. Many who refuse to worship it will be killed (Revelation 6:9).

The beast out of the sea (the Antichrist) and the beast out of the earth (the false prophet) will team up with Satan to form a counterfeit and unholy trinity.

> 15   And he had power to give life unto the image of the beast, that the image
> of the beast should both speak, and cause that as many as would not worship the
> image of the beast should be killed.

The second beast is allowed to seemingly impart life to the image of the first beast. It will speak.

Some interpret this to mean that a statute or other physical image of the beast will come to life. Others believe this is symbolic, referring to a public relations image of the beast through mass media.

Those who do not worship the image of the beast are threatened with death. Many Christians who refuse to worship the beast and his image will be beheaded (Revelation 20:4). The apostle Paul prophesied in 2 Thessalonians 2:3-12 that the Antichrist will go into the temple in Jerusalem and declare himself to be God. As previously mentioned, at the midpoint of the tribulation, he will attempt to influence all the religious activities of the world.

> 16   And he causeth all, both small and great, rich and poor, free and bond, to
> receive a mark in their right hand, or in their foreheads:
> 17   And that no man might buy or sell, save he that had the mark, or the name
> of the beast, or the number of his name.
> 18   Here is wisdom. Let him that hath understanding count the number of the beast:
> for it is the number of a man; and his number is Six hundred threescore and six.

Antichrist's mark, or name, or number of his name, will be forced upon people. Notice that his mark and name are not the same as his number.

The second beast, the false prophet, will require people to receive a mark on their right hands or foreheads in order to buy and sell. This is the mark of the beast. Even if Antichrist does not rule the entire world, it appears that he will dominate the world economy. Many people will die for refusing to take the mark (Revelation 13:7; 15:2-3; 20:4). This mark may mathematically represent the name of the Antichrist.

As previously mentioned, in scripture the number seven represents complete perfection. In contrast, the number six is incomplete and is a number representing humans. The number 666 falls completely short of divine perfection. Here, it also represents an imperfect system that is associated with Satan. The mark of the beast probably does not refer to one number. It may refer to a numbering system used to assign unique numbers to individuals.

The mark of the beast will mock the seal that God had previously placed on His followers (Revelation 7:2-3). God had previously marked His people so that angels of judgment would spare them. In a similar way, the Antichrist will mark his people in order to spare them from satanically inspired persecution aimed at God's followers.

Two Interpretations About the Mark of the Beast on Right Hands and Foreheads

1. **The mark of the beast will not be a literal mark.** Instead, the seal refers to decisions to follow the Antichrist and to reject the true God.

   A mark on the hand and forehead is figurative language for behaviors and attitudes (Exodus 13:8-9, 14-16; Deuteronomy 11:18; Revelation 14:1; 22:3-5). The "right hand" is figurative for actions and behaviors. The "forehead" is figurative for thoughts, decisions and attitudes. Thus the mark of the beast will not be a literal mark, such as a tattoo or an embedded computer chip.

2. **The mark of the beast will be a literal mark on right hands and foreheads.** God's visible seal on the 144,000 Christians in Revelation, chapter 7, will anger the Antichrist. This will motivate Antichrist to put the mark of the Beast, as identification, on the right hands or foreheads of his people (Revelation 13:16). Some speculate that the mark may include a computer chip buried in the skin and made visible only through the use of a scanner. This computer chip will act as a debit card.

   All major concerns today identify their customers with numbers instead of names. There is nothing wrong with these technologies; however, these are all forerunners of the technology that will be used for the mark of the beast.

It is possible that the mark of the beast could be literal and also contain the symbolism mentioned in the above scriptures. Regardless of which view is the most accurate, the result will be the same for those who receive this mark – eternal destruction (Revelation 14:9-11).

Through the mark, the beast system will be used to control much of the commercial operations of the world. Those that refuse the mark will be prevented from engaging in economic activities. Those that take the mark will knowingly be taking a loyalty oath to the Antichrist and his system, which is political, economic, and religious. Persons who receive this mark will seal their doom. They will have no further way to salvation (Revelation 14:9-11). Receiving the mark will include a conscious denial of all faith in the God of the Bible and in the Lord Jesus Christ.

CHRIST: *". . . the Lamb of God . . ."* John 1:29

Nineteen

Revelation – Chapter 14

Brief Summary

Chapter 14 gives information about 144,000 believers. Most prophecy teachers believe this is the same group that was previously mentioned in Revelation, chapter 7. The scene is in heaven at the midpoint of the tribulation. This gives us a glimpse into eternity and shows what awaits faithful believers.

This chapter also gives an overview of the events to follow in chapters 15 through 19. This preview will be summarized in the announcements of several angels who will be active on earth during the second half of the tribulation.

One angel will fly through the sky, preaching the gospel to the people on earth.

A second angel will announce the fall of Babylon, which includes the political, economic and religious system of the Antichrist. This system will be centered in a literal city.

A third angel will announce doom for those who worship the beast.

A fourth angel will give a preview of the judgment to come at the end of the tribulation, when Christ visibly returns to the earth. This is referred to as the "great winepress of the wrath of God."

Finally, other angels will assist in giving a preview of the Battle of Armageddon, which will occur at the end of the tribulation. The slaughter will be incomprehensible.

The Lamb and the 144,000 on Mount Zion

1 And I looked, and, lo, a Lamb stood on the mount Sion, and with him an hundred forty and four thousand, having his Father's name written in their foreheads.

2 And I heard a voice from heaven, as the voice of many waters, and as the voice of a great thunder: and I heard the voice of harpers harping with their harps:

3 And they sung as it were a new song before the throne, and before the four beasts, and the elders: and no man could learn that song but the hundred and forty and four thousand, which were redeemed from the earth.

4 These are they which were not defiled with women; for they are virgins. These are they which follow the Lamb whithersoever he goeth. These were redeemed from among men, being the firstfruits unto God and to the Lamb.

5 And in their mouth was found no guile: for they are without fault before the throne of God.

The 144,000 suddenly appear with "a Lamb" (Jesus) on Mount Zion. They are before the throne of God (verse 5). This is most likely the same group of 144,000 Jews that were mentioned in Revelation, chapter 7. The fact that both groups are 144,000 and have something written on their foreheads (Revelation 7:1-4; 14:1) is evidence that both of these chapters are referring to one and the same group. These Jews accepted Jesus Christ as their Messiah and refused to give their allegiance to the Antichrist.

Revelation 9:3-4 also refers to the 144,000 Jews who have the seal of God for their protection. As previously stated in the discussion about chapter 7, some believe that these seals will not be literal, visible marks, but refer to decisions to accept Jesus for salvation. Others believe these seals will be literal and visible marks.

The number 144,000 is significant. Similar to the number seven, the numbers 10 and 12 represent completeness in scripture. The number 10 is also a number of testimony. The number 144,000 is a multiple of 10 and 12. This number represents completeness and testimony.

Some believe that the number of 144,000 is not literal, but symbolic of the national conversion of Israel. According to this view, the 144,000 may represent the entire nation of Israel, or a specific group of Jewish converts within Israel. Whether or not the number of 144,000 is a literal number, it refers to the Jews who will be won to Christ during the tribulation.

Two Interpretations as to Why the
144,000 Suddenly Appear Before the Throne of God

1. **Some teach that this scene occurs after a midtribulation rapture of the 144,000.** When the Antichrist turns against the nation of Israel in the middle of the tribulation, and when the 144,000 have finished their earthly assignments, they will be caught up to heaven in a second rapture. Since Mount Zion is another name for Jerusalem (1 Kings 8:1; 1 Chronicles 11:5; 2 Chronicles 5:2), some believe that Jesus may meet the 144,000 in the air near the earthly Mount Zion to escort them back to heaven. Revelation 14:1 could also be referring to the heavenly mount Zion (Hebrews 12:22-23).

If this is a special rapture of this group of people, it will occur around the middle of the tribulation, after the seventh trumpet. The purpose is to deliver this group of believers from the wrath of the Antichrist.

2. **Others teach that the 144,000 standing before the throne of God have been martyred.** According to this view, the sealing of the 144,000 in Revelation 7:1-4 will only protect them from the wrath of God, not from the wrath of Satan and the Antichrist.

The 144,000 will sing a new song that only they will know. No one else can learn it. This implies that the 144,000 will have an experience that no other person or group has ever had.

Verse 4 tells us that the 144,000 ". . . were not defiled with women; for they are virgins. . . ." Some have concluded that the 144,000 are all male virgins. However, this group will probably be made up of both men and women. The term "virgin" can refer to either males or females. The phrase "not defiled with women; for they are virgins" may best be understood in a spiritual sense. This group remained pure and refused to partake of worldly sins after their conversions to Christ. They kept their marriage vows, or remained unmarried and sexually pure. Thus many of them will be virgins in a spiritual sense, free from fornication. This group will be close and consistent followers of Christ.

The 144,000 in Revelation, chapter 14, are referred to as "the first fruits unto God" (verse 4). If this is the same group mentioned in Revelation, chapter 7, some believe that this group will be the first to be saved during the seven-year tribulation. Others believe that the 144,000 in chapter 7 are merely the first Jews to be saved during the tribulation. In any event, the 144,000 mentioned in chapter 14 will be given a special position, standing near the throne of God (Revelation 14:1-5).

The state of perfection of the 144,000 refers to their condition in heaven. This will be after they have been caught up in a second rapture, or after they were martyred. They are forgiven and without fault because of their purified position in Christ.

An Angel Announces the Gospel to Persons on Earth

> 6   And I saw another angel fly in the midst of heaven, having the everlasting gospel to preach unto them that dwell on the earth, and to every nation, and kindred, and tongue, and people,
> 7   Saying with a loud voice, Fear God, and give glory to him; for the hour of his judgment is come: and worship him that made heaven, and earth, and the sea, and the fountains of waters.

An angel will fly through the sky, preaching the gospel to the people on earth. The fact that the words "everlasting gospel" are used shows that this angel is specifically preaching Christ to unbelievers. The gospel message of Christ is everlasting. It is good news to believers, but leads to judgment for those who refuse to believe. At this point in the tribulation, there will still be many who have not taken the mark of the beast and will be able to receive salvation.

Angels will be one of the vehicles through which the gospel will be preached during the last three and one-half years of the tribulation. This shows how desperate the circumstances on earth will become.

In verse 7, the message of this angel conveys three things:

(1)   "Fear God."
(2)   "Give glory to Him; for the hour of His judgment is come."
(3)   "Worship Him that made heaven, and earth, and the sea, and the fountains of waters."

This is a call to worship the true God rather than the Antichrist. It is a serious warning to those who are about to accept the mark of Antichrist. This angel flying through the air at the midpoint of the tribulation may receive the attention of millions of people.

A Second Angel Announces the Fall of Babylon

8   And there followed another angel, saying, Babylon is fallen, is fallen, that great city, because she made all nations drink of the wine of the wrath of her fornication.

The Book of Revelation refers to two Babylon's. The beast and the 10 kings will rejoice over the destruction of the Mystical Babylon that is discussed in Revelation, chapter 17. However, these kings will mourn over the destruction of the Babylon that is discussed in Revelation 18:9-19. This indicates that there are two Babylon's referred to in the Book of Revelation.

The first Babylon is a false religious system, represented as a prostitute (Revelation 17:1-6). This religious system will be destroyed by Antichrist and the 10 kings in the middle of the tribulation (Revelation 17:15-17). This first Babylon will be destroyed when the Antichrist gains great political power and the 10 kings give their kingdoms to the beast (Revelation 13:1-10).

The second Babylon is an economic and political system. It will also include a new religion that worships the Antichrist (Daniel 9:27; Matthew 24:15; 2 Thessalonians 2:3-4; Revelation 18:9-19, 22-23). Revelation 16:17-19 tells us that this system will be destroyed during the seventh vial, at the end of the tribulation. The destruction of this system of Babylon is fully described in chapter 18. The final destruction of this system actually occurs at Christ's Second Coming in Revelation 19:11-21.

The headquarters of these Babylon systems will be centered in a literal city.

Two Common Interpretations About the Headquarters City of the Babylon Systems

1.   **The headquarters of the Antichrist will be the city of Rome.** As mentioned in the discussion of Revelation, chapter 13, some teach that the seven heads of the beast refer to the Seven Hills of Rome. Revelation 17:9 states that the "seven heads are seven mountains, on which the woman sitteth." This refers to the city of Rome, the City of Seven Hills. Revelation 17:18 also refers to this woman as a "great city."

In New Testament times, the term "Babylon" was sometimes a code name for the city of Rome, as in 1 Peter 5:13. In the Book of Revelation, John may also have used the term "Babylon" as a code name for Rome. This was to avoid openly speaking out against the Roman Empire.

John was conveying that the system Antichrist will preside over will have its headquarters in the city of Rome.

2. **The headquarters of the Antichrist will be the ancient city of Babylon in Iraq,** which will be rebuilt. Some prophecies about the final destruction of the ancient city of Babylon have not yet been fulfilled.

Isaiah 13:19-20 indicates that after God destroys Babylon, like Sodom and Gomorrah, it will never be inhabited again. However, people are once again living in the ancient city of Babylon. Therefore, this city has not yet received the complete judgment of God. It will be rebuilt in oil-rich Iraq and become the capital city of Antichrist's kingdom.

A Third Angel Announces Doom for Those who Worship the Beast

9   And the third angel followed them, saying with a loud voice, If any man worship the beast and his image, and receive his mark in his forehead, or in his hand,

10   The same shall drink of the wine of the wrath of God, which is poured out without mixture into the cup of his indignation; and he shall be tormented with fire and brimstone in the presence of the holy angels, and in the presence of the Lamb:

11   And the smoke of their torment ascendeth up for ever and ever: and they have no rest day nor night, who worship the beast and his image, and whosoever receiveth the mark of his name.

The third angel will warn people not to worship the beast. This angel will announce that anyone who worships the beast and his image, or receives the mark of the beast, will be doomed to eternal torment. The "wrath of God" will be "poured out without mixture" (verse 10). That means that God's wrath will not be diluted or watered-down. Verses 10 and 11 are warning people about eternal torment in the lake of fire (Revelation 19:20; 20:10; 21:8). Angels may plead with the peoples of the world to repent.

Believers Killed by Antichrist Will Be Blessed

12   Here is the patience of the saints: here are they that keep the commandments of God, and the faith of Jesus.

13   And I heard a voice from heaven saying unto me, Write, Blessed are the dead which die in the Lord from henceforth: Yea, saith the Spirit, that they may rest

from their labours; and their works do follow them.

This is a word of encouragement for believers to remain true to God during persecutions. The two key ingredients for remaining faithful are consistent prayer and Bible study. Those in Christ who die for their faith during the tribulation will be especially blessed. The lifestyles of faith and obedience can produce wonderful fruit after death. Believers in the Lord Jesus Christ should always strive to store up treasures in heaven (Matthew 6:20). The peaceful rest experienced by the redeemed represents a sharp contrast to the judgment experienced by unbelievers. Those believers who remain faithful to Christ during the tribulation, even if it costs them their lives, will especially receive wonderful eternal blessings.

A Preview of Christ's Harvest at the End of the Tribulation

14   And I looked, and behold a white cloud, and upon the cloud one sat like unto the Son of man, having on his head a golden crown, and in his hand a sharp sickle.

15   And another angel came out of the temple, crying with a loud voice to him that sat on the cloud, Thrust in thy sickle, and reap: for the time is come for thee to reap; for the harvest of the earth is ripe.

16   And he that sat on the cloud thrust in his sickle on the earth; and the earth was reaped.

In verse 14, Christ is seen sitting on a white cloud. This refers to Christ's Second Coming when He will return on clouds (Daniel 7:13-14; Matthew 24:27-31; 26:64; Acts 1:9-11; Revelation 1:7). Verses 15 and 16 jump ahead to what will happen when Christ visibly returns to the earth at the end of the tribulation. Christ is seen here getting ready to gather a ripe harvest of His true believers. This is also a picture of judgment upon unbelievers who decide to follow the Antichrist. Christ will separate His true believers from those who refused to believe (Matthew 25:31-46), like a farmer harvesting his crops. In Joel 3:12-13, God's future judgment is described as a harvest. The sharp sickle in Joel 3:13 and Revelation 14:14-16 probably pictures the destruction of multitudes of people at the Battle of Armageddon (Isaiah 11:4; Zechariah 14:12; Matthew 13:30, 39; 2 Thessalonians 2:8; Revelation 19:17-21).

A Preview of the Coming Battle of Armageddon

17   And another angel came out of the temple which is in heaven, he also having a sharp sickle.

18   And another angel came out from the altar, which had power over fire; and

cried with a loud cry to him that had the sharp sickle, saying, Thrust in thy sharp sickle, and gather the clusters of the vine of the earth; for her grapes are fully ripe.

19   And the angel thrust in his sickle into the earth, and gathered the vine of the earth, and cast it into the great winepress of the wrath of God.

20   And the winepress was trodden without the city, and blood came out of the winepress, even unto the horse bridles, by the space of a thousand and six hundred furlongs.

John was given a preview of God's final judgment of the unbelievers. This is a preview of the Battle of Armageddon as described in Revelation 16:12-16 and 19:11-21.

The vine of the earth represents the people of the earth who are about to experience the wrath of God. These unbelievers will be thrown into a winepress. The treading of grapes in a winepress is used in scripture to represent God's wrath on the ungodly (Isaiah 63:3-6; Joel 3:12-13; Revelation 19:15). When Christ visibly returns at the end of the tribulation, all unbelievers in the world will be separated from the believers to be judged (Matthew 25:31-33). The believers who were in heaven will also return with Christ to the earth (Revelation 19:14; Zechariah 14:5). The wicked will not be allowed to enter Christ's kingdom. They will go into eternal punishment (Matthew 25:31-46).

A great slaughter will occur during the last days of the tribulation, "without the city." This indicates that a tremendous battle will occur near, but not in, Jerusalem. This will be the Battle of Armageddon (Revelation 16:16; 19:11-21; Isaiah 63:1-6; Joel 3:1-16; Zechariah 14:1-4,12). A furlong is about 660 feet (one-eighth of a mile).[49] The distance of 1,600 furlongs is about 200 miles. The Battle of Armageddon will cover an area that is this length.

Antichrist will command his military forces to invade the nation of Israel. Some teach that the armies of Antichrist will fight against invading armies from the east (Revelation 16:12). Others teach that these armies from the east will join with the Antichrist in an attempt to annihilate the nation of Israel. In any event, God will intervene in this battle (Revelation 19:11-21) and Antichrist's soldiers will be killed. The slaughter will be so great that the blood will be up to "the horse bridles" (Revelation 14:20). This means that the blood will be up to the average person's neck. Perhaps nuclear firepower will be used, or perhaps this will be miraculous power displayed by God.

Another preview of this Battle of Armageddon is given in Revelation 16:16-21. It tells us that great hail will fall. These hail stones will average a talent in weight, which can range from 75 to 100 pounds.[50] When these heavy pieces of ice fall and melt, much water will appear. This water will mix with the blood of those killed, producing a bloody liquid.

After the Battle of Armageddon, all unbelievers on the earth will be removed (Matthew 25:31-46). Christ will take over all the governments on earth. He will begin to rule over those believers who did not take the mark of the beast, but who survived the tribulation. Jesus will rule with a rod of iron for 1,000 years (Revelation 20:1-4). Those believers who have returned with Christ in their glorified bodies (Revelation 19:14; Zechariah 14:1-5) will rule and reign with Christ (Revelation 20:6). During this time the humans that are still in their earthly bodies will reproduce and replenish the earth (Isaiah 65:20). Some of those born during the Millennium will not accept Christ as Lord and Savior. However, people throughout the earth will be forced to worship Christ as Lord whether they want to or not (Revelation 19:15). At the end of the Millennium, the remaining unbelievers will be given one last opportunity to follow Satan (Revelation 20:7-9).

OLIVE OIL: Holy Spirit, Grace, Salvation, Matthew 25:1-4, Hebrews 1:9

Twenty

Revelation – Chapter 15

Brief Summary

This is another informational chapter. Before the next set of judgments from God occur, another scene in heaven is described.

The tribulation Christians who have gained victory over the beast are seen singing a song of praise and worship. Afterwards, seven angels come out of the heavenly temple and are given seven vials, or bowls, filled with the wrath of God.

The seventh trumpet judgment was originally announced in Revelation 11:15. It is an announcement that points ahead to the seven bowl (vial) judgments. These bowl judgments will be carried out by seven angels. The seven plagues from these bowls will be God's final judgments on earth during the closing stages of the tribulation. They are actually described in chapter 16, and continue until the Battle of Armageddon and Christ's return.

The Introduction of God's Final Judgments

    1   And I saw another sign in heaven, great and marvelous, seven angels having the seven last plagues; for in them is filled up the wrath of God.

This verse jumps ahead to chapter 16 by referring to the seven angels who will pour out seven bowls (vials) of judgment upon the earth. These plagues are full of "the wrath of God." The purpose of these plagues is to judge the people who have taken the mark of the beast.

161

These angels may be the same seven angels that sounded the trumpet judgments in Revelation 8:2, but this is not certain.

Verse 1 states that these are "the seven last plagues." During the second half of the tribulation, these will be the last judgments before Christ visibly returns to earth to set up His millennial kingdom. Probably far fewer people will be saved during the last half of the tribulation as compared to the first half. But, these judgments will hopefully inspire some to repent and turn to Christ, before they accept the mark of the beast.

The Sea of Glass Mixed With Fire

> 2   And I saw as it were a sea of glass mingled with fire: and them that had gotten the victory over the beast, and over his image, and over his mark, and over the number of his name, stand on the sea of glass, having the harps of God.
>
> 3   And they sing the song of Moses the servant of God, and the song of the Lamb, saying, Great and marvelous are thy works, Lord God Almighty; just and true are thy ways, thou King of saints.
>
> 4   Who shall not fear thee, O Lord, and glorify thy name? for thou only art holy: for all nations shall come and worship before thee; for thy judgments are made manifest.

Verse 2 mentions a sea of glass. As previously mentioned in our discussion about Revelation 4:6, some believe this sea of glass refers to a great mass of people. However, in chapter 15, a great crowd of believers is standing on this sea of glass. This sea is actually a beautiful pavement before God's throne, upon which God's followers are standing.

The presence of fire probably represents the Holy Spirit since fire is one of His symbols (Acts 2:3; Matthew 3:11-12; Luke 3:16-17). The fire may also represent God's wrath and judgment. Those who are martyred, or raptured, during the tribulation occupy this area. They did not abandon their faith in Christ when persecuted or killed by the Antichrist. These tribulation believers gained ultimate victory over the beast and are particularly blessed of God.

The redeemed in this group will have "the harps of God." Since musical instruments are used in heaven during praise and worship, they should not be excluded from the church, as some teach.

Verse 3 states that this group is singing "the song of Moses." Moses and the Israelites sang a song of redemption and deliverance following the crossing of the Red Sea (Exodus 15:1-18). Toward the end of his life, Moses sang another song of victory (Deuteronomy 32:1-43). Likewise, believers in heaven had previously sung a song to the Lamb (Revelation 5:9-12). Here in Revelation 15, the song of Moses and the song of the Lamb are combined. This new song celebrates the final deliverance of God's true believers from the power of Satan. This song of deliverance glorifies the Lord Jesus Christ.

This huge mass of people before the throne is worshipping God. The "King of saints" in verse 3 refers specifically to Jesus Christ. Since they are singing a song of Moses, some teach that these are Jewish believers in Jesus Christ. However, "the song of the lamb" is a song that all the redeemed can sing. This group is probably made up of both Jews and Gentiles who are saved during the tribulation. They are singing a song of victory.

Distribution of the Seven Vials to the Seven Angels

5   And after that I looked, and, behold, the temple of the tabernacle of the testimony in heaven was opened:

6   And the seven angels came out of the temple, having the seven plagues, clothed in pure and white linen, and having their breasts girded with golden girdles.

7   And one of the four beasts gave unto the seven angels seven golden vials full of the wrath of God, who liveth for ever and ever.

8   And the temple was filled with smoke from the glory of God, and from his power; and no man was able to enter into the temple, till the seven plagues of the seven angels were fulfilled.

In verse 5, the phrase "tabernacle of the testimony" was a Greek translation for the Hebrew "Tent of Meeting" in Exodus 40:34-35. Moses pitched the Tent of Meeting outside the camp before the tabernacle was built (Exodus 33:7). It was here that people brought their petitions and requests to the Lord.

John saw a temple in heaven. The heavenly temple that is mentioned in verse 5 is literal. Both the tabernacle of Moses and the temple of Solomon were patterned after the temple in heaven (Hebrews 8:5; 9:23-24). The testimony that comes from the heavenly temple indicates that the Lord is a covenant keeping God. Throughout the scriptures, God has initiated several covenants. People have always enjoyed the benefits of these covenants as long as they were obedient to the conditions God set forth.

The earthly tabernacle and temple were the places where the tablets of the Law were maintained. The seven angels come from the heavenly tabernacle to execute judgment. This indicates that God is sending these judgments because of the world's rejection of His laws and His word.

The angels that will execute these plagues are dressed like priests. This shows that they are free from impurities and injustices. The four heavenly beasts referred to are the same four beasts that are mentioned in Revelation 4:5-8. One of these creatures will give the seven golden vials (bowls) to the seven angels. These seven angels will carry out the judgments of the last half of the tribulation.

When King Solomon dedicated the first temple in Jerusalem, God's presence and glory became so intense that a cloud appeared and the priests could not stand to minister (2 Chronicles 5:13-14). In a similar manner, during this future event the heavenly temple will be filled with smoke from the glory of God. Smoke and a cloud are manifestations of God's presence, glory, and power (Exodus 19:18; 40:34-35; 1 Kings 8:10-11; Isaiah 6:1-4).

Whenever smoke is mentioned in the Book of Revelation, it is associated with God's judgment (Revelation 8:3-5; 9:2-3, 17-18; 14:11; 15:8; 18:9, 18; 19:2-3).

Verse 8 states that no one will be able to enter the heavenly temple until these final seven judgments have been completed. This signifies that no one will be allowed to intercede to stop these judgments. No one will be given access to the mercy seat to make petitions for the sinners who are about to receive these judgments. These last judgments will be without mercy.

The seventh trumpet in Revelation 11:15, which is also the third woe, announces events leading up to Christ's return. The seventh trumpet and third woe introduce the judgments of the seven vials, or bowls. We don't know whether these bowl judgments will begin at the same time or not. But, once each plague begins, it will continue until the last day of the tribulation, right up to the Battle of Armageddon.

BRIMSTONE: "...tormented with fire and brimstone..." Revelation 14:10

Twenty-One

Revelation – Chapter 16

Brief Summary

Chapter 16 continues the earthly story. It describes the seven vials, or bowls of wrath, which will be poured out. These will be among the last events before the Battle of Armageddon and the Second Coming of Christ. The seven bowl judgments described in this chapter are as follows:

First Bowl Judgment: Boils (terrible sores) on all who have received the mark of the beast

Second Bowl Judgment: The sea becomes blood, killing all plant life and creatures in the sea

Third Bowl Judgment: Freshwater supplies become blood

Fourth Bowl Judgment: Great heat from the sun

Fifth Bowl Judgment: An impenetrable darkness over Antichrist's kingdom, accompanied by physical pain

Sixth Bowl Judgment: The Euphrates River will dry up, making it much easier for advancing armies from the east to march westward toward the nation of Israel.

Seventh Bowl Judgment: The greatest earthquake in human history, moving all mountains and islands

We know that Antichrist will not insist on receiving widespread worship until the middle of the tribulation (Daniel 9:27; 2 Thessalonians 2:3-4). Since the vial or bowl judgments begin after Antichrist becomes an object of worship, these plagues begin at some point after the middle of the tribulation.

Whereas the trumpet judgments were partial, the bowl (vial) judgments will be more extensive. The previous trumpet judgments were calls to repentance. However, the vial judgments will occur when there is no more hope of repentance for those who have received the mark of the beast (Revelation 14:9-11).

The First Vial: Boils and Sores

1   And I heard a great voice out of the temple saying to the seven angels, Go your ways, and pour out the vials of the wrath of God upon the earth.
2   And the first went, and poured out his vial upon the earth; and there fell a noisome and grievous sore upon the men which had the mark of the beast, and upon them which worshipped his image.

Verse 1 tells us that these vial, or bowl, judgments consist of "the wrath of God."

This first plague is similar to the sixth plague in Egypt in the days of Moses (Exodus 9:9-11). Those who have received the mark of the beast and worship his image will develop terrible sores. There will be others who are still alive and who have not received this mark. This judgment only affects those who have received the beast's mark. This shows God's anger toward those who worship the beast's image. Some have speculated that these sores will result from nuclear radiation poisoning. However God chooses to initiate this plague; the people who have these sores will blaspheme God and refuse to repent (Revelation 16:11).

The Second Vial: The Sea Becomes Blood

3   And the second angel poured out his vial upon the sea; and it became as the blood of a dead man: and every living soul died in the sea.

This judgment is similar to the first Egyptian plague (Exodus 7:17-21). In Revelation 8:8-9, the second trumpet judgment turned one-third of the sea into blood. One-third of the creatures in the sea were killed. One-third of the ships on the sea were destroyed. Now with the second vial, the remaining waters of the sea become like blood. The sea will not become actual blood, but "as the blood of a dead man." Perhaps the sea becomes so polluted that its color looks like blood. In any event, all the living creatures in the sea will die. Their bodies will float to the top, giving off a horrible stench. This event will probably trigger many diseases for humans. Panic will be the result. This will also greatly affect commercial shipping.

As previously mentioned, the judgments described in chapter 8 may be poured out on what was the known world in John's time. This was primarily the Roman Empire surrounding the Mediterranean. The previous judgments may be partial because they are calls to repentance. Most of the judgments described in chapter 16 are much more extensive and worldwide.

The Third Vial: Rivers Become Blood

4   And the third angel poured out his vial upon the rivers and fountains of
waters; and they became blood.

The third vial turns drinking water into blood. This is similar to the third trumpet judgment in chapter 8 that turned one-third of the drinking water into blood. However, this time all domestic drinking water is poisoned. This will cause more diseases and more panic. If this plague is worldwide, it probably occurs at the very end of the tribulation, because the humans affected would not survive for very long.

5   And I heard the angel of the waters say, Thou art righteous, O Lord, which
art, and wast, and shalt be, because thou hast judged thus.
6   For they have shed the blood of saints and prophets, and thou hast given
them blood to drink; for they are worthy.

During the seven-year tribulation, many of the followers of God will be killed for their faith. Those who murder them will in turn be given "blood to drink." In other words, they will also experience bloody deaths. This also refers to the drinking waters turning to blood.

7   And I heard another out of the altar say, Even so, Lord God Almighty, true
and righteous are thy judgments.

The phrase "another out of the altar" may refer to another group of believers who were martyred during the tribulation. They are crying out for justice. God's judgments on sin and evil are justified. Since God is holy, He hates evil. God will judge all sins except those that are forgiven through faith in Christ's death on the cross.

The Fourth Vial: Great Heat

> 8   And the fourth angel poured out his vial upon the sun; and power was
> given unto him to scorch men with fire.
> 9   And men were scorched with great heat, and blasphemed the name of
> God, which hath power over these plagues: and they repented not to give him glory.

The fourth vial will produce great heat from the sun. This heat wave will be so intense that people will be scorched by it. Perhaps this will be the result of pollution from previous nuclear explosions and fallout, which will greatly damage the ozone layer in the atmosphere. If the earth's protective atmosphere is removed, this planet will quickly start to resemble a worldwide desert. Whatever the means that God uses, the ultraviolet rays of the sun will scorch people with heat and fire. This may also be accompanied by radiation poisoning.

Even now, heat waves cause many deaths. This future heat wave will be far worse than any previous heat wave the world has ever seen. During this time, drinking water will be desperately sought because of the heat. Since the drinking waters were spoiled during the judgment of the third vial, good water will be very difficult, if not impossible, to find.

God will be recognized as the source of this suffering; however, those whose hearts are turned against God will be so hardened that they will refuse to repent. Since people will realize that these judgments have come from God, they will curse Him. The heat will become unbearable, and many people will blaspheme God.

The Fifth Vial: Darkness

> 10   And the fifth angel poured out his vial upon the seat of the beast; and his
> kingdom was full of darkness; and they gnawed their tongues for pain,
> 11   And blasphemed the God of heaven because of their pains and their sores,
> and repented not of their deeds.

The fifth vial applies to the seat, or throne, of the beast. This refers to the geographic area under the authority of the Antichrist, or perhaps his headquarter city. If the Antichrist rules an area not much bigger than the Old Roman Empire, Europe will primarily be targeted with this judgment.

This will be a change from one extreme to another. The blinding brightness that will most likely accompany the great heat of the previous judgment will turn into impenetrable darkness. Some have speculated that this darkness over the kingdom of Antichrist will be the result of a nuclear winter. Perhaps some of these plagues will be the after effects of a nuclear war. Whatever the means that God uses, this darkness will coincide with, or immediately follow, the intense heat wave. And, there will be little or no drinking water. All this will continue to increase fear and suffering. Since the waters were previously turned to blood, rivers and other bodies of water may no longer be sources of electrical power to provide lighting.

This darkness was probably included in Christ's words in Matthew 24:29 and Mark 13:24. In those passages, Jesus mentioned the cosmic signs that will precede His Second Coming. Some of the Old Testament prophets also predicted that darkness will be associated with the judgments of God (Zephaniah 1:14-15; Amos 5:18).

The people who have taken the mark of the beast will probably still have their sores from the first vial. People will generally realize that these judgments are coming from God. Despite their suffering, they will persist in their rebellion against righteousness and will continue to blaspheme God.

The Sixth Vial: The Euphrates River Dried Up

> 12   And the sixth angel poured out his vial upon the great river Euphrates; and the water thereof was dried up, that the way of the kings of the east might be prepared.

The sixth vial will cause the Euphrates River to dry up. Since the other vials of judgment are literal, this bowl judgment of the Euphrates River drying up must also be literal.

This event will allow advancing armies from the east to continue their westward march. This ties in with the sounding of the sixth trumpet in Revelation 9:13-19, when demons from the Euphrates inspired the assembling of a vast army. This judgment may have a double meaning. In addition to a human army from the east, Revelation 16:12 may also refer to a continued invasion of a horde of demonic spirits from the area of the Euphrates.

Some teach that the invading armies from the east will fight against the armies of Antichrist in order to control Arab oil. Others teach that these armies from the east will join with the Antichrist in an attempt to annihilate the nation of Israel. In any event, God will intervene. The armies of the east and of Antichrist will be destroyed by the returning Christ at the Battle of Armageddon (Revelation 19:11-21).

Perhaps several Oriental nations will initially intend to wage war against the Antichrist, but demonic forces will inspire them to join forces with the Antichrist in opposition to the nation of Israel (Revelation 16:13-16). If the Antichrist is a Muslim, this military force could also be made up of armies from many Islamic nations who wish to join Antichrist in his destruction of the nation of Israel. The drying up of the Euphrates River will allow these armies from the east to quickly approach the Middle East. This is in preparation for what will be the Battle of Armageddon. This battle will probably occur during the last few days of the tribulation since the next judgment brings the tribulation to a close with the final destruction of Babylon.

Three Unclean Spirits Inspire Armies to Come to Armageddon

13   And I saw three unclean spirits like frogs come out of the mouth of the dragon, and out of the mouth of the beast, and out of the mouth of the false prophet.

14   For they are the spirits of devils, working miracles, which go forth unto the kings of the earth and of the whole world, to gather them to the battle of that great day of God Almighty.

15   Behold, I come as a thief. Blessed is he that watcheth, and keepeth his garments, lest he walk naked, and they see his shame.

16   And he gathered them together into a place called in the Hebrew tongue Armageddon.

Verses 13 through 16 are parenthetical. They are inserted between the sixth and seventh seals. John saw unclean spirits coming out of the dragon, the beast, and the false prophet (verse 13). These unclean spirits are demons that will work miracles to deceive many.

The "dragon" is Satan (Revelation 12:9). The "beast" is the Antichrist (Revelation, chapter 13:1-7). As previously mentioned, the Antichrist will have a false prophet who will lead a false religion (Revelation 13:11-15). The devil, the Antichrist, and the false prophet will form a kind of unholy trinity. They will be the leaders of a satanic system that is political, economic, and religious. These unclean spirits will be associated with this unholy trinity. The description of the unclean spirits coming out of the mouths of these evil rulers refers to the persuasive oratory that will deceive many. Deceit will be a key ingredient in their leadership (II Thessalonians 2:9-12).

These unclean spirits will work miracles of diplomacy through ambassadors and/or false prophets (verse 14). These spirits will seek the cooperation of the leaders of many nations; probably to help Antichrist annihilate the Jews by sending their armies to Armageddon (verse 16).

As previously mentioned in our discussion of chapter 13, this is evidence that the Antichrist will not rule the entire world. Even toward the end of the tribulation, Antichrist will be forced to rely on miracles of diplomacy to influence many nations. Deceived by satanic miracles, many national leaders will be demonized and will be inspired to send armies to the Middle East in preparation for the Battle of Armageddon. "That great day of God Almighty" refers to the day when God's judgments on the earth during the seven-year tribulation will be completed.

Verse 15 pronounces a blessing upon those faithful followers of Christ who are watching for His return. Christ will come as a thief, surprising the ungodly. Watching for the Lord Jesus Christ to suddenly appear and overthrow His enemies (2 Thessalonians 1:7-10) is an admonition to believers during the tribulation to remain spiritually true to God. God's faithful followers will not be spiritually vulnerable or ashamed when they visibly see Jesus.

Verse 16 ties in with verse 14. In verse 16, the King James Version includes the phrase "he gathered." This is translated as "they gathered" in several other versions (such as the Amplified, New International Version, Revised Standard Version, and the New King James Version). "They gathered" refers to demonic forces gathering armies from all over the world to march against the nation of Israel. Anti-Semitism will reach a level never before seen in history.

The Battle of Armageddon will be centered in the valley of Megiddo or Armageddon in Israel (Revelation 16:14-16; Zechariah 12:11). This valley is most likely the valley of Jezreel in north central Palestine. This is a strategic place for an invasion of Israel. However, this battle will cover a much larger area. The Battle of Armageddon will take place at the end of the seven-year tribulation. This battle will end at the moment of Christ's Second Coming (Revelation 19:11-21).

The Seventh Vial: A Great Earthquake and Hail

17   And the seventh angel poured out his vial into the air; and there came a great voice out of the temple of heaven, from the throne, saying, It is done.

18   And there were voices, and thunders, and lightnings; and there was a great earthquake, such as was not since men were upon the earth, so mighty an earthquake, and so great.

19   And the great city was divided into three parts, and the cities of the nations fell: and great Babylon came in remembrance before God, to give unto her the cup of the wine of the fierceness of his wrath.

20   And every island fled away, and the mountains were not found.

21   And there fell upon men a great hail out of heaven, every stone about the weight of a talent: and men blasphemed God because of the plague of the hail; for the plague thereof was exceeding great.

Verse 17 states that a "great voice" came out of the temple in heaven. Perhaps this will be God's voice. The phrase "it is done" means that God's wrath and the seven-year tribulation period are coming to an end. The armies will instantly be destroyed in battle. A great upheaval of nature will soon follow.

A great earthquake is mentioned in verse 18. In fact, it will be the greatest earthquake in human history.

Verse 19 mentions "the great city" that "was divided into three parts."

Two Interpretations of "The Great City."

---

1. "The great city" refers to Jerusalem (Revelation 11:8). Jerusalem will be divided into three parts.

2. "The great city" refers to the city that is the headquarters of the Antichrist. This city will be the center of the beast's economic, political, and religious system (Revelation, chapter 17). It is referred to as "Babylon."

As previously discussed, since "Babylon" was a code name used by early Christians to refer to Rome, some teach that this city is Rome. Others teach that this refers to the ancient city of Babylon in Iraq that will be rebuilt.

In any event, the headquarters city of Antichrist will be divided into three parts.

Verse 19 also states, "the cities of the nations fell," meaning that cities all over the world will be destroyed. This earthquake will change much of the earth. This vast upheaval of nature will make islands and mountains move and even disappear (verse 20). Some speculate that in addition to a great earthquake, volcanoes, and even an asteroid colliding with earth may be involved. There is the possibility that these events will also include a great war in which nuclear weapons are used.

Verse 21 tells us that at the end of the tribulation period, great hail will fall. As previously mentioned, these hail stones will average a talent in weight, which can range from 75 to 100 pounds. People who are in rebellion against God will still refuse to repent, and they will continue to blaspheme God.

God says, "It is done," in Revelation 16:17. This refers to the very end of the tribulation. However, chapters 17 through 19 give more details about the fall of Babylon, the return of Christ, and the Battle of Armageddon.

THE TRINITY

Twenty-Two

Revelation – Chapter 17

Brief Summary

Chapter 17 is an informational chapter. It describes a drunken harlot who rides a beast. This harlot is called "Babylon the Great." The picture of the harlot riding the beast is obviously symbolic.

The beast and the 10 kings will rejoice over the destruction of the mystical Babylon that is discussed in Revelation, chapter 17. However, these same kings will mourn over the destruction of a Babylon that is discussed in Revelation 18:9-19. This indicates that the Book of Revelation describes the destruction of two Babylon systems.

The first Babylon is a false religious system that has taken on various forms throughout human history. It is called "the woman" and the "great whore." The Antichrist will view this religious system as a competitor for worship. Consequently, this religious system will be destroyed by Antichrist and the 10 kings in the middle of the tribulation. Antichrist will replace the first Babylon religious system with another Babylon religious system.

In addition to being a new religion that worships the Antichrist, the second Babylon system will also be economic and political. This system will probably be centered in a literal city. It will be destroyed by Christ at His Second Coming. The destruction of this second Babylon system is fully described in chapter 18.

The Two Babylons

The first Babylon: A mystical religious system that will be destroyed by Antichrist in the middle of the tribulation

The first Babylon is a false religious system that is combined with political power, and is represented as a prostitute (Revelation 17:1-6). This false religious system has taken on various forms in many cultures throughout human history, such as witchcraft, demon worship, apostate Christianity, and other manifestations of the occult (Revelation 9:20-21; Matthew 24:24; 2 Thessalonians 2:9-12). It is called "the woman" and "the great whore" (Revelation 17:1-6, 9, 15-16, 18). The first Babylon is an all-encompassing religious system that will have a major influence in Antichrist's government during the first half of the tribulation. This religious system will be destroyed by Antichrist and the 10 kings in the middle of the tribulation (Revelation 17:15-16). Antichrist will replace this religious system with another religion that exalts himself (Daniel 9:27; Matthew 24:15; 2 Thessalonians 2:3-4). This will occur when the Antichrist gains great political power and the 10 kings give their kingdoms to the beast (Revelation 13:1-10; 17:17).

The Second Babylon: An Economic, Political and Religious System Introduced by the Antichrist, Reaching its Height During the Second Half of the Tribulation

The second Babylon is an evil political, economic, and religious system of the Antichrist. It will require worship of the Antichrist (Daniel 9:27; Matthew 24:15; 2 Thessalonians 2:3-4; Revelation 18:9-19, 22-23). Revelation 16:17-19 tells us that this system will be destroyed during the seventh vial at the end of the tribulation. The destruction of this system of Babylon is fully described in chapter 18. The final destruction of this system actually occurs at Christ's Second Coming in Revelation 19:11-21.

The headquarters of both Babylon systems will probably be centered in a literal city (Revelation 17:18).

The first Babylon will be destroyed by the 10 kings under the Antichrist (Revelation 17:15-16). However, the destruction of the second Babylon will be supernatural and occur in one day (Revelation 18:8). The destruction of the second Babylon will be associated with the earthquakes and hail of the seventh bowl judgment (Revelation 16:17-21).

The Great Harlot: Mystery Babylon

1   And there came one of the seven angels which had the seven vials, and talked with me, saying unto me, Come hither; I will shew unto thee the judgment of the great whore that sitteth upon many waters:

2   With whom the kings of the earth have committed fornication, and the inhabitants of the earth have been made drunk with the wine of her fornication.

3   So he carried me away in the spirit into the wilderness: and I saw a woman sit upon a scarlet coloured beast, full of names of blasphemy, having seven heads and ten horns.

4   And the woman was arrayed in purple and scarlet colour, and decked with gold and precious stones and pearls, having a golden cup in her hand full of abominations and filthiness of her fornication:

5   And upon her forehead was a name written, MYSTERY, BABYLON THE GREAT, THE MOTHER OF HARLOTS AND ABOMINATIONS OF THE EARTH.

6   And I saw the woman drunken with the blood of the saints, and with the blood of the martyrs of Jesus: and when I saw her, I wondered with great admiration.

In verse 1, an angel invites John to observe God's judgment poured out on a prostitute sitting upon many waters. The Bible sometimes portrays prostitution and adultery figuratively to represent religious apostasy (Isaiah 1:21; Jeremiah 3:9; Ezekiel 16:14-18, 32-41; James 4:4). Thus, this prostitute represents a unity of false religions. This will include so-called Christian movements that no longer accept the Bible as divinely inspired and have turned away from the gospel of Christ (2 Timothy 3:1-5; 4:3). These false religions persecute the true followers of Christ (Revelation 17:6).

Verse 15 explains that the waters the prostitute was sitting on represent the peoples of the earth. The influence of this harlot system is global. This satanic system of religions has dominated the peoples of the earth. That is why she is sitting on them. This harlot is also referred to as Babylon in verse 5. The whore, representing a satanic religious system, has had a vast influence over masses of people and various cultures to the point where she has been able to control entire nations.

Verse 2 states that this whore has committed fornication with "the kings of the earth." It is obvious that this woman is not a specific person, but a symbol of a religious system opposed to God. Verse 6 states that she is drunk "with the blood of the saints." This system has inspired persecution of God's true followers over a long period of time.

In verse 3, the Lord took John into the wilderness so he could view this scene from a proper perspective. John saw the whore sitting upon a beast. This blasphemous beast supports the whore. Although she will initially be part of Antichrist's kingdom, this harlot will be deceived by the beast she rides.

This beast represents a satanic governmental system. The harlot represents a false religious system that will be tied in with governments. The seven heads may represent seven great kingdoms in history that have supported this false religious system in various forms.

As previously mentioned, "horns" in scripture can represent kings and rulers (Daniel 7:24; Revelation 17:12). The 10 horns represent a confederacy of 10 kingdoms that will support the beast system of the Antichrist. The corrupt religious system, represented as a harlot, will seek to dominate Antichrist's system. This is why the Antichrist and his ten kings will eventually overthrow this harlot religious system (Revelation 17:16). Antichrist will then replace this false religious system with another false religious system that will be centered on himself (Daniel 9:27; 11:36-37; Matthew 24:15-21; 2 Thessalonians 2:1-12; Revelation 13:4; 14:9-11).

As previously mentioned, the term "beast" is used in the Book of Revelation to represent at least two, and possibly three, different things:

(1) A human being (the Antichrist) who comes out of the sea of people (13:1; 17:11)
(2) A political/governmental system opposed to God (Daniel 7:3-7, 17, 23; Revelation 17:12-17)
(3) Some believe the term "beast" may also refer to a supernatural being (a demon) that is allowed to come out of the bottomless pit (Revelation 11:7; 17:8). This demon will help inspire the beast system that Antichrist will set up.

Thus, the human beast out of the sea of humanity (Antichrist) and the beast government system are two different things. In addition, some believe that the beast from the bottomless pit is a demonic prince. If this is true, these three things are all represented in one symbol, the beast.

The gaudy clothing of the harlot described in verse 4 suggests her wealth and worldly glory. This harlot religious system will have access to a great deal of money. Her golden cup is beautiful on the outside, but full of abominations. This represents the spiritual condition of the apostate church and other false religions that practice immorality.

Roman prostitutes were required to identify themselves by wearing a tag with their names on their foreheads. In like manner, this harlot of false religions is identified with a name on her forehead (verse 5).

The word "mystery" in verse 5 indicates that the whore represents a mystical religion. The name "Babylon" comes from the word "Babel." In the Book of Genesis, the Tower of Babel symbolized human pride, self-glorification, and rebellion (Genesis 11:1-9). The foundation of this city, and successive Babylon systems, is disobedience to God. After God dispersed these people in Genesis, chapter 11, the initial mystery religion of Babylon spread in various forms throughout the world. The empires that supported this "Mystery Babylon" religious system were controlled by witchcraft, spiritism, astrology, and rebellion against God.

The religious system that is represented by the harlot covers a long period of history. The influence of this harlot-religious system has been responsible for the persecution and death of many believers in the true God. The woman's drunkenness shows the pleasure she has received in persecuting the followers of God over a long period of time. This false religious system, called Babylon, has recently become more and more prominent in so-called Christianity. The characteristics of this system include denial of the deity of Jesus Christ, His virgin birth, His resurrection, and the redemption that is available through Christ's sacrifice on the cross. Christ warned that religious deception will be a principle sign of the end times (Matthew 24:4-5, 11, 23-24; Mark 13:5-6, 21-22).

This false and blasphemous religious system will be a central part of Antichrist's government until the middle of the tribulation. This system will continue to persecute true followers of the Jesus Christ of the Bible until it is replaced by another evil system devised by the Antichrist.

The Beast That Carries the Harlot

> 7   And the angel said unto me, Wherefore didst thou marvel? I will tell thee the mystery of the woman, and of the beast that carrieth her, which hath the seven heads and ten horns.
>
> 8   The beast that thou sawest was, and is not; and shall ascend out of the bottomless pit, and go into perdition: and they that dwell on the earth shall wonder, whose names were not written in the book of life from the foundation of the world, when they behold the beast that was, and is not, and yet is.

Verse 8 states there are names not written in the Book of Life. This does not mean that God predestines some to be saved and some to be lost. It is God's will that all be saved (2 Peter 3:9). However, a person's name can be erased from the Book of Life (Psalm 69:28). The names of all believers will be written in God's Book of Life. The names of those who overcome will not be blotted out (Revelation 3:5).

The beast represents both the Antichrist (Revelation 13:1-8) and his kingdom. The phrase "was, and is not; and shall ascend out of the bottomless pit," means that the beast was alive, died, and was brought back to life from the "bottomless pit." Revelation 17:8 is related to Revelation 13:3 concerning the head that was wounded to death, but healed. Although this may refer to an assassination and resurrection of the Antichrist, it may also refer to a resurrected kingdom or governmental system that receives inspiration from the abyss.

In our discussion about Revelation, chapter 13, we mentioned two interpretations of the beast that had "one of his heads as it were wounded to death." These two interpretations are again included below.

Two Interpretations of the Head Wounded to Death

1. **The Antichrist will be given a deadly wound, that is, he will be assassinated.** Revelation 17:8 indicates that the beast, which was seen by people, and then not seen, will again appear after he comes up out of the abyss. This refers to the death and resurrection of the Antichrist.

Antichrist will be resurrected through Satan's supernatural power (Revelation 13:14). This may be Satan's method for deceiving much of the world (2 Thessalonians 2:9-10).

Some feel that Antichrist will portray a phony resurrection (Revelation 13:14). This will be inspired by the abyss. His alleged miraculous powers will convince many to follow and worship him (Revelation 13:3-4).

2. **One of the beast's heads (13:3), a great kingdom, will be wounded to death (come to an end) and then revived.** In other words, this deadly wound, said to be healed, refers to the resurrection of a former great empire thought to be extinct. This beast governmental system was once in existence, but went out of existence. Through Satanic powers, this system will be brought back into existence.

The beast in Revelation 17:8 cannot refer to the human Antichrist because the bottomless pit, or abyss, is not a place for human beings. It is a prison for certain demonic spirits (Luke 8:31; Revelation 9:1-11). There are certain Satanic princes confined there (Revelation 11:7; 17:8).

Another reason that Revelation 17:8 cannot refer to a literal resurrection of the Antichrist is because God alone, through Christ, has the power of resurrection (John 11:25). Satan cannot raise anyone from the dead.

The resurrection of the beast represents the persistence of evil. The "beast that was, and is not, and yet is" most likely refers to a resurrected kingdom that receives inspiration from the abyss.

In addition, the beast from the abyss (Revelation 17:8) may also refer to a demonic being that is released in order to help with the formation of Antichrist's government system. Some teach that this demon "was, and is not, and shall ascend out of the bottomless pit." This refers to the fact that this spirit was on the earth before John's lifetime, was imprisoned in the bottomless pit, but will be released again during Antichrist's reign.

It is often taught that the resurrection of a former kingdom refers to the revised Roman Empire. However, some teach that this resurrected kingdom will be literal Babylon, which is in modern day Iraq.

If the Antichrist is assassinated and brought back to life, this will be Satan's attempt to duplicate Christ's resurrection. However, this will be a poor imitation of the Lamb of God who died and rose from the dead. Regardless of which of the previous interpretations is correct, those who are unsaved will marvel and be astonished at the beast and his system.

> 9   And here is the mind which hath wisdom. The seven heads are seven mountains, on which the woman sitteth.
>
> 10   And there are seven kings: five are fallen, and one is, and the other is not yet come; and when he cometh, he must continue a short space.

The seven heads are seven mountains on which the woman sits. The two interpretations of the seven heads that were included in our discussion of chapter 13 are summarized in the following.

Two Interpretations About the Seven Heads

---

1. **The seven heads of the beast refer to the Seven Hills of Rome.** Revelation 17:9 states that the "seven heads are seven mountains, on which the woman sitteth." This refers to the city of Rome, the City of Seven Hills.

According to this view, the system that Antichrist will preside over will have its headquarters in Rome.

2. **The seven heads of the beast in Revelation 13:1 and 17:9 represent seven kingdoms, or empires, controlled by a recurring satanic system.** When the word "mountain" is used in scripture, and it is not referring to a specific geographic place, it refers to a great kingdom. Examples include Jeremiah 51:25 and Daniel 2:35. Each of the seven heads had a crown, indicating kingdoms (Revelation 12:3). The seven heads, which are mountains (Revelation 17:9) are referring to seven great kingdoms in world history. Most of these seven empires are in the past. These are kingdoms that God has used, or will use, to chasten Israel.

Revelation 17:10 tells us that by the Apostle John's time, five had fallen, one existed, and one was yet to come. This is referring to seven kingdoms in history.

In Daniel 2:29-45, five kingdoms predicted in Nebuchadnezzar's dream were as follows: Babylonia, Medo-Persia, Greece, Rome, and the future revised Roman Empire.

Revelation 17:3, and 17:7 refer to seven heads, which are seven mountains or kingdoms (Revelation 17:9-10). This list of seven kingdoms is as follows: Egypt, Assyria, Babylonia, Medo-Persia, Greece, Rome, and the future revised Roman Empire. John is considering two previous empires that Daniel's account did not consider (Egypt and Assyria).

The seven heads refer to seven empires controlled by a satanic beast system. The seventh kingdom, the revived Roman Empire, is yet to come and will be led by the Antichrist.

If there will be a revised Roman Empire, Antichrist's headquarters may be in the city of Rome. The harlot is seen sitting on the seven kingdoms. As previously stated, this harlot represents a satanic religious system that exerted tremendous influence throughout human history.

Five of these heads, or kingdoms, had fallen by John's day. One existed in John's day, and one was yet to come (Revelation 17:10). The seventh large satanic kingdom yet to come will include 10 kings. This future kingdom is represented by the feet of iron and clay on the image in Daniel 2:41-43.

Verse 10 tells us that the seventh kingdom will not last very long, and will only "continue a short space." Satan will be allowed to restore his past system of government, commerce, and false religion for a short time.

> 11   And the beast that was, and is not, even he is the eighth, and is of the seven, and goeth into perdition.

Revelation 17:11 may again suggest that Antichrist will die in the middle of the tribulation, and be resurrected.

The seventh head (seventh kingdom) will help to raise the Antichrist to prominence. The eighth kingdom, which will be the Antichrist's kingdom, will come out of the seventh kingdom. As previously stated, around the midpoint of the seven-year tribulation, Antichrist will gain absolute power over the confederation of the 10 kings. This is when the empire of the Antichrist (the large eighth satanic kingdom) will actually be set up (Revelation, chapter 13). The eighth kingdom of the Antichrist will continue for 42 months (Revelation 13:5). This eighth kingdom will include Satan's last attempts to destroy Israel. Satan's efforts to destroy the Jewish people included his use of the seven previous kingdoms.

> 12   And the ten horns which thou sawest are ten kings, which have received no kingdom as yet; but receive power as kings one hour with the beast.
>
> 13   These have one mind, and shall give their power and strength unto the beast.
>
> 14   These shall make war with the Lamb, and the Lamb shall overcome them: for he is Lord of lords, and King of kings: and they that are with him are called, and chosen, and faithful.

These 10 kings, represented by 10 horns, are not the same as the seven heads. In the last days, these 10 governmental leaders will pledge their countries to the beast and his system (Revelation 17:16-17). For a short time, these 10 kingdoms will be separate governments that are part of the seventh kingdom. When Antichrist gains more power over these countries, he will then consolidate them, forming what John refers to as the "eighth" kingdom (Revelation 17:11).

Verses 12-14 are discussing the 10 small kingdoms that will come under the rule of the Antichrist. These 10 kingdoms will be absorbed into the eighth large satanic kingdom that will be formed in the middle of the tribulation. The 10 smaller kingdoms will eventually join the Antichrist in making war with the lamb (Jesus). These kingdoms will persecute Christ's followers. This war on the lamb will conclude at the Battle of Armageddon (Revelation 16:16-19; 19:17-21; 20:1-3). The Lamb and His followers will be victorious.

> 15   And he saith unto me, The waters which thou sawest, where the whore sitteth, are peoples, and multitudes, and nations, and tongues.

As previously mentioned, the waters the prostitute was sitting on represent the peoples of the earth. This whore represents a satanic religious system that has had a vast influence over masses of people, and even some entire nations.

> 16 And the ten horns which thou sawest upon the beast, these shall hate the whore, and shall make her desolate and naked, and shall eat her flesh, and burn her with fire.

The ten kings will destroy the harlot. In other words, the Antichrist will turn these national leaders against the great religious system that is represented by the harlot. The institutions of this religious system will be destroyed.

During the first three-and-one-half years of the tribulation, the false harlot religions that were interwoven with the first seven kingdoms will coexist with the system of the Antichrist. In the middle of the tribulation, the Antichrist will set himself up to be worshipped as a god (Daniel 9:27). He will replace the religious system represented by the harlot with his own religious system. During the last three-and-one-half years of the tribulation, the Antichrist will fully implement his beast system, which will be political, economic, and religious. This does away with the seventh large satanic kingdom and institutes the eighth and final large satanic kingdom.

> 17 For God hath put in their hearts to fulfil his will, and to agree, and give their kingdom unto the beast, until the words of God shall be fulfilled.
> 18 And the woman which thou sawest is that great city, which reigneth over the kings of the earth.

Verse 18 refers to "the woman" as "that great city" that rules over the earth. In scripture, a city can represent a symbolic woman. For example, the city of New Jerusalem represents the Bride of Christ (Revelation 21:2; 21:9-10). Many believe that this woman represents the capital city of the kingdom of Antichrist. There has been a great deal of speculation about a literal city that will meet this description. As previously mentioned, some believe that this refers to the ancient city of Babylon in Iraq that will be rebuilt and repopulated. Others have claimed it refers to the city of Rome, Italy. Still others believe that the "great city" is not a literal city, but represents a satanic religious movement, without geographic borders.

Three Interpretations of the "Great City."

1. **The "great city" refers to Rome** where the headquarters of the Antichrist will be located.

In New Testament times, the term "Babylon" was sometimes a code name for the city of Rome, as in 1 Peter 5:13. In the Book of Revelation, John may have used the term "Babylon" as a code name for Rome. This was to avoid openly speaking out against the Roman Empire. Rome was seen as the enemy of faithful followers of Christ.

This city cannot refer to the ancient city of Babylon. Babylon will remain in ruins in fulfillment of prophecies in the Old Testament (Isaiah 13:19-22).

The fact that it has been slightly rebuilt as a tourist attraction does not make it the great city of the last days.

Rome will be the center of Antichrist's kingdom.

2. **The "great city" refers to the ancient city of Babylon in Iraq,** which will be rebuilt. This will be the headquarters of the Antichrist.

Some prophecies about the final destruction of the ancient city of Babylon have not yet been fulfilled.

Isaiah 13:19-20 indicates that after God destroys Babylon, like Sodom and Gomorrah, it will never be inhabited again. However, people are once again living in the ancient city of Babylon. Therefore, this city has not yet received the complete judgment of God.

Ancient Babylon will be rebuilt in oil-rich Iraq and become the capital city of Antichrist's kingdom.

The Antichrist will be able to economically bring all the industrialized nations to their knees by denying them oil from the Middle East. As previously stated in our discussion about Revelation 13, this is consistent with Islamic prophecy. Muslims believe an Islamic leader will arise who will convert the world to Islam. They believe he comes out of Iraq.

3. **This city, as well as this woman, is not a literal city, but a satanic religious movement.** Revelation 17:18 states that the woman is the great city. When used symbolically in scripture, a woman can represent a religious movement (Isaiah 54:5; Ezekiel 16:1-14; Hosea 2:16; Ephesians 5:25-27; Revelation 22:17).

Since this Babylon is described as a "mystery," it does not refer to a literal city, but to a mystical religious system.

Whichever interpretation is accurate, it is probable that the woman representing a satanic religious movement will have headquarters in a literal city.

Those who speculate that this city is Rome sometimes contend that the harlot is Roman Catholicism. However, the Roman Catholic Church is no more the harlot than any other great denominational structure. For example, it has been liberal protestant churches that have attempted to do away with the divine inspiration of scripture, the deity of Christ, His virgin birth, and His resurrection. The Catholic Church has retained these doctrines. The National Council of Churches and the World Council of Churches are actually some of the forerunners of this ecumenical harlot religious system, which will include apostate Christianity.

Whether or not Antichrist will rule the entire earth, he will attempt to bring all religions together that represent all the people of the world. It will consist of elements of all man made religious orders that will be in existence. The religious system that will be instituted by Antichrist probably resembles what is known as the New Age Movement. Antichrist will attempt to blend mysticism from all the religions of the world together, teaching religious tolerance. However, this system will have no tolerance for those who dissent, such as committed Christians and Jews.

THE TRINITY

Twenty-Three

Revelation – Chapter 18

Brief Summary

Chapter 18 is another informational chapter about the destruction of Babylon.

As was discussed in chapter 17, the beast and the ten kings will rejoice over the destruction of a false religious system referred to as Mystical Babylon (Revelation 17:16-17). However, these kings will mourn over the destruction of the Babylon that is discussed in Revelation 18:9-19. This indicates that there are at least two Babylon's referred to in the Book of Revelation.

Chapter 18 portrays the destruction of the second Babylon, which will be an economic/political/religious system that becomes fully manifest during the second half of the tribulation. The destruction of this system is described primarily in commercial and economic terms. Although this system will probably have its headquarters in a literal city, it will extend throughout all the nations that the Antichrist rules and influences.

The headquarters city and territories of the second Babylon system will be destroyed in "one hour" (Revelation 18:10, 17, 19). It will be burned with fire (Revelation 18:8), uninhabitable for humans (Revelation 18:2), and contain no activity (Revelation 18:22-23). This destruction may suggest divine miraculous catastrophes, or it may refer to nuclear war.

The first Babylon is religious in nature (Revelation 17:1-6) and will be destroyed by Antichrist and 10 kings in the middle of the tribulation (Revelation 17:15-16). This will occur when Antichrist gains great political power and seizes control over the 10 kings and their kingdoms (Revelation 13:1-10). This great apostate religious system, referred to as "Mystery Babylon," will be replaced by the religion of the Antichrist (Matthew 24:15; 2 Thessalonians 2:3-4).

The second Babylon will also be religious, as well as economic and political in nature (Revelation 18:9-19, 22-23). The "Babylon" introduced by the Antichrist will probably be headquartered in a literal city. As previously stated, some suggest that the capital city of this kingdom may be Rome. Others believe it will be the ancient city of Babylon rebuilt. Revelation 16:17-19 tells us that this Babylon will be destroyed by an earthquake during the seventh vial judgment, at the end of the seven-year tribulation. No doubt, a headquarters city is included in this destruction. This city will also be burned with fire (Revelation 18:8-10, 18; 19:3). Chapter 19 portrays the destruction of the governmental and military aspects of Antichrist's system (Revelation 19:17-21).

Indictment of Babylon

1   And after these things I saw another angel come down from heaven, having great power; and the earth was lightened with his glory.

2   And he cried mightily with a strong voice, saying, Babylon the great is fallen, is fallen, and is become the habitation of devils, and the hold of every foul spirit, and a cage of every unclean and hateful bird.

3   For all nations have drunk of the wine of the wrath of her fornication, and the kings of the earth have committed fornication with her, and the merchants of the earth are waxed rich through the abundance of her delicacies.

Verse 1 begins, "After these things." Chapter 18 takes place at some point after the whore's religious system is destroyed by the Antichrist (Revelation 17:15-16). As previously mentioned, "Mystery Babylon," will be replaced by the religion of the Antichrist (Matthew 24:15; 2 Thessalonians 2:3-4). Chapter 18 is a continuation of the seventh vial judgment against the system that Antichrist has set up (Revelation 16:17-21).

The final fall of Babylon was announced in Revelation 14:8. This announcement is repeated in 18:2.

The second Babylon is a governmental, commercial, and religious system that extends through nations. Many merchants of the earth will become rich from this system. This system is associated with demonic powers, wickedness, and self-centered luxuries. It is also a symbol of sinful pride and rebellion against God. Its depravity will be demonically inspired. After its destruction, these places will be uninhabitable for humans. Only demons will temporarily dwell in the city and territories of Babylon, until the final moment of the tribulation period.

The Verdict Against Babylon

4   And I heard another voice from heaven, saying, Come out of her, my people, that ye be not partakers of her sins, and that ye receive not of her plagues.

5   For her sins have reached unto heaven, and God hath remembered her iniquities.

6   Reward her even as she rewarded you, and double unto her double according to her works: in the cup which she hath filled fill to her double.

7   How much she hath glorified herself, and lived deliciously, so much torment and sorrow give her: for she saith in her heart, I sit a queen, and am no widow, and shall see no sorrow.

8   Therefore shall her plagues come in one day, death, and mourning, and famine; and she shall be utterly burned with fire: for strong is the Lord God who judgeth her.

In verse 4, the voice that is speaking is probably the voice of God because it refers to "my people."

Followers of the true God are told to separate themselves from the sins of Antichrist's Babylon system in order to avoid the judgment and destruction that will follow. This warning is directed at people who were not saved at the time of the rapture, but who accepted Jesus Christ as their personal savior during the tribulation. It may also be an appeal to Israelites to accept Jesus as their Messiah.

All Christians living prior to the tribulation should also take this warning seriously. We should apply this warning to our own lives, by separating ourselves from worldly and satanic influences.

The sufferings and judgments that God will send on the Antichrist's Babylon system will match the self-exaltations and luxurious lifestyles for which she will be known. In fact, God will repay those who participated in this system with a double penalty of judgment, according to their works. The wealth that results from the economic system of Babylon will be suddenly taken away. The headquarters of this Babylon system will cease to exist as a metropolis. The fact that it will be burned and destroyed with fire "in one day" may suggest divine miraculous catastrophes, or it may refer to nuclear war.

Sorrow Over the Destruction of Babylon

9   And the kings of the earth, who have committed fornication and lived deliciously with her, shall bewail her, and lament for her, when they shall see the smoke of her burning,

10   Standing afar off for the fear of her torment, saying, Alas, alas, that great city Babylon, that mighty city! for in one hour is thy judgment come.

11   And the merchants of the earth shall weep and mourn over her; for no man buyeth their merchandise any more:

12   The merchandise of gold, and silver, and precious stones, and of pearls, and fine linen, and purple, and silk, and scarlet, and all thyine wood, and all manner vessels of ivory, and all manner vessels of most precious wood, and of brass, and iron, and marble,

13   And cinnamon, and odours, and ointments, and frankincense, and wine, and oil, and fine flour, and wheat, and beasts, and sheep, and horses, and chariots, and slaves, and souls of men.

14   And the fruits that thy soul lusted after are departed from thee, and all things which were dainty and goodly are departed from thee, and thou shalt find them no more at all.

15   The merchants of these things, which were made rich by her, shall stand afar off for the fear of her torment, weeping and wailing,

16   And saying, Alas, alas, that great city, that was clothed in fine linen, and purple, and scarlet, and decked with gold, and precious stones, and pearls!

17   For in one hour so great riches is come to nought. And every shipmaster, and all the company in ships, and sailors, and as many as trade by sea, stood afar off,

18   And cried when they saw the smoke of her burning, saying, What city is like unto this great city!

19   And they cast dust on their heads, and cried, weeping and wailing, saying, Alas, alas, that great city, wherein were made rich all that had ships in the sea by reason of her costliness! for in one hour is she made desolate.

The second Babylon of the Antichrist, which will be a political/economic/religious system, will be destroyed "in one hour." As previously mentioned, this may suggest divine miraculous catastrophes, or it may refer to nuclear war.

Verse 10 implies that survivors living outside of the city and territories of the Antichrist's Babylon system will be afraid to enter these borders. Many, if not most, national leaders will be allied with the economic and religious system of the Antichrist. They will grieve and express sorrow over the destruction of this system.

In verse 11, many wealthy businessmen will weep over the destruction of the economic system of Babylon because they will no longer be able to profit from these markets. Their great riches will be gone, possibly suggesting an economic collapse that has worldwide affects. The fall of this economic system will affect all who enjoyed and depended on it.

The list of products in verses 12-13 shows the extreme materialism of this system. Most of this merchandise will consist of luxuries, not necessities. Some people are seen in this system merely as objects to be bought and sold. Verse 13 refers to slavery and probably includes human trafficking. At the very least, it refers to extremely cheap labor provided by persons whose lives are excessively controlled by exploitive businesses and corporations.

Since this Babylon system was known for its rich commerce, many greedy merchants throughout the world will mourn over her. Verse 15 again refers to merchants showing grief over this destruction and being afraid to go near the geographical territories that have been devastated. Perhaps this is a reference to radioactive nuclear fallout that is concentrated in these areas.

Verses 17-19 state that many ship owners and sailors, who were involved in trade by sea, will mourn over the sudden destruction of this economic system. This is a warning to all of us. God's people should not live for money. Christians can be prosperous without being greedily consumed with money and materialism.

The fact that trade by sea is mentioned would indicate that the city of Rome, which is closer to the sea, is a more likely candidate for the capital city of this system than is the ancient city of Babylon in Iraq.

Joy Over the Destruction of Babylon

> 20   Rejoice over her, thou heaven, and ye holy apostles and prophets; for God hath avenged you on her.

Although there is much sorrow on the earth about the destruction of this second Babylon system, there is a command for the heavenly world to rejoice. The people in heaven are told to rejoice over God's judgment on this wicked, satanic system of sinful pleasures, excessive luxurious lifestyles, and godless economic practices. Those who had been persecuted by the Antichrist's Babylon system will be avenged.

The Cause of the Destruction of Babylon

> 21   And a mighty angel took up a stone like a great millstone, and cast it into the sea, saying, Thus with violence shall that great city Babylon be thrown down, and shall be found no more at all.

22   And the voice of harpers, and musicians, and of pipers, and trumpeters, shall be heard no more at all in thee; and no craftsman, of whatsoever craft he be, shall be found any more in thee; and the sound of a millstone shall be heard no more at all in thee;

23   And the light of a candle shall shine no more at all in thee; and the voice of the bridegroom and of the bride shall be heard no more at all in thee: for thy merchants were the great men of the earth; for by thy sorceries were all nations deceived.

24   And in her was found the blood of prophets, and of saints, and of all that were slain upon the earth.

The destruction of Babylon is seen as being very violent. An illustration is given in verse 21 of an angel taking a stone, "like a great millstone," and casting it into the sea. A millstone represents action associated with sudden and total destruction (Jeremiah 51:63-64; Matthew 18:6; Luke 17:2). In the same manner, the economic/political/religious systems of Antichrist's Babylon system will be "thrown down" and will be "found no more." As previously mentioned, the final destruction of this Babylon system of the Antichrist is described in Revelation 19:17-21.

Verses 22-24 state that the city and territories of Antichrist's Babylon system will no longer contain activities of commerce and normal everyday human life. The activities of musicians and craftsmen will cease.

The first Babylon mentioned in Revelation 17 represents a satanic system of false religions that has influenced many great nations and empires throughout history. The second Babylon mentioned in Revelation 18 represents an economic/political/religious system that Antichrist will control during the second half of the seven-year tribulation. Both Babylon systems are associated with a reign of terror, and with the shedding of blood of Christian martyrs. These systems will be destroyed, never to be rebuilt.

JESUS CHRIST: Conquerer! Revelation 19:11-16

Twenty-Four

Revelation – Chapter 19

Brief Summary

Chapter 19 continues the heavenly story. After chapter 5, we discussed several chapters telling the earthly story, intermingled with informational chapters. Chapter 19 resumes the heavenly story, taking us back to the middle of the tribulation. We know this because chapter 19 begins soon after the Antichrist destroys the great whore, which is a religious system. This religious system is also the first Babylon mentioned in the Book of Revelation. The destruction of this system takes place in the middle of the seven-year tribulation, when Antichrist greatly increases his political power and influence.

The first 10 verses of chapter 19 explain what will be going on in heaven before Christ returns to the earth with his faithful believers. This includes rejoicing over the destruction of the first Babylon system of false religions. It also includes a description of the marriage supper of the Lamb, which takes place during the second half of the tribulation. Jesus is portrayed as the groom and the church as His bride.

In verse 11 there is a transition from the heavenly story back to the earthly story. At the end of the seven-year tribulation, Christ will gloriously and visibly return to the earth to defeat His enemies at the Battle of Armageddon. His faithful followers in heaven will also return with Him.

Antichrist and his false prophet will be totally defeated and judged.

The Marriage Supper of the Lamb

1   And after these things I heard a great voice of much people in heaven, saying, Alleluia; Salvation, and glory, and honour, and power, unto the Lord our God:

2   For true and righteous are his judgments: for he hath judged the great whore, which did corrupt the earth with her fornication, and hath avenged the blood of his servants at her hand.

3   And again they said, Alleluia. And her smoke rose up for ever and ever.

4   And the four and twenty elders and the four beasts fell down and worshipped God that sat on the throne, saying, Amen; Alleluia.

5   And a voice came out of the throne, saying, Praise our God, all ye his servants, and ye that fear him, both small and great.

6   And I heard as it were the voice of a great multitude, and as the voice of many waters, and as the voice of mighty thunderings, saying, Alleluia: for the Lord God omnipotent reigneth.

7   Let us be glad and rejoice, and give honour to him: for the marriage of the Lamb is come, and his wife hath made herself ready.

8   And to her was granted that she should be arrayed in fine linen, clean and white: for the fine linen is the righteousness of saints.

9   And he saith unto me, Write, Blessed are they which are called unto the marriage supper of the Lamb. And he saith unto me, These are the true sayings of God.

10   And I fell at his feet to worship him. And he said unto me, See thou do it not: I am thy fellowservant, and of thy brethren that have the testimony of Jesus: worship God: for the testimony of Jesus is the spirit of prophecy.

This scene pictures God receiving lavish praise in heaven. The word "Alleluia" that is used in these scriptures is derived from two Hebrew words meaning "praise" and "Lord." It means, "Praise the Lord." Those that have been redeemed are singing a song that refers to their salvation.

Great multitudes of people in heaven are praising God for the destruction of the great whore, or prostitute. As previously mentioned, this was a great false religious system that was destroyed at the midpoint of the tribulation. The armies of the 10 national leaders who pledged their loyalty to the beast have destroyed the great whore. They were eager to destroy the influence she had over many peoples.

At the whore's destruction, there is much rejoicing in heaven because a large part of the satanic system has been destroyed. Often after a deception has run its course, Satan will discard people that he has manipulated. In this case, Satan will use Antichrist to discard these false religious leaders.

During the last three-and-one-half years of the tribulation, the Antichrist will promote his own religious system, which will be centered on himself.

As previously stated in our discussion of chapter 4, the 24 elders may represent God's people from both the Old and New Testaments. Twelve of the elders may represent believers from the Old Testament and 12 of the elders may represent believers from the New Testament. We know that the names of the 12 tribes of Israel and the 12 apostles are written on the holy city, the New Jerusalem (Revelation 21:10-14).

In verse 5, the voice from the throne is probably an angel instructing all the hosts of heaven to praise our God.

The voice of many waters in verse 6 identifies huge companies of humans and angels praising God. This lavish praise is not merely a response to the downfall of the "Babylon" system. This celebration is focused on the marriage of the Lamb.

Verses 6 through 9 are describing the marriage supper of the Lamb. This marriage supper begins at about the time the harlot's religious system is destroyed on earth. Therefore, we conclude that the wedding of the Lamb and the marriage feast begin at midtribulation in heaven.

We saw in chapter 14 that the 144,000, after finishing their ministry, appear in heaven at the middle of the tribulation. They are then permitted to join the great company of believers who are praising God in heaven. Whether raptured or martyred, the 144,000 arrive in heaven in time for the marriage of the Lamb and the great marriage supper that follows.

John is shown the marriage of the Lamb to His bride. Jesus is the Lamb (John 1:35-36) and the Bridegroom (Matthew 22:1-14; John 3:26-29). In scripture, the nation of Israel is portrayed as God's wife (Isaiah 54:5-6; 62:5; Jeremiah 3:14; 31:32; Ezekiel 16:7-8; Hosea 2:16, 19). However, the church is represented as the bride of Christ (Romans 7:4; 2 Corinthians 11:2; Ephesians 5:23-32).

The Lamb's wife has made herself ready. Ephesians 5:27 states that the church, as the bride, will be glorious and presented to Christ without a spot or a wrinkle. This must occur after the Judgment Seat of Christ, which precedes the marriage supper of the Lamb.

All believers will stand before the judgment seat of Christ. This will occur after Christ comes for His church (Revelation 22:12). This is not a judgment of sin, for believers have had their sins judged and forgiven at the cross (Romans 8:1). It will not determine whether or not a believer will enter heaven. Instead, it will determine the degrees of rewards (2 Corinthians 5:10;

Romans 14:10; 1 Corinthians 3:11-15; Matthew 25:23; Luke 19:12-26). Believers on earth who survive the tribulation will be judged at Christ's glorious appearing. This will occur at the end of the tribulation when He brings rewards for His followers (Revelation 22:12). God judging His own people is also referred to in Psalm 50:3-6. The judgment seat of Christ is for believers. This is a separate event from the judgment of unbelievers, which takes place after the Millennium (Revelation 20:11-15).

Notice that the bride's clothing is extremely different from the clothing of the great prostitute, which is described in Revelation 17:4. Christ's bride is arrayed in fine white linen, representing the righteousness imparted to them by Christ (2 Corinthians 5:21; Romans 5:17; 10:4; 1 Corinthians 1:30).

We cannot earn our salvation through good works. Salvation is only available as a free gift through faith in God's grace (Ephesians 2:8-9). Good works do not produce salvation; good works should be the result of salvation. Although salvation assures us entry into heaven, salvation does not automatically produce heavenly rewards. This is why Jesus exhorted His followers to store up treasures in heaven (Matthew 6:20).

Verse 9 mentions "the marriage supper of the Lamb." This blessed event will be a literal supper, not just an analogy. The Greek word for "marriage" means "marriage feast." This banquet will be a celebration of the marriage between Christ and His bride.

Neither the bride nor the groom are invited guests. Instead, the friends of the bride and groom are invited as guests. Since the believers of the Church Age will be present as the bride, it will probably be all the Old Testament believers who are the invited guests. Since this event is called the marriage supper of the Lamb, referring to Christ's sacrifice for our salvation, the angels will not participate as guests at this feast.

John is so overwhelmed by this scene that in verse 10 he starts to worship the angel; however, the angel forbids him to do so. We should never idolize those messengers that God sends to His churches. The angel stated that he is also a fellow servant of God. This implies that throughout eternity, human believers will be equal with angels as fellow servants.

Verse 10 also states that "the testimony of Jesus is the spirit of prophecy." Every born-again believer has the testimony of Jesus. Whenever a Christian witnesses to others about Christ, he or she is entering into the spirit of prophecy. When we tell others about our great Lord, we are being consistent with scripture in proclaiming Christ as savior, king, and triumphant Lord. Since the New Testament times began, all true prophecy from God glorifies the Lord Jesus Christ, pointing people to Him. If a prophecy, spiritual manifestation, or religious teaching does not glorify the Jesus Christ of the Bible, it is not from the true God.

The Second Coming of Christ

11   And I saw heaven opened, and behold a white horse; and he that sat upon him was called Faithful and True, and in righteousness he doth judge and make war.

12   His eyes were as a flame of fire, and on his head were many crowns; and he had a name written, that no man knew, but he himself.

13   And he was clothed with a vesture dipped in blood: and his name is called The Word of God.

14   And the armies which were in heaven followed him upon white horses, clothed in fine linen, white and clean.

In verse 11, a transition is made from the heavenly story to the earthly story. It picks up the earthly story on the last day of the seven-year tribulation period. The rider on the white horse is a description of Jesus returning to earth. This event is also described in Zechariah, chapter 14. In this scene, Jesus no longer appears as a lamb, but as a warrior on a horse, symbolizing victory.

Jesus stated in Matthew 24:22 that unless The Great Tribulation was shortened, all mankind would perish. Christ's Second Coming immediately ends the seven-year tribulation.

The white horse rider in Revelation, chapter 6 represented the Antichrist; however, in chapter 19 we have no problem identifying this rider as Christ. Jesus is returning to earth to wage war in holiness and justice. We know that God is love (1 John 4:8), but he also judges. We need to help others meet God in His love. Anyone who puts this off will someday have to meet God in His wrath.

Jesus is called "Faithful and True." In righteousness, He judges and wages war. This is a sharp contrast to the blasphemous and deceitful system of the Antichrist that is described in Revelation, chapters 13 and 18.

Jesus will return to earth in flaming fire with His mighty angels (2 Thessalonians 1:7-8). He will also be accompanied by the redeemed (Zechariah 14:5; 1 Thessalonians 3:13; Jude 14-15). At the Second Coming, Christ will be visible (Matthew 24:27-30; Acts 1:9-11; Revelation 1:7). He will come in power and glory to judge His enemies (Psalm 96:13; Joel 3:11-12; Matthew 16:27; 24:29-31; Mark 13:24-26; Luke 21:27; Acts 17:31; Revelation 19:11-21).

Christ's visible Second Coming, at the end of the tribulation, will be accompanied by the sun and moon turning dark, and many meteorites falling (Matthew 24:29-30). Christ will instruct His angels to gather all the redeemed "from the four winds, from one end of heaven to the other" (Matthew 24:31).

Verse 12 describes Christ as having "many crowns," indicating He has unlimited authority. The Greek word used here for Christ's crowns is diademata, which refers to kingly crowns. This is in contrast to the Greek word stephanous, which denotes the "victors" crowns of the elders in Revelation 4:4. Christ's crowns are superior to any other crowns because He is the King of kings. He will establish His visible kingdom, taking control over all the earth (Zechariah 14:9).

Verse 12 also states that Christ will have "a name written, that no man knew." Names of people in the Bible often revealed something about the nature of persons. Some of the attributes of Christ are beyond our human ability to comprehend. Jesus has many names in scripture, but no one name that is known to us is adequate to describe Him.

Verse 13 states that Christ's robe will be dipped in blood. This is the blood He shed on the cross, not the blood of his enemies, because the battle has not yet begun. His robe will be dipped in blood to remind the world that redemption was available through His blood that was shed as a sacrifice for sins. Only Christ's blood can remove the guilt and stain of sin. Verse 13 also refers to one of Christ's titles, which is the "Word of God" (John 1:1). Christ reveals God to us.

Verse 14 refers to the fact that the human believers who were with Christ in heaven will return with Him to earth (Zechariah 14:5; 1 Thessalonians 3:13; Jude 14-15). Angels will also accompany Christ when He visibly returns to the earth (2 Thessalonians 1:7). The redeemed, along with the angels, will be riding white horses (Revelation 19:14). Two other scriptures indicate there are horses in heaven (2 Kings 2:11; 6:15-17).

Verses 8 and 14 both describe the glorified human believers clothed in white. This is a description of purity imparted to them by God.

As Christ descends, He will appear over Edom (Isaiah 63:1-6). The areas of ancient Edom, Moab, and Ammon will not be controlled by the Antichrist (Daniel 11:41). These three ancient countries are part of modern day Jordan. Edom is where many of the Jews will have fled to escape the Antichrist (Isaiah 16:1-5; Revelation 12:6,14). Jesus will appear over Edom, where many of the Jews are being protected. Christ will continue to descend until His feet touch the Mount of Olives, on the east side of Jerusalem (Zechariah 14:3-5). When His feet touch it, this mount will split in two. Most of Isaiah 63:1-6 is another description of the Battle of Armageddon.

Defeat of the Beast and the False Prophet at the Battle of Armageddon

The final verses of Revelation 19 deal with the Battle of Armageddon, which occurs at Christ's Second Coming. The word "Armageddon" only appears once in scripture (Revelation 16:16). It means "the mountain of Megiddo." This place is located in north central Palestine on the south side of the Valley of Megiddo (2 Chronicles 35:22; Zechariah 12:11). This place is also called the "Valley of Jehoshaphat" (Joel 3:1-2,12).

The purpose of the Battle of Armageddon will be to deliver Israel from total destruction by the Antichrist and the nations that are in league with him (Zechariah, chapter 14). Immediately afterwards, the nations that persecuted Israel will be judged and punished (Matthew 25:31-46). Christ will also set up His visible kingdom on the earth (Daniel 7:11-14; Revelation 20:4).

As previously discussed in our commentary about Revelation, chapter 7, many confuse the Battle of Armageddon with an earlier battle. Ezekiel 38 and 39 actually refer to a battle that occurs early in the tribulation, or perhaps just before the tribulation. The Battle of Armageddon is a second battle that occurs on the last day of the tribulation. Many confuse these two battles, referring to both of them as one battle: Armageddon.

During the second half of the tribulation, the Antichrist will persecute the Jews living in Israel. God will protect many of these Jews by diverting the Antichrist's attention. Antichrist will become distracted because of threats from the north and east (Daniel 11:44-45). The nations to the north and east will move against the Antichrist to bring an end to his conquests. This will keep him occupied during most of the last half of the tribulation and divert his attention from Israel. During this time, the Antichrist will lose much of the control he previously had over the nation of Israel.

Antichrist will eventually defeat the nations that oppose him. His territory will be expanded through conquest, causing other nations to cooperate with him. The nations under the influence of Antichrist will then be inspired by Satan to move their military forces against Israel, particularly against the remaining Jews that did not flee into the wilderness. Conquered Russia will be among these countries that comply with Antichrist's orders to move toward the Middle East. Antichrist will organize this invasion of Israel to annihilate the Jews in Palestine. The nations of the world will send armies that will gather in the Valley of Jehoshaphat (Joel 3:1-2, 9-17). As previously mentioned, this place is also referred to as the Valley of Armageddon (Revelation 16:16). In this last invasion, half of the city of Jerusalem will be destroyed (Zechariah 14:1-2). This invasion will immediately precede Christ's Second Coming.

The Jews will cry for their Messiah to come. Many Jews will turn to Christ (Romans 11:25-26). Were it not for the direct intervention of God, the Antichrist's armies would completely annihilate the Jews of the nation of Israel. The Jews will cry as they never have before for their Messiah to come.

> 15   And out of his mouth goeth a sharp sword, that with it he should smite the nations: and he shall rule them with a rod of iron: and he treadeth the winepress of the fierceness and wrath of Almighty God.
>
> 16   And he hath on his vesture and on his thigh a name written, KING OF KINGS, AND LORD OF LORDS.

Christ will intervene from heaven at the Battle of Armageddon (Zechariah 14: 3-5; Revelation 16:16-21; 19:11-21). The Jews living in Palestine will be delivered at the end of the tribulation. The nation of Israel will be converted to Jesus when He returns to defeat Antichrist (Romans 11:26-27; Revelation 19:11-20:6). The Battle of Armageddon will only last one day (Zechariah 14:1-7).

The sword that will come out of Christ's mouth is the Word of God (Ephesians 6:17; Hebrews 4:12). Although Christ will be accompanied by his followers in heaven, He will certainly not need help from this heavenly army. Christ alone will seize this victory, simply by speaking it into existence. This is the final stage of the seven bowl judgments that began in Revelation, chapter 16. The "rod of iron" represents the firmness by which Christ shall rule the nations.

The "winepress" mentioned in verse 15 is the same winepress of God's wrath that is mentioned in Revelation 14:19-20. The phrase, "he treadeth the winepress," symbolizes God's great judgment. This refers to the Battle of Armageddon. Christ will fight the nations that have sent armies against Jerusalem (Joel 3:9-16; Zephaniah 3:8; Zechariah 12:1-9; 14:2-4). Revelation 19:15 states that Christ will slay them with a sharp sword that comes out of His mouth. He will simply speak into existence the plague of Zechariah 14:12 on all the people that have come to fight against the nation of Israel. The vast demon driven armies will be destroyed at this battle. This will occur in the valley of Megiddo on the plains of Jezreel. Armageddon may actually refer to a larger war that ends with this battle in Palestine.

In Revelation, chapter 14, an angel predicted this battle. The angel stated that the blood would rise to the horses' bridles (Revelation 14:17-20). Another preview of this Battle of Armageddon was given in Revelation 16:16-21. It tells us that great hail stones will fall, averaging a talent in weight. As previously mentioned, a talent in weight can range from 75 to 100 pounds. When these heavy pieces of ice fall and melt, much water will appear. This water will mix with the blood of those killed, producing a bloody liquid.

Jesus is called "King of kings and Lord of lords." He is also called this in Revelation 17:14. Christ earned this title by the victory He purchased at the cross (Philippians 2:5-11). At His Second Coming, the wicked will mourn (Matthew 24:30).

> 17   And I saw an angel standing in the sun; and he cried with a loud voice, saying to all the fowls that fly in the midst of heaven, Come and gather yourselves together unto the supper of the great God;
>
> 18   That ye may eat the flesh of kings, and the flesh of captains, and the flesh of mighty men, and the flesh of horses, and of them that sit on them, and the flesh of all men, both free and bond, both small and great.
>
> 19   And I saw the beast, and the kings of the earth, and their armies, gathered together to make war against him that sat on the horse, and against his army.
>
> 20   And the beast was taken, and with him the false prophet that wrought miracles before him, with which he deceived them that had received the mark of the beast, and them that worshipped his image. These both were cast alive into a lake of fire burning with brimstone.
>
> 21   And the remnant were slain with the sword of him that sat upon the horse, which sword proceeded out of his mouth: and all the fowls were filled with their flesh.

In verses 17 and 18, an angel announces victory before the battle begins. Similar to the battle that occurred toward the beginning of the tribulation, the fowls are instructed to clean up the battlefield of Armageddon. Revelation 19:17 describes this as "the supper of the great God." This is a very harsh contrast to the description of the marriage supper of the Lamb in Revelation 19:1-9. Whereas the marriage supper of the Lamb is a joyous occasion, this battle will be extremely horrible.

The "beast" in verses 19 and 20 refers to the man who is the Antichrist (Revelation 13:1-8). As previously stated, many nations will be demonically influenced to send armies to the area of Armageddon. God will allow these armies to be gathered in order to defeat them. This war will end very quickly.

The Antichrist will receive swift judgment when Christ returns to the earth. As a matter of fact, Antichrist will be instantly destroyed "with the brightness of His coming" (2 Thessalonians 2:8). The Antichrist and the false prophet will be the first to be judged (Revelation 19:20). If the beast and the false prophet are killed in the Battle of Armageddon, their bodies may be resurrected before they are expelled from the earth. They will be "cast alive" into the Lake of Fire (Revelation 19:20; Daniel 7:11).

The remnant in verse 21 refers to the remainder of the armies assembled under the leadership of the Antichrist. They will be slain simply by Jesus speaking it. When Christ merely speaks, the battle is over. None of the soldiers who opposed Christ in this battle will survive.

Next, Jesus will judge the nations of the earth (Isaiah 11:1-4; Joel 3:12; Zechariah 14:1-15; Matthew 24:30; 25:31-46; 2 Thessalonians 1:7-9; Jude 14-15; Revelation 1:7; 19:11-21). God will destroy all the wicked throughout the earth (Jeremiah 25:29-33).

This will not be the final judgment of the dead. This judgment that occurs at the end of the tribulation will pertain to those persons still living on the earth. Judgment will be given based on how the surviving peoples of the world treated a group Jesus refers to as "my brethren" (Matthew 25:40, 45). In other words, this judgment will focus on the treatment that the peoples of the world gave to Christ's brethren, the Jews. Some believe that the Jewish brethren referred to in Matthew, chapter 25 specifically refer to the 144,000 Jews who will be witnesses for Christ during the tribulation (Revelation 7:1-8). During the tribulation, salvation available through Christ will be preached throughout the world to all nations (Matthew 24:14; Mark 13:10). The nations will be judged based on their acceptance or rejection of the gospel that was preached by the 144,000 Jewish evangelists. Acceptance or rejection of faith in Christ will be displayed by whether or not people gave these Jewish witnesses food, clothing, love, and visitation while they were persecuted and in prison (Matthew 25:31-46).

Jesus will enter Jerusalem. He will be recognized as the King of kings and Lord of lords. His kingdom will then be visibly established on the earth (Daniel 7:13-14; Luke 1:32). Jesus will rule the earth with a rod of iron (Revelation 2:27; 12:5; 19:15). This phase of His reign will last 1,000 years (Revelation 20:4-6). During Christ's millennial reign, the remainder of God's promised blessings to Israel will be literally fulfilled. The whole earth will be fertile and prosperous.

The millennial reign of Christ starts out with only saved believers on the earth. All the unsaved will be removed from the earth at the end of the seven-year tribulation (Matthew 25:31-46). No unsaved person will be on the earth at the start of Christ's thousand-year reign. However, many will be born during the Millennium (Isaiah 65:20, 23) to those believers who survive the tribulation and will still be in their physical bodies. Unfortunately, many who are born during the Millennium will not accept Christ and will rebel against God at the end of this thousand-year period (Revelation 20:7-10).

CHRIST LIVING IN MAN: The hope of glory, Colossians 1:27

Twenty-Five

Revelation – Chapter 20

Brief Summary

This chapter describes Satan's imprisonment in the bottomless pit for 1,000 years. During this Millennium, Christ will visibly reign on the earth, along with those who were previously saved and who have received their glorified bodies. These believers in Christ are called blessed because they are part of the "first resurrection."

During the millennial reign of Christ, the earth will be exceedingly fruitful, prosperous and peaceful. The Book of Revelation does not include a detailed description of these thousand years. But various descriptions are given of this era by several Old Testament prophets.

At the end of the thousand years, Satan will be released for a short time. He will be allowed to deceive those who were born during the Millennium, but never accepted Christ. They will rebel against God and foolishly surround His capital city of Jerusalem. God will devour them with fire. Then, Satan will be cast into the Lake of Fire forever.

Immediately following the Millennium, the Great White Throne Judgment will take place. Believers have no part in this particular judgment. It will be for all the unsaved who have ever lived. At this event, all the unsaved on earth and in Hades will be transferred to hell, which is the Lake of Fire. This is the "second death."

Satan Bound for One Thousand Years

1   And I saw an angel come down from heaven, having the key of the bottomless pit and a great chain in his hand.

2   And he laid hold on the dragon, that old serpent, which is the Devil, and Satan, and bound him a thousand years,

3   And cast him into the bottomless pit, and shut him up, and set a seal upon him, that he should deceive the nations no more, till the thousand years should be fulfilled: and after that he must be loosed a little season.

After the Battle of Armageddon, one of God's holy angels will come down from heaven with a key to the bottomless pit. The angel will bind the devil with "a great chain" and cast him into the abyss (Revelation 20:1-3). This may be the same angel of God who used a key to unlock the bottomless pit, releasing an army of demons in Revelation 9:1-3.

Satan will be bound for a thousand years. Whether Satan's angels will also be cast into the bottomless pit at this time is not stated; however, they will not be active on the earth during the Millennium. It is reasonable to conclude that Satan's angels will also be banished to the abyss during this time. Since satanic forces will not be able to deceive people during the Millennium, the majority of people on the earth born during the Millennium will probably become believers in Christ.

After Christ's thousand-year reign on the earth, Satan will be released for a short time. He and his evil angels will attempt to deceive the nations one last time (Revelation 20:7-8). Afterwards, they will be cast into the Lake of Fire (Revelation 20:9-10). This will result in the final destruction of all evil (Revelation 20:12-15).

The First and Second Resurrection

4   And I saw thrones, and they sat upon them, and judgment was given unto them: and I saw the souls of them that were beheaded for the witness of Jesus, and for the word of God, and which had not worshipped the beast, neither his image, neither had received his mark upon their foreheads, or in their hands; and they lived and reigned with Christ a thousand years.

5   But the rest of the dead lived not again until the thousand years were finished. This is the first resurrection.

6   Blessed and holy is he that hath part in the first resurrection: on such the second death hath no power, but they shall be priests of God and of Christ, and shall reign with him a thousand years.

In Revelation 20:4, John saw people sitting on thrones. Some teach that the people sitting on these thrones will be the tribulation martyrs. However, these persons may be the 24 elders who were mentioned earlier, sitting on thrones (Revelation 4:4; 5:8; 11:16). Christ's immediate disciples will occupy 12 of these thrones (Matthew 19:28; Luke 22:30). God will delegate authority to those sitting on thrones to act as judges. They will be reigning with other redeemed people (Daniel 7:9,22,27; Revelation 2:26-27; 3:21; 5:9-10; 20:4,6).

The martyred believers of the tribulation will be given special recognition. These martyrs are mentioned in the fifth seal (Revelation 6:9-11). The term "beheaded" in Revelation 20:4 probably represents all Christian martyrs during the seven-year tribulation. These martyrs will be resurrected to reign with Christ during the Millennium.

Christ and His followers will visibly and literally reign together on the earth for a thousand years. We will soon discuss this in detail.

Verse 6 tells us that those who take part in the first resurrection are blessed. The first resurrection refers to the resurrection of God's people (Isaiah 26:19; Daniel 12:2,13; John 11:25-26; 14:19).

The wicked dead will not participate in the first resurrection. The second resurrection only involves the wicked dead, and will occur immediately after the Millennium (Revelation 20:5). The first resurrection of believers will probably have three phases.

(1)   The first phase of the first resurrection is commonly referred to as the rapture. The phrase "rapture of the church" refers to the catching up of all true believers in Christ to meet the Lord in the air (1 Thessalonians 4:14-18; 1 Corinthians 15:51-55). The Lord will descend from heaven to take out of the world, in an instant, all the dead and living in Christ. The physical bodies of the dead in Christ shall rise. The soul and spirit of every deceased Christian will be reunited with his or her resurrected glorified body. Those believers alive on the earth at the rapture will also have their physical bodies transformed. Since this event will involve "the dead in Christ" (1 Thessalonians 4:16), it probably will not include Old Testament believers.

(2)   The second phase of the first resurrection will probably occur on the last day of the tribulation (Revelation 20:4-6). This phase will involve the resurrection of the physical bodies of those believers who were saved after the rapture and martyred during the seven-year tribulation (Revelation 20:4). The physical bodies of the Old Testament believers will most likely be resurrected at this time to join their souls and spirits (Daniel 12:1-3).

(3)   The third phase of the first resurrection will include those believers who were saved after the rapture and survived the tribulation. These believers will remain in their physical bodies throughout the Millennium. This phase will also include persons born in physical bodies during the Millennium who accept Christ (Isaiah 65:20-23).

Those saved persons still in their physical bodies during the Millennium will be given glorified bodies after the Millennium. This is a promise to all the redeemed (Romans 8:23; 1 Corinthians 15:51-54).

As previously stated, the second resurrection refers to the resurrection of the wicked dead (Daniel 12:2; Revelation 20:11-15). This resurrection will occur at the Great White Throne Judgment, immediately after the Millennium (Revelation 20:5). This judgment only involves unbelievers. The unsaved will live throughout eternity, in total separation from God. This is referred to as the second death (Revelation 20:14; 21:8). Blessed are those who are able to participate in the first resurrection and not the second resurrection (Revelation 20:6).

The Millennial Reign of Christ on the Earth

A "thousand years" is mentioned six times in the first seven verses of Revelation, chapter 20. This thousand-year reign of Christ on the earth is often referred to as "the Millennium." More details about this period of time are actually given in the Old Testament. The Messiah's visible rule on the earth was prophesied (Psalm 2:6-9; Isaiah 9:6; 11:4; Jeremiah 3:17; Daniel 7:13-14; Micah 4:1-3; Zechariah 9:10; 14:4-9; Revelation 2:26-27).

The redeemed that died, or were raptured before the Millennium, will be in glorified bodies and return with Christ to reign with Him (Revelation 19:11-14). Initially, they will be ruling over saved persons that survived the tribulation and are still in their physical bodies. However, many more people will be born during the Millennium (Isaiah 65:20, 23).

Three Positions Regarding the Millennial Reign of Christ[51]

1. **Premillennialism.** The 1,000 years is a literal time period, during which Christ will visibly reign on the earth. Christ will visibly return before the Millennium. That is why this view is called premillennial.

There will be a seven-year tribulation period immediately before Christ's return.

During the Millennium, all of God's covenant promises to Israel will be literally fulfilled.

Satan will be bound during the Millennium. He will be released for a short time at the end of the thousand years before his final defeat and removal from the earth.

The eternal order will begin 1,000 years after Christ returns.

2. **Postmillennialism.** The 1,000 years is interpreted symbolically as the Church Age. The thousand years are not literal years. Christ will not visibly return to the earth until after the Millennium. That is why this view is called postmillennial.

The church will usher in this age through preaching, evangelism, and societal reforms. Satan's power is bound when the gospel is preached.

After the whole world becomes Christianized, Christ will return.

The covenant promises to Israel are seen as being fulfilled in the church.

The eternal order will begin when Christ returns, immediately after a symbolic millennial Church Age.

3. **Amillennialism.** This view holds that there will be no literal millennial kingdom on the earth. Christ rules over a spiritual kingdom in the hearts of believers. Millennial prophecies will be fulfilled in eternity.

The covenant promises to Israel are seen as being fulfilled in the church.

According to this view, Satan was bound and limited by the power of the gospel, soon after the first coming of Christ.

The eternal order will begin when Christ returns, immediately after the Church Age.

Postmillennialism is ridiculous, because it holds that human efforts can usher in a utopia on earth that will cause Christ to return. There is also no justification for the amillennial position, which contends that the 1,000 years are symbolic, not literal. Nothing in the context of Revelation, chapter 20, indicates that this 1,000-year period should not be taken literally. In addition, the idea that Satan is not active on the earth during the Church Age is unbiblical (1 Peter 5:8; Ephesians 6:11).

The premillennial view is the correct position. After Christ visibly returns, He will usher in the Millennium. Christ and His followers who have received their glorified bodies will rule and reign with Him in this earthly kingdom for a literal time period of 1,000 years. As previously noted,

Satan will be bound during the Millennium (Revelation 20:2-3). There will be no political parties, labor unions, police or crime. The form of government will not be democratic but theocratic. God will reign through His son, Jesus Christ (Revelation 11:15; 20:6). This will be an age in which God's righteousness will be displayed (Isaiah 11:5; 32:1; Jeremiah 23:6; Daniel 9:24).

People will be born during the Millennium (Isaiah 65:20). Most will probably accept salvation through Christ. Unfortunately, some persons born during the Millennium will reject Christ and become rebellious toward God. This rebellion will be suppressed until the devil is released at the end of the thousand years (Revelation 19:15; 20:7-9). Death will be much more infrequent than it is today, but it will still occur during the Millennium (Isaiah 65:20). Capital punishment may exist during this time (Isaiah 11:3-4).

Concerning the Millennium, Dwight J. Pentecost has written the following:

> ". . . this age will see the complete fulfillment of all the covenants that God made with Israel. . . . The promises in the Abrahamic covenant concerning the land and the seed are fulfilled in the millennial age (Isa. 10:21-22; 19:25; 43:1; 65:8-9; Jer. 30:22; 32:38; Ezek. 34:24, 30-31; Mic. 7:19-20; Zech.13:9; Mal. 3:16-18). Israel's perpetuity, their possession of the land, and their inheritance of blessings are directly related to the fulfillment of this covenant. . . . The promises in the Davidic covenant concerning the king, the throne, and the royal house are fulfilled by Messiah in the millennial age (Isa. 11:1-2; 55:3, 11; Jer. 23:5-8; 33:20-26; Ezek. 34:23-25; 37:23-24; Hos. 3:5; Mic. 4:7-8). The fact that Israel has a kingdom, over which David's Son reigns as King, is based on the Davidic covenant. . . . The promises in the Palestinic covenant concerning the possession of the land are fulfilled by Israel in the millennial age (Isa.11:11-12; 65:9; Ezek. 16:60-63; 36:28-29; 39:28; Hos. 1:10-2:1; Mic. 2:12; Zech. 10:6). . . . The promises of the new covenant of a new heart, the forgiveness of sin, the filling of the Spirit are fulfilled in the converted nation in the millennial age (Jer. 31:31-34; 32:35-39; Ezek. 11:18-20; 16:60-63; 37:26; Rom. 11:26-29). All the spiritual blessings Israel receives are fulfillment of this covenant."[52]

There are many scriptures in the Old Testament that give us a glimpse of the visible worldwide reign of Messiah during the Millennium. Here are a few examples:

Worldwide peace will exist under the reign of the Prince of Peace. There will be no need of armies or navies. Implements of destruction will be made into tools of agriculture (Isaiah 2:2-4; 9:6-7; 54:13; Hosea 2:18; Micah 4:3-4; Zechariah 9:10).

The whole earth will become exceedingly fertile, fruitful, and prosperous (Isaiah 35:1-2, 6-7; 51:3; 65:21-23; Ezekiel 34:26-27; 36:30, 35; Zechariah 8:12; Romans 8:19-23). God will provide for the needs of His followers, even before they ask Him (Isaiah 65:24).

The span of life will be greatly lengthened. As previously mentioned, death will be rare during the Millennium, but it will still occur (Isaiah 65:20). Since Satan, who previously had the power of death, will be bound during the Millennium (Revelation 20:1-2), death will be very infrequent. There will be no temptations and no sickness (Isaiah 29:17-19; 33:24; 35:5-6). However, death will not be totally done away with until the final judgment after the Millennium (Revelation 20:14).

The believers living in their glorified bodies during the Millennium will be immortal; however, death will still be a possibility for people who are living in their physical bodies. Most of these natural people will live until the end of the thousand years. Those in their physical bodies that do not rebel with Satan at the end of the Millennium will also receive glorified bodies and live with God forever. The promise of glorified bodies is for all the redeemed (Romans 8:23; 1 Corinthians 15:51-54).

Wild animals will be domesticated and will pose no threat to people or to each other (Isaiah 11:6-9; 65:25; Hosea 2:18).

All mankind will know the Lord, and the whole earth will be filled with the glory of the Lord, who will be king over all the earth. The knowledge of the Lord has greatly increased during the Church Age. However, this prophesied expansion of true spiritual knowledge will reach complete fulfillment during Christ's millennial reign (Isaiah 2:2-3; 11:9; 54:13; Micah 4:1-2; Zechariah 14:9,17; Malachi 1:11).

Israel will worship Christ, and Jerusalem will be the center of our Lord's administration (Isaiah 2:2-4; 24:23; Jeremiah 3:17; Micah 4:2,8; Zephaniah 3:9-20; Zechariah 8:22-23; 14:16-17). The Lord's administration will be holy (Zechariah 14:20-21). Jerusalem will be a place of joy, with no more sadness (Isaiah 65:18-19).

Those who are saved and in their glorified bodies will be ruling the earth with Christ (Daniel 7:18, 27; Revelation 2:26-27; 5:10; 20:6). We are going to be administrators of God's kingdom. The martyred saints of the seven-year tribulation period are particularly mentioned with honor (Revelation 20:4).

There will be a millennial temple with water flowing out of it. Christ Himself will build this temple when He returns to earth to set up His kingdom (Zechariah 6:12-13). Christ's earthly throne will be located in this temple (Ezekiel 43:5-7). There will be priests in this temple as there were in the temple of the Old Testament. The priesthood will be for offerings, not for salvation. These offerings will act as memorials and object lessons to show people throughout the earth what has been accomplished through Christ. In chapters 43-46 of Ezekiel, most of the feasts that were observed by the Jews are mentioned. These offerings and feasts will be observed during the Millennium. Ezekiel described a vision the Lord gave him of water flowing from under the threshold of the millennial temple of God, which becomes a huge river (Ezekiel 47:1-10). God also showed Zechariah this river, which will constantly flow to the Mediterranean Sea and the Dead Sea (Zechariah 14:8). Although this will be a literal river, it also represents God's blessings flowing from Jerusalem during the Millennium. The Lord showed Ezekiel that there will be fruit bearing trees along the banks of this river (Ezekiel 47:12).

The light of the sun will be increased sevenfold during the Millennium, and the light of the moon will be as bright as the light of the sun is today (Isaiah 30:26).

There will be missionaries during the Millennium. The Jewish people will become great missionaries of the Gospel of Jesus Christ (Isaiah 66:18-21; Zechariah 8:22-23). The gospel message will be shared with the unsaved who will be born during the Millennium. Since Satanic forces will not be present and worldly influences will be suppressed, most will get saved – some will not.

Some believe that during the Millennium, the Lord will establish resurrected King David as a ruler over Israel. The scriptures used to support this view include Jeremiah 30:9; Ezekiel 34:23-24; 37:24-25; and Hosea 3:5. However, others believe these scriptures will be fulfilled by Christ Himself.

Finis Dake contends that the Old Testament law of Moses will be reinstituted during the Millennium and into eternity.[53] Scriptures used to support this view include Isaiah 2:2-4; Micah 5:2; and Ezekiel 40:1-48:35. According to this view, the prophets who wrote these passages only knew about the law of Moses. When they prophesied about the law in the eternal kingdom, they could have only had the law of Moses in mind. When God gave the law to Moses, God emphasized that this law was eternal and was to be observed forever.

On the other hand, Dwight J. Pentecost convincingly argues that the sacrificial system during the Millennium will have major differences from the law of Moses and will not be a return to the Mosaic law.[54] For example, the dimensions and furnishings of the millennial temple given by Ezekiel will be different from any of the previous Jewish temples or tabernacles. The millennial temple will contain no Ark of the Covenant, no Mercy-seat, no Golden Candlesticks, no Shewbread, no veil, and no unapproachable Holy of Holies. The sacrifices during the Millennium will not be for the forgiveness of sins, but will serve as memorials and object lessons of the death of Christ on the cross. Whereas sacrifices under the Old Covenant looked forward to a perfect and final sacrifice for sins, sacrifices during the Millennium will serve as reminders of Christ's sacrifice on the cross. These sacrifices will serve a purpose similar to that of communion during the Church Age.

Since death will be done away with after the Millennium (Revelation 20:14), any acting out of sacrifices in eternity will not include the death of animals. Although there will be a temple of God in Jerusalem during the Millennium (Ezekiel 40:1-46:24), there will be no temple after the Millennium in the new earth (Revelation 21:22). This indicates that there will not be a sacrificial system after the Millennium.

Most premillennialists seem to believe that during the Millennium, the resurrected and raptured believers will freely interact with those still in their mortal bodies. This will be similar to the Lord Jesus Christ, after His resurrection, interacting with His disciples in His resurrected body.

Others believe that during the Millennium, the resurrected believers will rule and reign with Christ from the city of New Jerusalem. Although they will return with Christ at His Second Coming, the resurrected believers will primarily remain in the city of New Jerusalem during the Millennium. According to this view, the city of New Jerusalem will be suspended above the earth, and will not descend to the earth until after the millennium (Revelation 21:2). This view holds that only people in their natural bodies will be living on earth during the Millennium.[55] All of this is debatable.

After the thousand-year Millennium, Jesus will hand over His kingdom to the Heavenly Father (1 Corinthians 15:24-26). Then, God's final and everlasting kingdom will begin (Revelation 21:1-22:5).

Satan is Released for a Short Time

7   And when the thousand years are expired, Satan shall be loosed out of his prison,

8   And shall go out to deceive the nations which are in the four quarters of the earth, Gog and Magog, to gather them together to battle: the number of whom

is as the sand of the sea.

    9   And they went up on the breadth of the earth, and compassed the camp of the saints about, and the beloved city: and fire came down from God out of heaven, and devoured them.

    10   And the devil that deceived them was cast into the lake of fire and brimstone, where the beast and the false prophet are, and shall be tormented day and night for ever and ever.

After 1,000 years, Satan will be loosed for a short time and will attempt to deceive the nations. He will be allowed to deceive many people who still have not accepted Christ by the end of the Millennium.

As previously mentioned, during the Millennium there will still be people in their natural physical bodies that will be reproducing. Many of those born during this thousand-year period will eventually decide to rebel against Christ's lordship.

Nations will continue to exist after the seven-year tribulation (Revelation 20:8). During the Millennium, whole nations will probably turn to Christ. Other nations may largely reject Christ. Before the Millennium, the terms "Gog" and "Magog" refer to the leader of people living far to the north of Israel, primarily in Russia (Ezekiel 38 and 39). Toward the end of the Millennium, Gog and Magog probably will represent those people from all the nations who will rebel against God (Revelation 20:8). The phrase "four quarters of the earth" means that rebellious people will exist throughout the earth.

The expression "as the sand of the sea" does not mean that Satan will be able to deceive the majority of people. During the conditions of the Millennium there will be a huge population explosion. The human population will certainly exceed the entire population of human history prior to the Millennium. Most of the people living during the Millennium will be Christians. That means that ultimately there will be more people who are saved than will be in hell.

The "beloved city" is the city of Jerusalem, which will be the center of our Lord's administration. Many of these rebels will attempt to surround and capture Jerusalem. A full battle will not result because God will consume them with fire in an instant.

After this brief rebellion, Satan will then be cast into the Lake of Fire where he will be tormented forever (Revelation 20:10). The prophet Isaiah predicted this event. Chapter 14 of the Book of Isaiah has a double application, referring both to the judgment of an ancient king of

Babylon and to the final judgment of Satan. This passage in Isaiah tells us that when Lucifer receives his final judgment, he will no longer rule over anything (Isaiah 14:9-17).

The Great White Throne Judgment

11   And I saw a great white throne, and him that sat on it, from whose face the earth and the heaven fled away; and there was found no place for them.

12   And I saw the dead, small and great, stand before God; and the books were opened: and another book was opened, which is the book of life: and the dead were judged out of those things which were written in the books, according to their works.

13   And the sea gave up the dead which were in it; and death and hell delivered up the dead which were in them: and they were judged every man according to their works.

14   And death and hell were cast into the lake of fire. This is the second death.

15   And whosoever was not found written in the book of life was cast into the lake of fire.

As previously stated, the Great White Throne Judgment includes the wicked dead of all ages. All of the unsaved will be resurrected to appear at this judgment. This judgment will occur after the Millennium, and after Satan is cast into the Lake of Fire (Revelation 20:10). The Great White Throne Judgment may take place in heaven, since that is where God's throne is located. God's throne will later be relocated to the earth (Revelation 21:1-5). Christ will be the one sitting on the great white throne, judging the unsaved (John 5:22). This event does not include believers, because they were previously evaluated and given rewards at the judgment seat of Christ (2 Corinthians 5:10).

God's Book of Life contains the names of all believers who have put their trust in the true God to save them (Daniel 12:1; Luke 10:20; Philippians 4:3; Revelation 21:27). The names of those who have not accepted the true God are not written in the Book of Life (Revelation 13:8; 17:8; 20:15). This does not mean that God predestines some to be saved and some to be lost. It is God's will that all be saved (2 Peter 3:9). However, a person's name can be erased from the Book of Life (Exodus 32:32; Psalm 69:28). But, the names of those who overcome will not be blotted out (Revelation 3:5).

Verse 12 makes a distinction between "the books" and "the Book of Life." The Book of Life contains the names of all persons that are saved (Revelation 3:5; 13:6-8; 17:8; 21:27). On the other hand, Revelation 20:12 indicates that "the books" contain records of each unsaved person's works.

This implies that there will be various degrees of punishment for the unsaved according to their works (Luke 12:47-48).

Only unbelievers will be judged at the Great White Throne Judgment. The physical bodies of the unsaved dead will be resurrected at this time. Their souls and spirits, which were in Hades, will join their resurrected bodies. Since their names are not recorded in the Book of Life, they will be consigned to eternal punishment in the Lake of Fire, which is hell.

This judgment of the wicked dead is also called "the resurrection of damnation" (John 5:29) and the "second death" (Revelation 2:11; 20:6, 14; 21:8). The first death was spiritual death that came to the human race through Adam's disobedience (Genesis 2:17; Romans 5:12; 1 Corinthians 15:21-22). The second death will be eternal separation from God (Revelation 20:14-15). Jesus stated that there will be weeping and gnashing of teeth (Matthew 22:13; 25:30). The apostle Paul described the final condition of the unsaved as "everlasting destruction" (2 Thessalonians 1:8-9). These descriptions are not symbolic, but literal.

Hebrews 9:27 says, "And it is appointed unto man once to die, but after this the judgment." Concerning the inevitability of judgment from God, C.M. Ward has written the following:

> *"There must be a final audit. Everyone intuitively believes it. The price of privilege is responsibility."* [56]

God originally prepared hell for the future punishment of Satan and his fallen angels (Matthew 25:41). It was not intended for humans. Unfortunately, many people will join Satan and his fallen angels in hell (Matthew 13:41-42, 49-50; Revelation 20:15). Many would like to believe that hell is simply a place of execution, where people will be annihilated and cease to exist. Sadly, it is a place of everlasting punishment (Matthew 18:8; 25:41, 46; Mark 9:43-44, 46, 48). The Antichrist and his false prophet are examples of this. The Antichrist is a man (2 Thessalonians 2:3; Revelation 13:18). At the end of the tribulation, the Antichrist and false prophet will both be cast alive into the Lake of Fire (Revelation 19:20). One thousand years later, the devil will also be cast into the Lake of Fire, joining the beast and the false prophet (Revelation 20:10). Notice that after 1,000 years, both the beast and false prophet, who are human, will still not be burned up or annihilated. As humans in hell, the unsaved will continue to live in torment throughout eternity.

Revelation 20:11 states that the earth and heaven fled from the face of God. This may refer to the destruction of the heavens and earth as we know them (Isaiah 51:6; 2 Peter 3:7, 10-12; Revelation 21:1). In 2 Peter 3:7, it indicates that the earth will be cleansed with fire at this final judgment. Some believe this means that the current earth and sky will cease to exist. However, this language appears to be figurative because the earth will remain forever and will never be annihilated (Ecclesiastes 1:4; Psalm 104:5). The current material universe will be renovated to cleanse it from every stain of sin, but this current universe will continue to exist.

Many contend that 2 Peter 3:7-12 refers to events at the end of the tribulation, not events after the Millennium. The reason is that 2 Peter 3:4 asks the question, "Where is the promise of His coming?" This is not referring to the end of the Millennium, since Christ will have visibly returned a thousand years earlier. If 2 Peter 3:7-12 is associated with the Second Coming of Christ, then it may also refer to a renovation of the heavens and the earth at the beginning of the Millennium.

Revelation 20:14 tells us that death will also be cast into the Lake of Fire. The last enemy to be destroyed will be death (1 Corinthians 15:26). When Christ's millennial reign is completed and death is finally destroyed, Jesus will present the kingdom to God the Father (1 Corinthians 15:24-28).

At the Great White Throne Judgment, all unbelievers will be transferred from Hades to the Lake of Fire. The Lake of Fire is another name for hell. Revelation 20:14 states in the King James Version that "death and hell were cast into the Lake of Fire." Since the Lake of Fire and hell are the same place, the King James Version seems to indicate that hell will be cast into hell. This doesn't make sense.

In Revelation 20:14, the word translated "hell" is actually the word "Hades." Hell and Hades are two different places. Hades is a place where the wicked dead currently go at death. "Hades" is often mistranslated as "hell" in the King James Version (such as in Luke 16:23). The New King James Version renders a more accurate translation of Revelation 20:14: "Death and Hades were cast into the Lake of Fire." In other words, at the Great White Throne Judgment, the inhabitants of Hades will be cast into hell, which is also referred to as the Lake of Fire. This will include anyone whose name is not found in the Book of Life. This is the second death.

HOLY SPIRIT: Matthew 3:16-17

Twenty-Six

Revelation – Chapter 21

Brief Summary

The Apostle John saw a "new heaven" and a "new earth." God also reveals a "New Jerusalem." This city will descend from heaven to the earth, prepared as a bride beautifully dressed for her husband. Redeemed believers that make up this city are the bride of Christ. Believers will live in this city, in paradise, throughout eternity. There will be no night in the New Jerusalem. The light in the city will come from God Himself.

The city will have 12 gates with an angel at each gate. The names of the 12 tribes of Israel will be written on the 12 gates. These represent Old Testament believers.

There will be 12 foundations on the walls with the names of the 12 apostles of Christ. These represent New Testament believers.

God will dwell among believers on the new earth. There will be no pain or sorrow in this paradise. The redeemed will have wonderful access to God and enjoy perfect and glorious fellowship with Him.

The New Heaven, the New Earth, and the New Jerusalem

> 1   And I saw a new heaven and a new earth: for the first heaven and the first earth were passed away; and there was no more sea.

The apostle Peter tells us that the world as we know it shall be destroyed with fire and there will be "new heavens and a new earth" (2 Peter 3:7,10-13). Isaiah also prophesied about the new heavens and the new earth (Isaiah 65:17; 66:22), blending his predictions of the Millennium with the Age of Eternity. God will shake the material universe (Hebrews 12:26-28). The creation will then be liberated from the contamination of sin (Romans 8:20-21). This will happen during, or immediately after, the Great White Throne Judgment (Revelation 21:1-2). The new earth will be far superior to the old earth.

The heavens that will pass away are those surrounding the earth in the material universe, not the heaven where God lives. God's dwelling place does not need to be replaced. In fact, heaven, where God lives, is the place from which the New Jerusalem will be transferred to the earth (Revelation 3:12; 21:2,10).

In 2 Peter 3:10, the day of the Lord is mentioned in connection with the renovation of the heavens and earth. The day of the Lord refers to God's judgment against unbelievers (Isaiah 13:6, 9; Jeremiah 46:10; Joel 1:15; 2:1, 11, 31; Zephaniah 1:14; 1 Thessalonians 5:2-3; 2 Peter 3:10). It is also associated with a time of spiritual restoration (Joel 2:28-32; Acts 2:17-21). The day of the Lord refers to more than a single day. The day of the Lord most likely refers to a time of judgments toward the end of the seven-year tribulation, and concludes with the cleansing of the heavens and earth immediately after the Millennium.

Jesus said, "Heaven and earth shall pass away" (Matthew 5:18; 24:35). He was not talking about an annihilation of the earth. This refers to the earth's purification. The earth will remain forever and will never be annihilated (Ecclesiastes 1:4; Psalm 104:5). Instead, the material universe will be renovated to cleanse it from every stain of sin and to adapt it to new conditions. This renovation of the earth will end the day of the Lord (2 Peter 3:10) and begin the day of God (2 Peter 3:12-13).

Currently, the earth's surface is covered by two-thirds water; however, according to Revelation 21:1, the new earth will have much less water. The result will be that almost the entire earth's surface will be habitable.

2   And I John saw the holy city, New Jerusalem, coming down from God out of heaven, prepared as a bride adorned for her husband.

3   And I heard a great voice out of heaven saying, Behold, the tabernacle of God is with men, and he will dwell with them, and they shall be his people, and God himself shall be with them, and be their God.

4   And God shall wipe away all tears from their eyes; and there shall be no more death, neither sorrow, nor crying, neither shall there be any more pain: for the former things are passed away.

5   And he that sat upon the throne said, Behold, I make all things new. And he said unto me, Write: for these words are true and faithful.

This city, called the New Jerusalem, already exists in heaven (Galatians 4:26). After the Millennium and the Great White Throne Judgment, this city will descend from heaven to the earth, prepared as a bride beautifully dressed for her husband (Revelation 21:9-10). Since it takes people to make up a city, the bride of Christ refers to the company of redeemed believers that will dwell in the city. The bride is a city, which includes all the inhabitants of the city. She is called "the bride," and "the Lamb's wife" (Revelation 21:9).

Some teach that only believers from the Church Age will live in the New Jerusalem. This is not accurate. In Hebrews 11:8-10, we are told that Abraham "looked for a city . . . whose builder and maker is God." Other Old Testament believers also looked forward to living in this city (Hebrews 11:16). This is referring to the New Jerusalem, built by God Himself (Hebrews 12:22; Revelation 3:12; 21:2,10). Thus, Old Testament believers will also inhabit the city of New Jerusalem.

Some teach that the bride of Christ will only include those believers that excelled in their service to God, from both the Old and New Testament eras.

Perhaps the voice referred to in verse 3 is the voice of Christ. The voice declares that God will leave heaven to dwell forever with redeemed people in this holy city. God Himself will pack up, so to speak, and move to the earth. Our Lord will live, or tabernacle, with us on the new earth forever (Revelation 21:3; 22:3-5). This city on earth will be the headquarters of God's eternal kingdom. Verse 4 tells us that the effects of sin, such as sorrow, pain, unhappiness and death, will be gone forever. We will probably remember things worth remembering. However, believers will not remember things that would cause them sorrow or regret (Isaiah 25:8; 65:17). For example, after the Millennium, we may be unable to recall any of our loved ones who rejected Christ. In verse 5, God Himself declares that He will make all things new. The redeemed will experience an eternity that will be more exciting and wonderful than we can imagine.

> 6   And he said unto me, It is done. I am Alpha and Omega, the beginning and the end. I will give unto him that is athirst of the fountain of the water of life freely.
>
> 7   He that overcometh shall inherit all things; and I will be his God, and he shall be my son.
>
> 8   But the fearful, and unbelieving, and the abominable, and murderers, and whoremongers, and sorcerers, and idolaters, and all liars, shall have their part in the lake which burneth with fire and brimstone: which is the second death.

The one who states that "I am Alpha and Omega" is the same one who "sat upon the throne" in verse 5 – Almighty God. Christ also referred to Himself as the "Alpha and Omega" in Revelation 1:8-11 and 22:12-13. This title belongs to both the Heavenly Father and to Jesus. This is one example from scripture asserting that Jesus is Almighty God.

Here, the Lord is repeating His offer of everlasting life. The scriptures sometime use water as a symbol of the blessings of eternal life in Christ (John 4:7-14; 7:37-38). People are desperate to satisfy their spiritual thirst. Only God can satisfy this need through Jesus Christ.

Water is also one of the symbols of the refreshing work of the Holy Spirit (John 7:38-39). God will give "the water of life freely" to those who humbly ask.

Verse 8 reveals that none of the unsaved will be on the earth from this point on. There will be several classes of people that will not be allowed to enter God's eternal kingdom. The list of those who will not be allowed to enter includes the following:

(1) Fearful or cowardly – who fear the disapproval of people more than they value loyalty to God
(2) Unbelieving – who choose to be disbelieving and refuse to accept Christ
(3) Abominable – those who practice sin as a lifestyle and are disgusting in God's sight
(4) Murderers
(5) Whoremongers, that is, fornicators
(6) Sorcerers – the Greek word translated here as "sorcerers" is pharmakeus. This refers to the practice of magic arts and the use of drugs for spell-giving potions.
(7) Idolaters who worship, or are devoted to, things others than the true God
(8) Liars who practice deception

This does not mean that those who have committed these sins can never be saved. However, those who continue to practice these sins show that they are not saved. These will have their part in the Lake of Fire. The classes of unbelievers mentioned in verse 8 are similar to the list of persons described elsewhere that will not be allowed to enter God's kingdom (1 Corinthians 6:9-10; Galatians 5:19-21; Ephesians 5:5). They will experience eternal torment and separation from God. The visions given to John do not allow any room for doubt concerning the final judgment for those in rebellion against God (Revelation 20:14-15). There will be no second chance for those who have been cast into the Lake of Fire.

9   And there came unto me one of the seven angels which had the seven vials full of the seven last plagues, and talked with me, saying, Come hither, I will shew thee the bride, the Lamb's wife.

10   And he carried me away in the spirit to a great and high mountain, and shewed me that great city, the holy Jerusalem, descending out of heaven from God,

The angel again points out the bride of the Lamb to John. As in verse 2, the city of New Jerusalem is again referred to as Christ's bride. The bride is not just the buildings of a city. It takes people to inhabit a city. Therefore, the bride is made up of believers. Verses 11 through 27 provide more of a description of the physical city.

The "high mountain" referred to is probably the actual site of the New Jerusalem. This future city will include the area of the historical Jerusalem and Israel that is sometimes referred to as a mountain (Isaiah 2:2; Ezekiel 40:2). Jerusalem and Israel are also referred to as Mount Zion (Psalm 48:1-2; Micah 4:1-2). Although the temple mount is not huge, Mount Zion is very significant in terms of spiritual symbolism. It represents the temple area, God's kingdom and the New Jerusalem (Hebrews 12:22).

11   Having the glory of God: and her light was like unto a stone most precious, even like a jasper stone, clear as crystal;

12   And had a wall great and high, and had twelve gates, and at the gates twelve angels, and names written thereon, which are the names of the twelve tribes of the children of Israel:

13   On the east three gates; on the north three gates; on the south three gates; and on the west three gates.

14   And the wall of the city had twelve foundations, and in them the names of the twelve apostles of the Lamb.

The greatest characteristic of the city of New Jerusalem will be the presence and glory of God (verse 11). The glory of God will provide light throughout the city. This light is likened to a jasper stone. Jasper can be red due to the presence of iron, but it can also be brown, yellow or green.[57] However, here it is described as "clear as crystal." This may be a comparison to a diamond, representing purity and holiness.

The wall is symbolic of the security that believers will enjoy in this city. The city will have 12 gates with an angel at each gate. The names of the 12 tribes of Israel will be written on the 12 gates.

As mentioned at the beginning of this book, in scripture the number 12 and multiples of 12 often represent divine authority, administration, and governmental perfection. Some examples are found in Matthew 19:28; Numbers 1:5-16; and 1 Kings 4:7. Two examples earlier in the Book of Revelation are the 24 thrones with 24 elders (4:4), and the 144,000 witnesses (14:1). In the last two chapters of the Book of Revelation, the descriptions and measurements of the city of New Jerusalem include many multiples of 12:

- 12 gates (21:12,21)
- 12 angels (21:12)
- 12 tribes of Israel (21:12)
- 12 foundations (21:14)
- 12 apostles (21:14)
- 12,000 furlongs (21:16)
- 144 cubits (21:17)
- 12 pearls (21:21)
- 12 types of fruit (22:2)

The repetition of multiples of 12 emphasizes that the redeemed will spend eternity in a perfect home, under the perfect leadership and administration of God.

Verse 12 tells us that the gates will have the names of the 12 tribes of Israel. These were the primary means by which God revealed Himself in the Old Testament. Likewise, the 12 foundations on the walls will bear the names of the 12 apostles (verse 14). These were the primary means by which the preaching and teaching of the gospel of Christ was initially spread in the New Testament. Each time the believers enter the city, they will be reminded of the role that Israel and the apostles played in God's message of redemption.

The listing of the 12 tribes of Israel and the 12 apostles incorporate believers from all ages. Verses 12 through 14 emphasize the unity of God's people of the Old Testament and the New Testament. The believers are fellow citizens who have benefited spiritually from the prophets of the old covenant and the apostles of the new covenant (Ephesians 2:19-21). The names of the 12 tribes and 12 apostles on the gates and foundations show that believers from both the Old and New Testament eras will live in this city. The followers of God from all ages will be perfectly united.

15   And he that talked with me had a golden reed to measure the city, and the gates thereof, and the wall thereof.

16   And the city lieth foursquare, and the length is as large as the breadth: and he measured the city with the reed, twelve thousand furlongs. The length and the breadth and the height of it are equal.

17   And he measured the wall thereof, an hundred and forty and four cubits, according to the measure of a man, that is, of the angel.

The base of the city lies on the earth. Each of the four sides at the base will be an equal length of 12,000 furlongs. As previously stated, a furlong is about 200 meters, or one-eighth of a mile. Thus, this city will be about 1,500 miles long, 1,500 miles wide, and 1,500 miles high. A land area of 1,500 miles square in the United States would reach from the Rocky Mountains to the Appalachian Mountains, and from the Canadian border to the Gulf of Mexico. The size of this city indicates that it will have more than enough space for the believers of all ages.

The city of Los Angeles covers a land area of about 500 square miles. The New Jerusalem will cover a land area of about 2,250,000 square miles. This does not include the height of the city. As a cube, the New Jerusalem would contain about 3,375,000,000 cubic miles!

Some speculate the shape of this city will be a pyramid, like a mountain peak, 1,500 miles high. This passage also allows for this possibility. Whatever the shape, the city of New Jerusalem will be able to accommodate billions of people.

God will perfect the earth and atmosphere, replacing it with a whole new dimension. We will not be limited by the laws of physics of this current world. In our glorified bodies, we will have instant access to any place we choose. We also will not be limited to the borders of the New Jerusalem. This vast city will be a kind of headquarters that we will be able to enter and leave.

Verse 17 tells us that the wall encompassing this city will be 144 cubits wide. A standard cubit was about 18 inches.[58] That means that these walls will be about 216 feet thick.

18   And the building of the wall of it was of jasper: and the city was pure gold, like unto clear glass.

19   And the foundations of the wall of the city were garnished with all manner of precious stones. The first foundation was jasper; the second, sapphire; the third, a chalcedony; the fourth, an emerald;

20   The fifth, sardonyx; the sixth, sardius; the seventh, chrysolyte; the eighth, beryl; the ninth, a topaz; the tenth, a chrysoprasus; the eleventh, a jacinth; the twelfth, an amethyst.

21   And the twelve gates were twelve pearls; every several gate was of one pearl: and the street of the city was pure gold, as it were transparent glass.

This city will be incredibly beautiful. All the foundations will be garnished with various precious and beautiful stones of various colors. These precious materials magnify the glory and beauty of the city. These materials also represent purity and durability because this city will last forever.

Each separate gate will be made from a single pearl. The main street of the city will be pure gold, not just paved with gold. This gold will be transparent. Any of our words are inadequate to describe the good things God has prepared for us (1 Corinthians 2:9-10).

22   And I saw no temple therein: for the Lord God Almighty and the Lamb are the temple of it.

23   And the city had no need of the sun, neither of the moon, to shine in it: for the glory of God did lighten it, and the Lamb is the light thereof.

Verse 22 tells us that no temple will exist throughout eternity. A temple will no longer be needed. There will be no designated place of worship because God will no longer live in heaven. God will move His residence to the earth, and His presence will envelop the entire city. One could think of this city and the entire earth as one big place of worship. We will not need a house of worship because we will be worshipping God in His direct presence. God Himself will be the temple. His personal presence will be very strong throughout the city of New Jerusalem and the new earth.

There will be no night in this city (Revelation 21:25). The light in the city will come from God Himself and the Lamb. In 1 John 1:5, it states that "God is light, and in Him is no darkness." This glorious light of God will surpass the sun (Isaiah 60:19-20). This does not mean there will be no night in other areas of the earth. Day and night, as well as light from the sun and moon, will continue eternally (Genesis 8:22; Psalm 89:35-37; 148:3-6; Isaiah 66:22-23). In other parts of the earth there will still be a need for light from the sun and moon.

24   And the nations of them which are saved shall walk in the light of it: and the kings of the earth do bring their glory and honour into it.

25   And the gates of it shall not be shut at all by day: for there shall be no night there.

26   And they shall bring the glory and honour of the nations into it.

27   And there shall in no wise enter into it any thing that defileth, neither whatsoever worketh abomination, or maketh a lie: but they which are written in the Lamb's book of life.

Two Interpretations About "Nations" and "Kings" Throughout Eternity

1. **Many nations will exist on earth throughout eternity.** God will continue to separate people by nations. The redeemed will populate and develop the earth, using boundaries. Kings will also exist throughout eternity. These leaders will visit the city to give glory and honor to God.

2. **There will be no nations throughout eternity.** The Greek word used here for "nations" can also be translated "Gentiles." This probably refers to non-Jews who accepted Christ. The "kings" are probably former governmental leaders who received Christ. These persons will not be kings in eternity.

The pearly gates of the city will never be shut because there will be no night in the city. The redeemed will be allowed to enter and leave the city. Traffic to and from the city will be constant.

Some believe that the city of New Jerusalem will be in midair; however, references to its foundations tend to go against this theory. Also, the fact that people who dwell on the earth will be able to pass in and out of the city seems to imply that it will be located on the earth.

The New Jerusalem will be God's headquarters for the entire earth, and probably the universe.

Verse 27 is another warning to the unsaved. Those whose names are not written in the Lamb's Book of Life (Revelation 3:5; 20:12-15) will not be able to enter the city of New Jerusalem, or any other part of the new earth. The unsaved will be in the Lake of Fire (Revelation 20:15). The new earth and the New Jerusalem will be perfect and holy, made up of those who have been perfected in Christ Jesus.

As previously mentioned, good works alone are not enough to gain salvation and spend eternity with Christ. Salvation is a free gift of God that cannot be earned (Ephesians 2:8-9). Salvation requires faith in Christ and in His death on the cross. His sacrifice on the cross makes it possible for us to ask forgiveness for our sins (1 John 1:9). Only those who have experienced their sins forgiven through Christ Jesus will be admitted into God's eternal kingdom (John 3:16; Romans 10:9-10).

Twenty-Seven

Revelation – Chapter 22

Brief Summary

This chapter gives a final description of the new earth and ends with an assurance that Christ will return.

The redeemed will be able to eat from the tree of life, which is a symbol of eternal life in Christ. Believers will enjoy intimate fellowship with God on the new earth throughout eternity. The curse that God pronounced on the earth in Genesis, chapter 3, will cease to exist. Sin and death will be removed forever.

As in the first chapter, a blessing is given for those who take heed to obey the sayings of this book. A warning is also given for those who reject the messages of this book. In addition, a strong command is given that the Word of God is not to be tampered with. Anyone who adds or takes away from the words of this book will receive the judgments and plagues described in this book. This does not just apply to the Book of Revelation, although the emphasis is there. It also includes the rest of the written Word of God, since the Book of Revelation is tied into both the Old and New Testaments.

The Book of Revelation closes with an invitation to accept the flowing waters of salvation through Christ Jesus. This last chapter of the Bible warns all of us to be prepared for the promised return of Christ. Three times in this chapter, Jesus promises that He will return suddenly. He may return at anytime. The Apostle John closes with a prayer, asking that Christ will return quickly.

The River of Life and the Tree of Life

1   And he shewed me a pure river of water of life, clear as crystal, proceeding out of the throne of God and of the Lamb.

2   In the midst of the street of it, and on either side of the river, was there the tree of life, which bare twelve manner of fruits, and yielded her fruit every month: and the leaves of the tree were for the healing of the nations.

There will be an abundant supply of water in the city of New Jerusalem. A pure river of life will proceed from the throne of God (verse 1). As previously mentioned, the scriptures sometimes use water to represent abundant life and eternal blessings in Christ (John 4:7-14). Water also represents the Holy Spirit and the spiritual life that He imparts (Isaiah 32:15; 44:3; Joel 2:28-29; Zechariah 12:10; John 7:37-39; Revelation 22:17). The river coming from the throne represents continual grace, power, and glory flowing from God and the Lamb.

God's throne will probably be located at the top of the City of New Jerusalem, 1,500 miles above the land surface. If this is true, the river coming from God's throne will gradually flow 1,500 miles from the top to the bottom of the city.

God and the Lamb of God, who is Jesus, share an everlasting throne. The fact that Christ equally shares honor, glory, and power with the Heavenly Father is another indication of Christ's deity. Jesus is Almighty God.

The tree of life in the Book of Genesis refers to the wonderful spiritual life that will be given to believers throughout eternity. After Adam and Eve sinned, they were forbidden to eat from this tree (Genesis 3:22-24). But throughout eternity, believers will have access to the tree of life because their sins have been removed by Christ's death on the cross. This tree represents the fact that God will supply all our needs, including perfect and continual health.

On each side of the pure river grows the trees of life, bearing a different fruit each month of the year. These trees will constantly be in bloom, showing that there will be no winters in the new earth. The main boulevard of the city will be surrounded by only one species of tree – the tree of life.

Occasionally people wonder whether or not we will eat in eternity. We know that we will eat in heaven at the marriage supper of the lamb (Revelation 19:1-10). We will eat during the Millennium. And, we will eat fruit in the New Jerusalem (Revelation 2:7). God has made provision for us to eat throughout eternity, not because we will be hungry, but because these will be blessed experiences, and God wants us to have these experiences.

The leaves of these trees are "for the healing of the nations." The word "healing" can also be translated "health." In other words, there will be no sickness or dissension. These health giving leaves symbolize the absence of anything that brings physical or spiritual harm, and the preservation of perfect health. These leaves represent perpetual spiritual life, divine health, and harmony. We will never again need deliverance from sickness or pain because the curse will be lifted. And, there will be no lack of unity because past relationships of tension will be healed.

As previously mentioned, the city of New Jerusalem will have 12 gates (Revelation 21:12). This implies at least 12 major boulevards in this city. Perhaps the description of one of the streets in Revelation 22:2 is representative of all 12 boulevards, each paved with gold, with a river and many trees of life on each side.

The trees and rivers will add to the pleasures and enjoyment of life for the redeemed. The residents of the New Jerusalem will enjoy the fruit of these trees because this has been promised to the overcomers (Revelation 2:7; 22:14).

The Curse of Sin Shall Cease to Exist

> 3   And there shall be no more curse: but the throne of God and of the Lamb shall be in it; and his servants shall serve him:
> 4   And they shall see his face; and his name shall be in their foreheads.
> 5   And there shall be no night there; and they need no candle, neither light of the sun; for the Lord God giveth them light: and they shall reign for ever and ever.

There will be no more divine curse (verse 3). The curse put on the earth by God in Genesis 3:14-19 will be removed. Nothing that is cursed can exist in God's presence. Sin, sickness, death, temptation, and sadness will not exist. The fact that the earth will no longer be cursed is proven by God's willingness to relocate His throne there. The throne of God and of the Lamb will be in the city. The redeemed will be servants of God in the midst of His presence and glory. Those things that were lost in the third chapter of the Book of Genesis will be perfectly restored.

The Problems Introduced in the First Three Chapters of Genesis Will Be Resolved in the Last Three Chapters of the Book of Revelation.

In Genesis 3, intimate fellowship with God was lost.

In Revelation 21, intimate fellowship with God will be restored, and God will dwell with us.

In Genesis 3, the first Adam transferred dominion of the earth to Satan.	In Revelation 20, Satan will be bound. Jesus, the Second Adam, will set up His throne on the earth.
In Genesis 3, people were driven from the garden and lost access to the tree of life.	In Revelation 22, we will be able to eat from the tree of life, which is a symbol of eternal life in Christ.
In Genesis 3, the earth was cursed with suffering and hardship.	In Revelation 21, the curse will be removed: there will be no pain and suffering.
In Genesis 3, death entered the world.	In Revelation 20, death will be removed. The new heaven and earth will not have death.

Verse 4 promises that the redeemed will enjoy seeing God face to face. The removal of the curse will allow the redeemed to have wonderful access to God's awesome presence. God will live among His people, and we "shall see his face." In our glorified bodies, we will be able to stand in God's presence and see Him face to face! Jesus promised that the pure in heart will see God (Matthew 5:8). This promise will be completely fulfilled. We shall see Him as He really is (1 John 3:2).

God's "name shall be in their foreheads." Whether or not this is a literal mark, it indicates that God will honor His followers. God will identify with us and mark us as His prized possessions. God will take delight in His redeemed because they will reflect the character traits given to them by Christ (Revelation 3:12).

Verse 5 again mentions that the light in the city will come from God Himself (Revelation 21:23). This was previously mentioned in our study of Revelation, chapter 21. The statement that "there shall be no night there" may apply only to the city of New Jerusalem, not the rest of the earth. Day and night will never pass away (Genesis 8:22; Psalm 89:35-37; 148:3-6; Isaiah 66:22-23). Night will probably still exist on the earth outside of the city. The city will have no need of light from the sun or moon; but the sun, moon, and stars will probably continue to shine for the other parts of the earth.

We will reign with God throughout eternity. Perhaps our activities will include travel to other galaxies and planets.

Jesus is Coming

> 6   And he said unto me, These sayings are faithful and true: and the Lord
> God of the holy prophets sent his angel to shew unto his servants the things which
> must shortly be done.
> 7   Behold, I come quickly: blessed is he that keepeth the sayings of the
> prophecy of this book.

In verse 6, the phrase "things which must shortly be done" refers to the great spiritual conflict described in the prophecy of the Book of Revelation. The prophecy of future things given to the Apostle John began in chapter 4. The prophecy that began in that chapter is now coming to a close.

Jesus states in verse 7, "Behold, I come quickly." Christ made this statement almost 2,000 years ago. The word "quickly" is probably better translated "suddenly." Christ will come back without warning, surprising many.

We are urged to live our lives knowing that Christ may return at anytime. A blessing is promised to those who keep the sayings of this book (Revelation 1:3; 22:7). Therefore, we must separate ourselves from worldly practices and fleshy desires. Our priorities must conform to the priorities of God as revealed in His word, and as revealed by the Holy Spirit working in our lives.

> 8   And I John saw these things, and heard them. And when I had heard and seen, I
> fell down to worship before the feet of the angel which shewed me these things.
> 9   Then saith he unto me, See thou do it not: for I am thy fellowservant, and of thy
> brethren the prophets, and of them which keep the sayings of this book: worship God.

As in Revelation 19:10, John is so overwhelmed by what he sees and hears that he starts to worship the angel/messenger; however, he is forbidden to do so. We should never idolize those messengers that God sends to His churches.

Every person worships something. The possibilities include money, possessions, pleasures, power, entertainers, philosophies, and technologies, to name a few. We must only worship God and devote ourselves to Him. Only then will we have the proper priorities, values, and attitudes. Only then will our relationships with God and other people be the most fulfilling.

The angel (messenger) in verses 8 and 9 may refer to a redeemed man because he calls himself a "fellowservant" of the prophets. This does not mean that redeemed people become angels. It must be remembered that the Greek word for "angel" is the same as "messenger". This angel or messenger that John is speaking to may be a redeemed human who had been one of the prophets.

> 10   And he saith unto me, Seal not the sayings of the prophecy of this book:
> for the time is at hand.

In the Old Testament, Daniel was told to seal his prophecies of the end times until "the time of the end" (Daniel 12:4,9). The messages that God gave Daniel were not for Daniel's time. In Revelation 22:10, John is told not to seal this prophecy because the time is at hand. God wants His followers to be prepared for Christ's return.

The seal of Daniel's prophecy has since been lifted in recent generations with the tremendous explosion of knowledge and the dramatic fulfillment of end-time Bible prophecy. John's prophecy was not to be sealed because it is to serve as a warning to Bible believing churches. The general messages of the Book of Revelation should be proclaimed to all believers and all churches.

> 11   He that is unjust, let him be unjust still: and he which is filthy, let him be
> filthy still: and he that is righteous, let him be righteous still: and he that is holy, let
> him be holy still.
> 12   And, behold, I come quickly; and my reward is with me, to give every man
> according as his work shall be.

A warning is given for those who reject the messages of this book. The conditions in which people will exist throughout eternity will be determined by their spiritual conditions at their deaths. Those who reject the Apostle John's prophecy will continue in their sins. Believers must persevere in righteousness until Christ returns.

In verse 12, Christ Himself promises to return. When Jesus comes again to receive His own, He will bring His rewards with Him (Matthew 25:13-23). After being raptured (1 Thessalonians 4:14-18; 1 Corinthians 15:51-52), believers will receive rewards according to their faithful service to Christ (2 Corinthians 5:10; 1 Corinthians 3:11-15; Matthew 25:23; Luke 14:14; 2 Timothy 4:8).

As previously mentioned, the judgment of believers is actually a distribution of rewards. This event is only for the redeemed. This is not a judgment of sin. Believers have already had their sins judged when they accepted Christ's sacrificial death on the cross (Romans 8:1). Rewards will be dispensed for stewardship of opportunity and energy used in serving Christ. This judgment of the believers occurs during the seven-year tribulation, and perhaps at the beginning of the Millennium for the believers who have survived the tribulation. In addition, there will probably be a further distribution of rewards at the end of the Millennium for those believers saved during the Millennium.

The judgment of believers for the distribution of rewards is a separate event from the Great White Throne Judgment that is described in Revelation, chapter 20. The Great White Throne Judgment is for all the unsaved who have ever lived. Thank God that believers do not have to worry about the Great White Throne Judgment. After experiencing salvation through Christ Jesus, believers only need to concern themselves with the eternal rewards that come from serving Christ

> 13   I am Alpha and Omega, the beginning and the end, the first and the last.

The title of "the first and the last" is one of the titles that Jehovah God used in the Old Testament to describe Himself (Isaiah 44:6; Isaiah 48:12).

- In Revelation 22:13, Jesus applied the title of "the first and the last" to Himself. The context in Revelation 22:12-13 indicates that Jesus is speaking, not the Heavenly Father.
- In Revelation 1:17, Christ also applied the title of "the first and the last" to Himself. Revelation 1:18 makes it clear that Christ was speaking, not the Heavenly Father.
- Jesus also applied the title of "the first and the last" to Himself in Revelation 2:8.

Since God is "the first" and "the last" (Isaiah 44:6; 48:12), and since Jesus is "the first and the last" (Revelation 1:17-18; 2:8; 22:13), the correct conclusion is that Jesus is God. Jesus is not a lesser-created being. He is Almighty God. We look to Christ Jesus for our salvation. It is only through Him that we can live in God's eternal kingdom.

> 14   Blessed are they that do his commandments, that they may have right to the tree of life, and may enter in through the gates into the city.
> 15   For without are dogs, and sorcerers, and whoremongers, and murderers, and idolaters, and whosoever loveth and maketh a lie.
> 16   I Jesus have sent mine angel to testify unto you these things in the churches. I am the root and the offspring of David, and the bright and morning star.

A final blessing is pronounced in verse 14 over those who keep the truths of this book. The Lord's true followers will be given the right to the tree of life (representing eternal fellowship with God) and will be welcomed to enter the city of New Jerusalem. Believers will enjoy these privileges because our sins have been forgiven through Christ's death on the cross. Those who have rejected God will not be given the privilege of dwelling in God's eternal kingdom.

In verse 16, Jesus Himself affirms the authenticity of this book. The remaining verses of the Bible focus on the Lord Jesus Christ. As part of the Godhead, Jesus always existed. This is beyond human comprehension. But as a human, Jesus was a direct descendant of King David (Matthew

1:6-17). The prophet Isaiah predicted the coming of the Messiah, describing Him as "a rod out of the stem of Jesse" (Isaiah 11:1). Jesse was the father of David. Isaiah also described the coming Messiah as "a branch" growing "out of his roots" (Isaiah 11:1).

Jesus calls Himself "the offspring of David." He is referring to Himself as the Messiah of Israel. This is also what was meant by two other titles of Christ: "the Lion of the tribe of Judah" and "the Root of David" (Revelation 5:5).

Revelation 2:28 promises that faithful believers will be given the morning star as their ultimate reward. A morning star appears just before dawn when the night is the coldest and darkest. When the world is in its darkest hour spiritually, Christ will suddenly appear to visibly usher in the kingdom of God on earth. The morning star is Christ (Revelation 22:16). As "the bright and morning star," Christ is the light of salvation. Christ will usher in the visible manifestations of God's glorious eternal kingdom on the earth.

> 17   And the Spirit and the bride say, Come. And let him that heareth say, Come. And let him that is athirst come. And whosoever will, let him take the water of life freely.
> 18   For I testify unto every man that heareth the words of the prophecy of this book, If any man shall add unto these things, God shall add unto him the plagues that are written in this book:
> 19   And if any man shall take away from the words of the book of this prophecy, God shall take away his part out of the book of life, and out of the holy city, and from the things which are written in this book.

Jesus makes one final appeal in verse 17, inviting everyone to receive His living water. Verse 17 also includes the last mention of the Holy Spirit in the Bible. The Holy Spirit is inspiring the bride (true believers) to invite all who want the flowing waters of salvation to come to Christ. Everyone is encouraged to accept Christ as their savior and Lord, before it is too late. All who do not yet have a personal relationship with God are invited to partake of the streams of living water available through Christ and the Holy Spirit (John 7:37-39). Jesus Christ is the source of eternal water that imparts spiritual life.

In verses 18 and 19, God gives a strong admonition that the Word of God is not to be tampered with. As previously mentioned, this warning does not just apply to the Book of Revelation, although the emphasis is there. It also includes the rest of the written word of God, since the Book of Revelation is tied into both the Old and New Testaments.

Those who knowingly tamper and distort the primary doctrines of the Bible – particularly concerning salvation through Jesus Christ – will lose their place in the Book of Life and forfeit their eternal life in the holy city, the New Jerusalem. Whoever adds or takes away words from this book will also receive the judgments and plagues mentioned in this book. Believers can never afford to have a careless attitude toward God's Holy Scriptures.

20   He which testifieth these things saith, Surely I come quickly. Amen. Even so, come, Lord Jesus.

21   The grace of our Lord Jesus Christ be with you all. Amen.

By using the term "Amen," the Apostle John is showing his agreement with and desire for Christ's return. John is also showing his agreement with Christ's invitation for all to receive eternal spiritual life through Jesus. The grace of God is unmerited favor and mercy imparted to those who believe on the Lord Jesus Christ.

The Book of Revelation is actually a book of comfort and hope. It reminds us that no matter what happens, God is in control. It illustrates that evil will eventually be abolished. And, it encourages the faithful followers of Christ by reminding them that they will receive rewards beyond their comprehension.

The Bible ends with a promise from Jesus that He is coming again. He can come at any moment. John responds, "Come, Lord Jesus." We must always be ready and prepared for His sudden return. This last book of the Bible ends with a prayer that Christ will return quickly. This is our blessed hope (Titus 2:13).

"Come, Lord Jesus"

Appendix A

Different Views About When the Rapture Will Occur In Reference to the Seven-Year Tribulation

There is much disagreement as to whether the rapture of the church will occur at the beginning, middle, or end of the seven-year tribulation. In addition, some believe there will be more than one rapture. The following is not a complete study of this subject, but only a brief overview.

The Midtribulation Rapture View

The midtribulation rapture view holds that the church will be preserved during the first three-and-one-half years of the tribulation, and then removed around the middle of the tribulation. Revelation 14:1 mentions 144,000 believers that suddenly appear before the throne of God in heaven around the middle of the tribulation. This may imply that a rapture has just taken place.

How do we know that this scene in Revelation, chapter 14, occurs in the middle, or past the middle, of the tribulation? This is concluded from the following:

(1) Daniel 9:27 states that the Antichrist will break his seven-year covenant with Israel in the middle of the seven years.

(2) Matthew 24:15 also refers to the time when Antichrist will turn against the Jews. Therefore, the events in Matthew, chapter 24, after verse 15 unfold during the second half of the tribulation.

(3) Signs in the sun, moon, and stars occur after the midpoint of the tribulation (Matthew 24:29). These signs are part of the sixth seal (Revelation 6:12-14).

(4) The 144,000 suddenly appear before God's throne (Revelation 14:1) after the sixth seal, at the middle, or past the middle, of the tribulation.

There are various interpretations of this midtribulation event:

- Some believe there will only be one rapture of the church, which will occur at midtribulation. It will include all true believers who have survived on the earth up to that time.
- Others believe that there will be two raptures: a pretribulation rapture and a second rapture at midtribulation:

  (1) Some believe that this second midtribulation rapture will be a partial rapture, only including the 144,000. The reason is that the 144,000 are the only ones specifically mentioned in Revelation 14:1.

(2)   Others believe this second midtribulation rapture will include all persons who will be saved after the beginning of the tribulation and have survived up to that time. According to this view, the 144,000 are only mentioned in this midtribulation rapture because they will receive special recognition. In addition to the 144,000, this midtribulation rapture includes other believers who have gained victory over the beast (Revelation 15:2-4).

Midtribulationists deny the doctrine of imminence. This is the belief that the rapture can take place at any time. Belief in a midtribulation rapture teaches that many signs involving the first half of Daniel's 70th week must occur prior to the rapture.

This view sometimes includes the idea that the tribulation is only three-and-one-half years in length. In other words, the tribulation only consists of the second half of Daniel's 70th week, the second half of this seven-year period. This is what Jesus referred to as the "great tribulation" (Matthew 24:21).

Midtribulationists contend that 2 Thessalonians 2:1-3 indicates the rapture cannot occur until after the Antichrist is revealed. Midtribulationists contend that the Antichrist will not be revealed (recognized by the Jews for who he really is) until the middle of the tribulation (Daniel 9:27). Since the rapture cannot occur until after the Antichrist is revealed, and the Antichrist is revealed at the midpoint of the tribulation, the rapture supposedly cannot occur until at least the middle of the tribulation.

Some scriptures that indicate Christians will experience tribulation are used to argue that the church will go through the first half of the tribulation. Examples include Matthew 24:9-11; Mark 13:9-13; Luke 23:27-31; John 15:18-19; and 16:1-2, 33.

In 1 Corinthians 15:52, it states that the rapture will be accompanied by "the last trump." Midtribulationists believe that the "last trump" is the seventh trumpet of judgment in Revelation 11:15-19. According to this view, the rapture cannot take place until the seventh trumpet, which is sounded in the middle of the seven-year tribulation.

Revelation 3:10 states, "I also will keep thee from the hour of temptation, which shall come upon all the world." In addition, 1 Thessalonians 1:10 and 5:9 state that the church has not been appointed to suffer wrath. The midtribulation rapture view contends that the church will have to endure the wrath of Satan and the Antichrist during the first half of the tribulation (the seals and trumpets). However, the church will be removed just prior to the wrath that comes directly from God in the second half of the tribulation.

The Prewrath Rapture View

A view similar to the midtribulation rapture view is sometimes called the prewrath rapture. Those who embrace this teaching believe that the rapture of the church will occur at some point during the second half of the tribulation. According to this view, the church will have to endure the wrath of Satan and the Antichrist until some point past the midpoint of the tribulation. However, the church will be exempt from the wrath that comes directly from God during the latter part of the tribulation. This judgment from God is also referred to as the "Day of the Lord" (Joel 2:10-11, 30-31; Acts 2:19-21). According to this view, the rapture occurs after the sixth seal and just before the seventh seal. Thus, the rapture of the church occurs just prior to the wrath that comes directly from God, known as the Day of the Lord.[59]

The Day of the Lord (wrath of God) judgments begin at the opening of the seventh seal in Revelation 8:1, just after the church is taken out of the way. According to this view, the Day of the Lord begins at some point during the second half of the tribulation. This conclusion is based on the following:

(1) Signs in the sun, moon, and stars are part of the sixth seal in Revelation 6:12-14. These signs are also mentioned in Joel 2:10-11, 30-31; Acts 2:19-21; and Matthew 24:29.

(2) The signs of the sixth seal mentioned in Matthew 24:29 occur after the midpoint of the tribulation (after Antichrist desecrates the Jewish temple – Matthew 24:15 and Daniel 9:27).

(3) Since the sixth seal begins after the midpoint of the tribulation, judgments directly from God under the seventh seal must also begin after the midpoint of the tribulation.

(4) Therefore the seventh seal, which introduces the seven trumpets and the Day of the Lord judgments, will occur at some point during the second half of the tribulation.

(5) The rapture will occur just prior to the wrath that comes directly from God, at some point during the second half of the tribulation.

Those who teach this view contend that the church will be raptured immediately before God begins to pour out His wrath on the earth, known as the Day of the Lord. Accordingly, the rapture will occur between the sixth and seventh seals, during the second half of the tribulation.

The Posttribulation Rapture View

Posttribulationists deny the doctrine of imminence, which is the belief that the rapture can take place at any time. Belief in a posttribulation rapture teaches that many signs involving the entire tribulation must occur prior to the rapture and Second Coming of Christ.

This view holds that there will only be one rapture of the church at the end of the seven-year tribulation. The purpose of the rapture is to deliver the church from the Battle of Armageddon (Revelation 16:13-16; 19:11-21). According to this view, Christ's Second Coming (Revelation 19:11-14) and the catching up of believers (Matthew 24:29-31; 1 Thessalonians 4:13-18) are the same event, or perhaps only separated by a few minutes or hours. The surviving believers will be caught up at the end of the tribulation and will immediately return with Christ to the earth.

The posttribulation rapture view contends that the Olivet Discourse (Matthew 24-25) only refers to Christ's Second Coming at the end of the tribulation, not to an earlier rapture. The Olivet Discourse addresses the persecution of the Jews in Israel primarily during the second half of the tribulation. Therefore, in the Olivet Discourse, Christ was only referring to His coming at the end of the tribulation.

Some scriptures that indicate Christians will experience tribulation are used to argue that the church will go through the entire tribulation. Examples include Matthew 24:9-11; Mark 13:9-13; Luke 23:27-31; John 15:18-19; and 16:1-2, 33.

In 1 Corinthians 15:52, it states that the rapture will be accompanied by "the last trump." Post-tribulationists believe that the "last trump" is the seventh trumpet of judgment in Revelation 11:15-19. According to this view, the rapture cannot take place until the seventh trumpet, which is sounded toward the end of the seven-year tribulation.

Revelation 20:4-6 mentions "the first resurrection" that takes place just prior to the Millennium at the end of the tribulation. Since this is the first resurrection, this eliminates the possibility of a previous rapture with a previous resurrection.

Revelation 3:10 states, "I also will keep thee from the hour of temptation, which shall come upon all the world." The posttribulation rapture view holds that the church will be preserved, but not removed, during the temptations of the entire tribulation period.

The Pretribulation Rapture View

Pretribulationists embrace the doctrine of imminence, which teaches that no additional prophecies need to be fulfilled before the rapture of the church. The early church also believed that Christ could return at any time (1 Corinthians 15:51-52; Philippians 3:20; 1 Thessalonians 1:9-10; 4:16-17; 5:5-9; 1 Timothy 6:13-14; Titus 2:13; James 5:8-9; Revelation 22:20).

Many signs were given to Israel that would shortly precede the visible return of Christ at the end of the tribulation. However, no signs were given to the church that would shortly precede the rapture. Instead, the church is commanded to watch for Christ. Pretribulationists believe that the church will not participate in the seven-year tribulation.

Chapters 4 and 5 of the Book of Revelation take place in heaven at the beginning, or just prior to, the tribulation. Chapter 6 takes place on earth at the beginning of the tribulation. In chapters 4 through 19, nothing is said about the church on earth, although it is mentioned as being in heaven. Many believe that Revelation 4 and 5 picture the raptured church with God in heaven just before the tribulation. If the church were left on earth during the tribulation, this surely would have been mentioned. Therefore, many believe the rapture will take place just before the beginning of Revelation, chapter 4.

According to the pretribulation rapture view, if the church were not raptured until the middle, second half, or end of the tribulation period, this would conflict with 1 Thessalonians 1:10 and 5:9. These scriptures state that the church has not been appointed to suffer wrath. This includes the wrath of Satan, the wrath of the Antichrist, the wrath of the Lamb, and the wrath of God throughout the tribulation. Also, the seals and trumpets are all part of God's judgments from which the church will be spared. In 1 Thessalonians 4:16-18, we are exhorted to receive comfort as we look forward to the rapture. But, this cannot comfort us if we must first look forward to a terrible, horrible wrath. Therefore, the rapture must occur prior to, or at the beginning of, the seven-year tribulation.

Although some scriptures indicate Christians will experience suffering and persecution, this does not prove that the church will go through any part of the seven-year tribulation. For example: Matthew 24:9-11; Mark 13:9-13; and Luke 23:27-31 address Israel, not the church. Other scriptures that address the church, such as John 15:18-19; 16:1-2, 33, are discussing tribulation in a general sense. These passages are not specifically talking about Daniel's 70th week (seven-year tribulation).

Revelation 3:10 states, "I also will keep thee from the hour of temptation, which shall come upon all the world." The pretribulation rapture view holds that this is a promise that the church will be removed, by rapture, at the beginning of the seven-year tribulation. If the church remains on earth during part or all of the tribulation and is kept safe, then who are the martyrs for Christ under the fifth seal (Revelation 6:9-11)? Pretribulationists believe these martyrs for Christ will be persons saved after the rapture, who will die for their faith. Revelation 3:10 is referring to a pretribulation rapture.

Pretribulationists contend that the first seven seals of judgment come directly from God, and are not merely humans committing acts of atrocities against other humans. These are all part of the wrath of God that the church will avoid through rapture. Whenever judgment was poured out directly from God, such as the Genesis Flood or the destruction of Sodom and Gomorrah, God always delivered His people first. The blessed hope of the rapture (Titus 2:13) would not be a blessed hope if it occurs in the middle, or end, of the tribulation.

It is true that Revelation 20:4-6 mentions "the first resurrection," which takes place just prior to the millennium, at the end of the tribulation. However, this does not disprove a previous rapture and a previous resurrection. 1 Corinthians 15:20-23 states that we will be resurrected "every man in his own order." This indicates that the first resurrection will include different groups and different events. The first resurrection includes at least three phases.

(1)   The first phase of the first resurrection will be a pretribulation rapture of the church (1 Thessalonians 4:14-18). Since this event involves "the dead in Christ," it probably will not include Old Testament believers.

(2)   The second phase of the first resurrection will occur on the last day of the tribulation (Revelation 20:4-6). This phase will include the resurrection of those who were saved and died during the tribulation, along with the Old Testament believers (Daniel 12:1-3).

(3)   The third phase of the first resurrection will include believers who survive the tribulation, along with those who will be born during the Millennium and accept Christ. This third phase of the first resurrection will occur 1,000 years after the tribulation. We know that believers in their physical bodies during the Millennium will eventually be given glorified bodies because this is a promise to all the redeemed (Romans 8:23; 1 Corinthians 15:51-54).

Although the above groups are raised at different times, they are all part of the first resurrection. The first resurrection includes all believers. The second resurrection refers to all unbelievers resurrected after the Millennium. This is known as the "second death" (Revelation 20:6; 14-15).

The date of the rapture cannot be predicted. However, many that will be saved during the tribulation will know almost the precise time of the Lord's visible Second Coming by calculating the beginning and ending of the seven-year tribulation.

• If the church is not raptured until the end of the tribulation period, believers could set a definite time for the rapture – seven years after the Antichrist enters into a covenant with Israel (Daniel 9:27).

• If the church is not raptured until midtribulation, believers could predict the time of the rapture: about three and one-half years after the Antichrist enters into a covenant with Israel (Daniel 9:27).

But, it is unscriptural to set dates for the rapture (Matthew 24:36) because the time of the rapture is a secret (Matthew 24:37-44). In order for the time of the rapture to remain a secret, it must occur before, or at the very beginning of, the seven-year tribulation. Since Christ stated that no one will know the day or hour of His return (Matthew 24:36, 42, 44, 50; 25:13), these statements were referring to a pretribulation rapture, not Christ's visible Second Coming.

The view that the rapture occurs at the end of the seven-year tribulation leaves no time for the marriage supper of the Lamb. This banquet occurs during the tribulation period (Revelation 19:1-9) and before Christ's Second Coming (Revelation 19:11-14).

If all of the surviving believers are raptured and given glorified bodies at the end of the tribulation, there would be no one left in their physical bodies to reproduce during the Millennium. All of the surviving unbelievers will be removed from the earth at the beginning of the Millennium (Matthew 13:40-43, 25:31-46). The Millennium starts out with only believers. Persons who are saved after the rapture, and who survive the tribulation, will enter the Millennium in their physical bodies and will reproduce (Isaiah 65:20). But, human reproduction would not be an option if all believers were given glorified bodies in a rapture at the end of the tribulation.

Jesus promised that when He returns, He would bring rewards according to the works of each believer (Revelation 22:12). Revelation 4:4 shows that the 24 elders have already been given their rewards, as seen by their white robes and golden crowns. This indicates that the first phase of Christ's return, the rapture (1 Thessalonians 4:16-17), and the judgment seat of Christ for most believers (2 Corinthians 5:10) have occurred prior to the fourth chapter of Revelation. This is consistent with the teaching of a pretribulation rapture that occurs between chapters 3 and 4 of the Book of Revelation.

2 Thessalonians 2:1-3 indicates that the coming of our Lord cannot occur until after the Antichrist is revealed. Pretribulationists contend that this scripture is not referring to the rapture of the church, but to the visible Second Coming of Christ at the end of the tribulation. The visible Second Coming of Christ will occur seven years after the Antichrist is revealed. Therefore, 2 Thessalonians 2:1-3 does not teach against a pretribulation rapture.

The "last trump" that is mentioned in reference to the rapture in 1 Corinthians 15:52 refers to the end of the Church Age. This is not the sounding of the seventh trumpet toward the middle, or end, of the tribulation. According to this view, "the last trump" of the Church Age is a different trumpet from the trumpets of judgment during the tribulation. The trumpet that signals the rapture is "the trump of God" (1 Thessalonians 4:16), whereas the seventh trumpet is an angel's trumpet (Revelation 11:15). These are two separate trumpets that signal two separate events.

As previously noted, many who believe in a pretribulation rapture also believe in a second rapture in the middle of the tribulation. Some believe this second rapture will be partial, only involving the 144,000 Jews mentioned in Revelation 7:1-8 and 14:1-5. Others believe this second rapture will include all believers who were saved after the first rapture, and survived up to that point.

Appendix B

Brief Summary of the Prophetic Feasts of Israel

It is commonly taught that the four spring feasts (Passover, Unleavened Bread, First Fruits, and Pentecost) were fulfilled in Messiah's first coming and the founding of the church. It is also commonly taught that the three autumn feasts (Trumpets, Atonement, and Tabernacles) will be fulfilled during the tribulation and at Messiah's Second Coming.[60] There are also two additional feasts that are not part of the Mosaic Law, and take place during winter months. These additional two feasts (Dedication/Hanukkah and Purim/Esther) symbolize the deliverance of the Jewish people from persecution of the Antichrist.

THE SPRING FEASTS:

Passover

Date: Fourteenth day of the month of Nisan, also known as the month of Abib.

This month overlaps March and April. Nisan (Abib) is the first month of the Jewish religious calendar.

Description: Passover meal, the Seder (Say der), was to remind the Israelites of their miraculous deliverance from Egypt (Exodus 13:3-4; 34:18; Deuteronomy 16:1). It was the tenth plague of the firstborn sons that delivered Israel from the bondage of slavery. This plague is described in Exodus, chapter 11 and 12:1-14. The instructions for celebrating this feast are given in Exodus 12:15-20, 43-48; Leviticus 23:5; Numbers 9:1-14; 28:16; and Deuteronomy 16:1-7.

Every household would select a lamb on the tenth day of the month of Nisan (also called the month of Abib). This was the first month of the Jewish religious calendar. On the fourteenth day of this month, these lambs were slain. Each family would eat their lamb together with bitter herbs and unleavened bread (bread made without yeast). During the seven days following Passover, only unleavened bread was to be eaten.

Prophetic Significance: Passover foreshadowed redemption through the crucifixion of the Messiah.

When the death angel saw the blood of the lamb on the doorpost, He would pass over that household, leaving their firstborn alone (Exodus 12:12-13). Jesus was crucified as the "Lamb of God who takes away the sin of the world" (John 1:29). When God sees the blood of Jesus, the lamb of God, covering us, His wrath and judgment pass over us.

Participating in communion (the Lord's supper) is a remembrance of Christ's sacrifice as the perfect Passover Lamb (Luke 22:20; 1 Corinthians 5:7). This sacrifice of Messiah was prophesied in Isaiah 53.

In scripture, leaven symbolizes sin (Luke 12:1; 1 Corinthians 5:8). Unleavened bread symbolizes purity and is a picture of Jesus, who is without sin. To prevent bubbling and air holes, it became traditional to punch holes in the bread (to pierce it). It also became traditional to grill this bread, which left stripes. During the meal, this bread is broken. This bread is a wonderful picture of Christ the Messiah – pure, pierced, with stripes and broken for us.

Jesus came the first time as the suffering servant of Isaiah 53, and gave Himself as the perfect and final sacrificial lamb. He removes the sins of those who believe in Him.

Feast of Unleavened Bread

Date: Fifteenth through the twenty-first day of the month of Nisan, also known as the month of Abib.

This month overlaps March and April. Nisan (Abib) is the first month of the Jewish religious calendar.

Description: The Feast of Unleavened Bread is referred to in I Corinthians 5:6-8. The Passover meal signaled the beginning of the Feast of Unleavened Bread (Exodus 12:15-20; Leviticus 23:6-8; Numbers 28:17-25; Deuteronomy 16:3-8). The Feast of Unleavened Bread was celebrated on the day after Passover. It lasted from the 15th to the 21st day of the month of Nisan. During this time, only unleavened bread could be eaten (Exodus 13:3-10).

Unleavened bread, like Passover, reminds us about the deliverance of the Israelites from Egypt. The Israelites had to eat in haste because they had to be ready for travel at a moment's notice. They did not have time for the bread to rise, which required them to prepare the bread without yeast.

In scripture, leaven represents sin. Before the feasts of Passover and Unleavened Bread, all leaven had to be removed from the houses of the Israelites. This required a great amount of house cleaning. Everything in the house was thoroughly washed and scrubbed. Searching the house for leaven (yeast) was symbolic of searching for and removing all hypocrisy and wickedness from their lives. This cleaning implied that their lives and homes were set apart for God. The purging of leaven from the household was necessary before celebrating the feasts of Passover and Unleavened Bread.

Prophetic Significance: Jesus fulfilled this feast as the one who had no leaven (sin) in Him (2 Corinthians 5:21; 1 John 3:5). The Feast of Unleavened Bread was a visual aid of the holiness of the coming Messiah.

He who knew no leaven (sin) became leaven (sin) for us. This feast also referred to the Messiah as the source of our spiritual nourishment. Jesus is the Bread of Life (John 6:32-35, 47-51, 53-58).

Communion with Christ, the unleavened bread, will result in separation from evil.

Christ, the bread of life, provides believers with right standing and peace with God. This was accomplished at Messiah's first coming when He purchased our salvation through His crucifixion.

Feast of First fruits

Date: Sixteenth day of the month of Nisan, also known as the month of Abib.

This month overlaps March and April. Nisan (Abib) is the first month of the Jewish religious calendar.

Description: One of the first sheaves of the spring barley harvest was presented to the priests, along with a lamb as a burnt offering. This acknowledged that the fruit (harvest) of the ground came from the Lord (Leviticus 23:9-14; Numbers 28:26). This occurred in connection with the Feast of Unleavened Bread. It was an act of dedicating the coming harvest to the Lord.

Prophetic Significance: The Feast of First Fruits is fulfilled in Christ's resurrection. Christ rose from the dead on the feast of first fruits. 1 Corinthians 15:20 says Jesus became the first fruits of those who have died. It means the whole crop is not in yet. We are part of the crop yet to be harvested! Christ became the first of many millions of believers whose bodies will someday be resurrected.

Feast of Weeks

Also called Feast of Harvest and the Day of Pentecost

Date: Sixth day of the month of Sivan.

This month overlaps May and June. Sivan is the third month of the Jewish religious calendar.

Description: Whereas Passover, the Feast of Unleavened Bread and the Feast of First Fruits were observed at the start of the spring barley harvest, the Feast of Weeks took place at the beginning of the summer wheat harvest (Deuteronomy 16:9-12; Leviticus 23:15-22). The Feast of Weeks (Pentecost) was celebrated 50 days after the Feast of First Fruits. Pentecost means "50." This was a thanksgiving offering for the wheat harvest (Exodus 23:16; 34:22; Numbers 28:26-31).

The Feast of Weeks was only observed for one day, which was a day of rest. This feast expressed gratitude and joy for the Lord's blessings on the harvest.

Two loaves of bread baked with leaven were presented to the Lord at the tabernacle. This signified that the daily bread for the people was provided by God (Leviticus 23:15-21). This involved a wave offering by the priest to the Lord. There were also other sacrifices presented with this offering. On this day of joy, the Israelites were to remember the poor by leaving the gleanings in the fields for the needy (Leviticus 23:22).

This feast also commemorated the giving of the law at Mount Sinai. The Jews have traditionally believed God gave Moses the law on the Day of Pentecost.

Prophetic Significance: Pentecost represented the promise of God's Holy Spirit under the new covenant.

The two loaves were baked with fine flour and leaven. The fine flour represents perfect righteousness and is seen as a type of Jesus. The two loaves also represent Jews and Gentiles, both with the leaven of sin in their lives. Both can receive forgiveness through Messiah, the bread of life (John 6:32-35, 47-51, 53-58).

This feast pointed ahead to the gift of the Holy Spirit being poured out on Messiah's followers. Fifty days after Jesus' resurrection, the Holy Spirit was sent on the Day of Pentecost to empower Christ's disciples to fully serve God (Acts 2:1-4).

As previously mentioned, the Jews have traditionally believed God gave Moses the law on the Day of Pentecost. Some see this as the birthday of the nation of Israel. Similarly, the Day of Pentecost is often viewed as the birthday of the church.

Since the Jews have largely rejected their Messiah, the complete fulfillment of this feast for the nation of Israel will not occur until Christ's millennial reign on the earth.

THE AUTUMN FEASTS:

Feast of Trumpets

Also known as Rosh Hashanah

Date: First day of the month of Tishri. This month overlaps September and October.

Tishri is the seventh month of the Jewish religious calendar and the first month of the Jewish secular calendar.

Description: Trumpet blasts signaled the beginning of the secular new year.

The main purpose of the Feast of Trumpets was to prepare the people for the Day of Atonement (Yom Kippur) 10 days later (Leviticus. 23:23-25). These ten days of repentance and Yom Kippur make up the high holy days. God wanted Israel to think about spiritual things, especially about their covenant relationship with Him.

This day was marked by the blowing of trumpets all day, as well as the offering of sacrifices (Numbers 29:1-6). The trumpets were blown to call people to repent and to remind them that the holy days were arriving. The type of trumpet blown was a ram's horn (the shofar). This was to remind the people of the ram sacrificed in place of Isaac (Genesis 22:13).

At this time, Jewish tradition reminds the people of God's Book of Life, and their desire to have their names recorded and retained in the Book of Life.

Prophetic Significance: The Feast of Trumpets represents the preparation of Israel for national repentance and their acceptance of Jesus as their Messiah.

The Jews called God the "horn of their salvation." This meant that God was their deliverer who would fight their battles for them and save them from their enemies. Jesus is referred to as the horn of salvation (Luke 1:68-71). As the commander of the army of God and the horn of our salvation, Jesus has defeated our Satanic enemies and the sin in men's hearts.

The Feast of Trumpets relates to the Christian's spiritual warfare. Our strength and power comes through Christ – the horn or trumpet of our salvation. Jesus' voice is likened to the sound of a trumpet (Revelation 1:10). We are to put on the armor of God as He leads us into spiritual warfare (2 Corinthians 10:3-4; Ephesians 6:10-18).

God does have a Book of Life (Revelation 20:15). This book is called "the Lamb's Book of Life" (Revelation 21:27). This is referring to the Lamb of God – Jesus (John 1:29). The only way to have one's name written in the Book of Life is through faith in the Jewish Messiah – Jesus (John 3:16; 10:27-30).

The Feast of Trumpets will be completely fulfilled at the end of the tribulation when the armies of Antichrist are persecuting the Jews and attacking Jerusalem. This will prepare the Jews of Israel to turn to Jesus as their Messiah in national repentance.

Day of Atonement

Also known as Yom Kippur

Date: Tenth day of the month of Tishri. This month overlaps September and October

Tishri is the seventh month of the Jewish religious calendar, and the first month of the Jewish secular calendar.

Description: The main idea of this occasion was the covering of sin by making an equivalent payment. Yom means "day" and Kippur means "atonement" or "covering." The word atonement refers to reconciliation between God and man. This provided a comprehensive sacrifice for all sins that may not have been atoned for throughout the preceding year. This was also the most solemn day of the entire year (Leviticus 16:1-34; 23:26-32; Numbers 29:7-11). It reminded the people of God's future day of judgment.

The tenth day of the month of Tishri was a day of national cleansing and repentance from sin. No work was permitted on this day. It was also a day of godly sorrow, godly repentance, and confession of sins. All the people were required to fast on this solemn day (Leviticus 16:31). This was the only regular day of fasting in the Bible. It was a time of mourning with a contrite heart before God.

Only the high priest would officiate on this day. The other priests were not even allowed in the tabernacle, but were treated as other members of the congregation. For this occasion, the high priest laid aside his special garments and dressed in white linen. The offerings included two rams as burnt offerings for himself and the congregation. In addition, a bullock was sacrificed to cover the sins of the high priest, and two goats were a sin offering for the people.

Blood from the bullock and one of the goats was applied to the mercy seat on the Ark of the Covenant. By the sprinkling of blood, the high priest sanctified all three divisions of the tabernacle: the Holy of Holies, the holy place, and the outer sanctuary at the altar of burnt offering. In this way, the three divisions of the tabernacle were properly cleansed on the Day of Atonement for the nation.

Placing his hand on a live goat, the high priest confessed the sins of the nation. Then another person would take the goat into the wilderness and release it. This "scapegoat" symbolically carried the sins of the nation away from the people (Leviticus 16:8-10, 20-22).

After confessing the sins of the people, the high priest returned to the tabernacle and changed into his normal official clothes. At the altar in the outer court, he offered two more burnt offerings, one for himself and another for the nation of Israel.

Prophetic Significance: The Day of Atonement represents the salvation of the nation of Israel when the Jews will recognize Jesus as their Messiah. This will occur toward the end of the tribulation.

On the Day of Atonement, a scapegoat was used. The sins of the nation were confessed over it. The goat was then sent away into the desert, symbolizing that their sins were being removed (Leviticus 16:20-22). This scapegoat foreshadowed Christ, who took upon himself the sins of the whole world. Whereas the Old Testament system of sacrifices and scapegoats were inadequate, Christ's crucifixion made the forgiveness of sins available once and for all (Isaiah 53:6,11-12; Romans 3:21-26). The sacrifices on the Day of Atonement provided a covering over sin, but not a permanent taking away of sin. As the perfect and final sacrifice, Jesus has successfully dealt with all of the purification issues before God (Romans 5:6-11; 6:23; 2 Corinthians 5:21; 1 Peter 1:18-19; 1 John 2:1-2).

Christ fulfilled the typology of the Day of Atonement (Hebrews 9:6-10:18). Jesus went into the heavenly Holy of Holies with His own blood, which He shed for the sins of the world. The blood of Jesus did what the blood of bulls and goats could never do. His blood did not just temporarily cover sins, it removed them permanently, for those who believe.

Since the animal sacrifices of the Old Testament looked forward to Christ's perfect sacrifice for our sins, there is no more need for animal sacrifices (Hebrews 9:11-15).

When Jesus died on the cross, the thick veil in the temple was ripped from top to bottom (Matthew 27:50-51; Luke 23:44-46). This showed that God had removed all barriers between man and God's presence in the Holy of Holies.

Toward the end of the seven-year tribulation, the Jews of the nation of Israel will accept Jesus as their Messiah and great scapegoat, who has taken away the sins of believers.

Feast of Booths or Tabernacles

Also called the Ingathering

Date: Days 15-21 of the month of Tishri. This month overlaps September and October.

Tishri is the seventh month of the Jewish religious calendar, and the first month of the Jewish secular calendar.

Description: This feast reminded the Israelites of God's faithfulness and protection during their 40-year wilderness journey. For seven days the people left their houses and lived in temporary booths, tents, or shelters made from tree branches. This reminded them of God's goodness to His people during their 40 years in the desert when they had no permanent dwellings (Leviticus 23:33-43; Nehemiah 8:14-17). There were also other sacrifices presented during this feast (Numbers 29:12-38).

The Feast of Booths or Tabernacles was also called the Feast of Ingathering (Exodus 23:16; 34:22), because it celebrated the conclusion of the harvest of summer fruits and nuts. The fruit of the land had been reaped, so the people could now rest from their harvest labors and rejoice (Deuteronomy 16:13-15).

Every seventh year during the Feast of Tabernacles, a public reading of the law was commanded (Deuteronomy 31:9-13).

In Israel, Torah is usually celebrated on the 22nd day of Tishri. In other places, it is celebrated on the 23rd day of Tishri. This is a celebration of the receiving of the Torah, or the Pentateuch (the first five books of the Bible).

Prophetic Significance: The Feast of Tabernacles foreshadows the beginning of Messiah's visible millennial reign on the earth. Jesus will visibly dwell (tabernacle) with His believers on earth.

Jesus, the Word, (John 1:1) became flesh and dwelt (tabernacled) among us (John 1:14). Jesus is the tabernacle or dwelling place of God (Colossians 2:9). God dwells in our midst through Jesus Christ (Matthew 18:20).

On the last day of the Feast of Tabernacles, it became traditional for the Jews to march around the temple with torches and set these lights around the walls of the temple. This practice recognized that Messiah would be a light to the Gentiles (Isaiah 49:6; Luke 2:32), making salvation available to all nations.

It was also a tradition on the last day of this feast for a priest to carry water from the pool of Siloam to the temple. This looked forward to the time when Messiah will make the whole earth know the Lord, "as the waters cover the sea" (Isaiah 11:9). This will be completely fulfilled during Christ's future millennial reign on the earth (Isaiah 2:2-4; 24:23 23; Jeremiah 3:17; Micah 4:2-3; Zechariah 8:22-23; 14:9; Revelation 20:1-4). During the Millennium, all believers will celebrate the Feast of Tabernacles (Zechariah 14:16-19).

The Feast of Tabernacles was just prior to the rainy season. This was a time of thanksgiving for the rain God was going to send. Many see the symbolism of the coming Messiah who would give them living waters of life (John 7:37-39) from the Holy Spirit.

When Jesus, the Jewish Messiah and savior of the world, dwells (tabernacles) with us on the earth, it will be a glorious age.

THE WINTER FEASTS:

Feast of Dedication

Also called the Festival of Lights and Hanukkah

Date: Days 25-30 of the month of Kislev, and the first two days of the month of Tevet.

This feast falls within December. Kislev and Tevet are the ninth and tenth months of the Jewish religious calendar.

Description: This was a commemoration of the purification of the temple in the Maccabean era (166-164 B.C.), between the Old and New Testaments. An ancient king from Syria, Antiochus Epiphanes, greatly persecuted the Jews for their religion. The Jews finally won their independence from the Syrians and restored their temple worship. The temple was ceremonially purified after Antiochus Epiphanes, who sacrificed a pig on the altar, had defiled it.

In the temple, oil was found and dedicated for sacred use in the burning of the temple lamps. There was only enough oil to keep the lamps burning for about one day. According to Jewish tradition, these lamps continued to supernaturally burn for eight days. This feast is referred to in John 10:22 as the Feast of Dedication. Today, it is referred to as the Feast of Lights or "Hanukkah." This is an eight-day feast commemorating the cleansing of the temple from defilement by the Syrians and deliverance from an evil foreign king.

Prophetic Significance: It is symbolic of Christ purifying the temple, when He drove out the moneychangers. Traditionally, Hanukkah centers on lighting a candlestick of nine candles, called a menorah. Each night another candle is lit, until all nine are lit. Hanukkah, or the Festival of Lights, reminds us that Jesus is the light of the world (John 8:12; 9:5; 12:46).

The story behind Hanukkah reminds believers in Christ to be faithful to God, even in times of persecution (Matthew 5:10-12).

The ancient king, Antiochus Epiphanes, is a type and shadow of the Antichrist in his desecration of the Jewish temple and in his persecution of the Jews. When Christ returns at the end of the tribulation, he will cleanse Israel from the defilement of the Antichrist. Christ Himself will build a new temple in Jerusalem from which He will rule and reign during the Millennium (Zechariah 6:12-13; Ezekiel, chapters 43-46).

Feast of Purim

Also called the Feast of Lots and the Feast of Esther

Date: Fourteenth and fifthteenth days of the month of Adar.

This month overlaps February and March. Adar is the twelfth month of the Jewish religious calendar.

Description: This feast celebrates God's protection of the Jewish people. It commemorates the foiled plot of Haman to kill all the Jews living in the Persian Empire. This celebration is a day of joy, feasting, and giving presents. Mordecai established this feast (Esther 9:18-32).

This occasion was to remember an event that occurred to the Jews living in Persia. The name comes from the Babylonian word pur, meaning "Lot." The pur was something similar to dice. Hamon used the "pur" to determine the day the Jews were to be destroyed (Esther 3:7). It is a two-day festival celebrating God's deliverance of His people from Haman's plot to kill the Jews.

The Feast of Purim reminds us that God can overrule the laws of chance. God's people should never see themselves as victims of fate or chance.

During this holiday, the story of Esther is read in Jewish synagogues. Whenever Haman is mentioned, everyone boos. Whenever Mordecai is mentioned, everyone cheers.

In Jewish leap years, when there is an extra month of Adar, Purim is always celebrated during the second month of Adar.

Prophetic Significance: Jesus, the groom, protects His bride – the church – from the judgments of the world.

Esther is a type of the church. She represents the bride of Christ who is being prepared to come into the presence of the King of kings. Esther's obedience and submissive attitude during the process of being chosen and during her reign reflect the desired character of the bride of Christ.

Haman's hatred for the Jews, and his plot to annihilate them, make him an Old Testament type of the future Antichrist who will seek to destroy all Jews and Christians (Revelation 13:15).

Mordecai is a type of the Holy Spirit, whose rule always brings peace and prosperity to God's kingdom. Mordecai's watchful, nurturing care for Esther parallels the relationship of the Holy Spirit to us. The aim of Mordecai was to exalt the king and to bring the bride into relationship with him. In the same way, the key ministry of the Holy Spirit is to exalt Jesus and to bring the church into relationship with Christ.

The preparations of Esther to come into the presence of the king reveal the processes of God bringing the church into His presence. The queen found favor with the king and her petition was granted. As we totally surrender to the Holy Spirit, we gain the heart of our king. This causes Him to extend His royal scepter to us as we stand in His presence with petitions.

As God delivered the Jews from Haman, at the end of the tribulation God will deliver the surviving Jews who accept Jesus as Messiah from the Antichrist

Appendix C

Accepting Christ as Your Personal Savior

Jesus is the only name by which people can be saved. Speaking about Jesus Christ, Acts 4:12 states: "Neither is there salvation in any other: for there is none other name under heaven given among men, whereby we must be saved." How can you know your sins are forgiven and that you will spend eternity with God?

- **Realize that all people have sinned and need forgiveness.**

  Romans 3:23: "For all have sinned, and come short of the glory of God."

- **Believe that Christ died as a substitute sacrifice for our sins, so that we can receive God's free gift of salvation.**

  Romans 5:8: "But God commendeth his love toward us, in that, while we were sinners, Christ died for us."

  Romans 6:23: "For the wages of sin is death; but the gift of God is eternal life through Jesus Christ our Lord."

- **Ask Christ to forgive your sins, and confess Him as your Lord and Savior.**

  Romans 10:9-10: "That if thou shalt confess with thy mouth the Lord Jesus, and shalt believe in thine heart that God hath raised him from the dead, thou shalt be saved. For with the heart man believeth unto righteousness; and with the mouth confession is made unto salvation."

  I John 1:9: "If we confess our sins, he is faithful and just to forgive us our sins, and to cleanse us from all unrighteousness."

Believe on the Lord Jesus Christ. Confess that you are a sinner and accept His forgiveness. Become involved in a good Bible believing church. Read the Bible daily. A good place to start is the Gospel of John.

Revelation 3:20 states the following: "Behold, I stand at the door, and knock: if any man hear my voice, and open the door, I will come in to him, and will sup with him, and he with me."

Jesus is knocking on the door of your heart, asking you to invite Him in.
If you have not already done so, ask Jesus Christ into your heart today.

Notes

1. *The Popular Encyclopedia of Bible Prophecy*, General Editors: Tim LaHaye and Ed Hindson (Eugene, Oregon: Harvest House Publishers, 2004), 1.
2. Finis Jennings Dake, *God's Plan for Man* (Lawrenceville, Georgia: Dake Bible Sales, Inc., 1949), 22.
3. Charles Beach and Leonard Albert: *Lay Coordinator's Manual* (Cleveland, Tennessee: Pathway Press, 1980), 105-107.
4. Ibid., 109-111.
5. Ibid., 112-113.
6. Robert Gundry, *A Survey of the New Testament* (Grand Rapids, Michigan: Zondervan, 2003), 507.
7. Edward Hindson, *The Book of Revelation, Unlocking the Future* (Chattanooga, Tennessee: AMG Publishers, 2002), 14.
8. Robert Gundry, *A Survey of the New Testament* (Grand Rapids, Michigan: Zondervan, 2003), 508-509.
9. Gary Cohen, *Understanding Revelation* (Chicago, Illinois: Moody Press, 1978), 53-54.
10. Edward Hindson, *The Book of Revelation, Unlocking the Future* (Chattanooga, Tennessee: AMG Publishers 2002), 14.
11. Tim LaHaye, *Revelation Unveiled* (Grand Rapids, Michigan: Zondervan, 1999), 19.
12. Ed, F. Vallowe, *Biblical Mathematics* (Columbia, South Carolina: The Olive Press, 1998), 53-59, 80-84, 98-101.
13. Ibid., 60-65.
14. Ibid., 74-79.
15. Dwight J. Pentecost, *Things to Come* (Grand Rapids, Michigan: Zondervan, 1958), 55.
16. Ibid., 46.
17. Finis Jennings Dake, *Revelation Expounded* (Lawrenceville, Georgia: Dake Bible Sales, Inc., 1950), 22.
18. *Nelson's Illustrated Bible Dictionary*, General Editor: Herbert Lockyer Sr. (Nashville, Tennessee: Thomas Nelson Publishers, 1986), 804.
19. Ibid., 652-653.
20. Ibid., 345.
21. *Compact Bible Dictionary*, Ronald F. Youngblood, F.F. Bruce & R.K. Harrison (Nashville, Tennessee: Nelson Reference & Electronic, 2004), 439.

22. Edward Hindson, *The Book of Revelation, Unlocking the Future* (Chattanooga, Tennessee: AMG Publishers, 2002), 35-36.

23. *Nelson's Illustrated Bible Dictionary,* General Editor: Herbert Lockyer Sr. (Nashville, Tennessee: Thomas Nelson Publishers, 1986), 820. and Jimmy Swaggart, The Book of Revelation (Baton Rouge, Louisiana: Jimmy Swaggert Evangelistic Association, 1980), 20.

24. Tim LaHaye, *Revelation Unveiled* (Grand Rapids, Michigan: Zondervan, 1999), 64, and *Dake's Annotated Reference Bible,* Finis Jennings Dake (Lawrenceville, Georgia: Dake Bible Sales, Inc., 1991) page 287 in New Testament section.

25. Merrill F. Unger, *Archaeology and the New Testament* (Grand Rapids, Michigan: Zondervan, 1972), 279-280.

26. Robert Gundry, *A Survey of the New Testament* (Grand Rapids, Michigan: Zondervan, 2003), 516.

27. Merrill F. Unger, *Archaeology and the New Testament* (Grand Rapids, Michigan: Zondervan, 1972), 285.

28. Robert Gundry, *A Survey of the New Testament* (Grand Rapids, Michigan: Zondervan, 2003), 517.

29. Ibid., 517.

30. Merrill F. Unger, *Archaeology and the New Testament* (Grand Rapids, Michigan: Zondervan, 1972), 270-272.

31. Ibid., 264-265.

32. Robert Gundry, *A Survey of the New Testament* (Grand Rapids, Michigan: Zondervan, 2003), 517.

33. *The Popular Encyclopedia of Bible Prophecy,* General Editors: Tim LaHaye and Ed Hindson (Eugene, Oregon: Harvest House Publishers, 2004), 67-68.

34. Ibid., 357-358.

35. Ibid., 381.

36. *Nelson's Illustrated Bible Dictionary,* General Editor: Herbert Lockyer Sr. (Nashville, Tennessee: Thomas Nelson Publishers, 1986), 571.

37. Ed, F. Vallowe, *Biblical Mathematics* (Columbia, South Carolina: The Olive Press, 1998), 98-101.

38. Ibid., 91-93.

39. *The Popular Encyclopedia of Bible Prophecy,* General Editors: Tim LaHaye and Ed Hindson (Eugene, Oregon: Harvest House Publishers, 2004), 119-120.

40. Ibid., 119-120.

41. John Hagee, *Jerusalem Countdown* (Lake Mary, Florida: FrontLine, 2006) 17.

42. Ibid., 104-108.

43. *Nelson's Illustrated Bible Dictionary,* General Editor: Herbert Lockyer Sr. (Nashville, Tennessee: Thomas Nelson Publishers, 1986), 581-582.

44. Dwight J. Pentecost, *Things to Come* (Grand Rapids, Michigan: Zondervan, 1958), 322-323.

45. Finis Jennings Dake, *God's Plan for Man* (Lawrenceville, Georgia: Dake Bible Sales, Inc., 1949), 934-935.

46. Finis Jennings Dake, *Revelation Expounded* (Lawrenceville, Georgia: Dake Bible Sales, Inc., 1950), 155-157.

47. Perry Stone and Joe Van Koevering, "God's Prophetic Alerts," *God's News Behind The News* (July – August 2003), 6.

48. Perry Stone and Joe VanKoevering, "The Antichrist Jew or Gentile?" *God's News Behind The News* (September-October 2003), 6.

49. *Nelson's Illustrated Bible Dictionary,* General Editor: Herbert Lockyer Sr. (Nashville, Tennessee: Thomas Nelson Publishers, 1986), 1098.

50. *The Student Bible Dictionary,* General Editors: Karen Dockrey, Johnnie Godwin, Phyllis Godwin (Uhrichsville, Ohio: Barbour Publishing, Inc., 2000), 244

51. *The Popular Encyclopedia of Bible Prophecy,* General Editors: Tim LaHaye and Ed Hindson (Eugene, Oregon: Harvest House Publishers, 2004), 232-235.

52. Dwight J. Pentecost, *Things to Come* (Grand Rapids, Michigan: Zondervan, 1958), 476-477.

53. Finis Jennings Dake, *Revelation Expounded* (Lawrenceville, Georgia: Dake Bible Sales, Inc., 1950), 279.

54. Dwight J. Pentecost, *Things to Come* (Grand Rapids, Michigan: Zondervan, 1958), 512-531.

55. Ibid., 532-546, 577-579.

56. C.M. Ward, *What You Should Know About Prophecy* (Springfield, Missouri: Gospel Publishing House, 1975), 112.

57. *Nelson's Illustrated Bible Dictionary,* General Editor: Herbert Lockyer Sr. (Nashville, Tennessee: Thomas Nelson Publishers, 1986), 571.

58. Ibid., 1098.

59. Marvin Rosenthal, *The Pre-wrath Rapture of the Church* (Nashville, Tennessee: Thomas Nelson Publishers, 1990), pages 35 and 60.

60. *The Popular Encyclopedia of Bible Prophecy,* General Editors: Tim LaHaye and Ed Hindson (Eugene, Oregon: Harvest House Publishers, 2004), 107-108.

Bibliography

Beach, Charles and Albert, Leonard. *Lay Coordinator's Manual.* Cleveland, Tennessee: Pathway Press, 1980.

Cohen, Gary. *Understanding Revelation.* Chicago, Illinois: Moody Press, 1978.

Compact Bible Dictionary, Ronald F. Youngblood, F.F. Bruce & R.K. Harrison (Nashville, Tennessee: Nelson Reference & Electronic), 2004.

Dake, Finis Jennings. *God's Plan for Man.* Lawrenceville, Georgia: Dake Bible Sales, Inc., 1949.

Dake, Finis Jennings. *Revelation Expounded.* Lawrenceville, Georgia: Dake Bible Sales, Inc., 1950.

Dake's Annotated Reference Bible, Finis Jennings Dake (Lawrenceville, Georgia: Dake Bible Sales, Inc., 1991)

Gundry, Robert. *A Survey of the New Testament.* Grand Rapids, Michigan: Zondervan, 2003.

Hagee, John. *Jerusalem Countdown.* Lake Mary, Florida: FrontLine, 2006.

Hindson, Edward. *The Book of Revelation, Unlocking the Future.* Chattanooga, Tennessee: AMG Publichers, 2002.

LaHaye, Tim. *Revelation Unveiled.* Grand Rapids, Michigan: Zondervan, 1999.

Nelson's Illustrated Bible Dictionary, General Editor: Herbert Lockyer Sr. (Nashville, Tennessee: Thomas Nelson Publishers), 1986.

Pentecost, J. Dwight. *Things to Come.* Grand Rapids, Michigan: Zondervan, 1958.

Rosenthal, Marvin. *The Pre-wrath Rapture of the Church.* Nashville, Tennessee: Thomas Nelson Publishers, 1990.

Swaggart, Jimmy. *The Book of Revelation.* Baton Rouge, Louisiana: Jimmy Swaggert Evangelistic Association, 1980.

The Popular Encyclopedia of Bible Prophecy, General Editors: Tim LaHaye and Ed Hindson (Eugene, Oregon: Harvest House Publishers), 2004.

The Student Bible Dictionary, General Editors: Karen Dockrey, Johnnie Godwin, Phyllis Godwin (Uhrichsville, Ohio: Barbour Publishing, Inc.), 2000.

Unger, Merrill F. *Archaeology and the New Testament.* Grand Rapids, Michigan: Zondervan, 1972.

Vallowe, Ed, F. *Biblical Mathematics.* Columbia, South Carolina: The Olive Press, 1998.

Ward, C.M., *What You Should Know About Prophecy.* Springfield, Missouri: Gospel Publishing House, 1975.

Made in the USA
Lexington, KY
08 December 2015